Towards
Medical

Challenging the dominant account of medical law as normatively and conceptually subordinate to medical or bioethics, this book provides an innovative account of medical law as a rhetorical practice. The aspiration to provide a firm grounding for medical law in ethical principle has not yet been realized. Rather, legal doctrine is marked, if anything, by increasingly evident contradiction and indeterminacy that are symptomatic of the inherently contingent nature of legal argumentation. Against the idea of a timeless, placeless ethics as the master discipline for medical law, this book demonstrates how judicial and academic reasoning seek to manage this contingency, through the deployment of rhetorical strategies, persuasive to concrete audiences within specific historical, cultural and political contexts. Informed by social and legal theory, cultural history and literary criticism, John Harrington's careful reading of key judicial decisions, legislative proposals and academic interventions offers an original, and significant, understanding of medical law.

John Harrington is Professor of Global Health Law at Cardiff Law School, UK.

Towards a Rhetoric of Medical Law

John Harrington

Routledge
Taylor & Francis Group

LONDON AND NEW YORK

First published 2017
by Routledge
2 Park Square, Milton Park, Abingdon, Oxon, OX14 4RN

and by Routledge
711 Third Avenue, New York, NY 10017

First issued in paperback 2017

Routledge is an imprint of the Taylor & Francis Group, an informa business

British Library Cataloguing-in-Publication Data
A catalogue record for this book is available from the British Library

Library of Congress Cataloging-in-Publication Data
Names: Harrington, John, 1969–
Title: Towards a rhetoric of medical law : against ethics /
John Harrington.
Description: New York, NY : Routledge, 2016. | Includes
bibliographical references and index.Identifiers:
LCCN 2016011368| ISBN 9781138854055 (hbk) |
ISBN 9781315722429 (ebk)
Subjects: LCSH: Medical laws and legislation. | Medical ethics. |
Medical laws and legislation–Great Britain. | Medical ethics–Great
Britain.
Classification: LCC K3601 .H37 2016 | DDC 344.04/1014–dc23
LC record available at http://lccn.loc.gov/2016011368

ISBN 13: 978-1-138-48193-0 (pbk)
ISBN 13: 978-1-138-85405-5 (hbk)

Typeset in Baskerville
by Wearset Ltd, Boldon, Tyne and Wear

Tiomnaím an leabhar seo do m'athair agus mo mháthair John is Greta Harrington agus do m'athair críonna Tom Nealon.

Contents

	Acknowledgements	ix
1	Rhetoric	1
2	Paradox	17
3	Space	42
4	Time	69
5	Utopia	90
6	Progress	117
7	Art	140
8	Ethics	162
	Index	185

Acknowledgements

The genesis of this book can be traced to my first position, as a researcher and lecturer, at the Free University of Berlin under the late Professor Dieter Giesen, a pioneer of comparative medical law. My engagement with German civil law methods there suggested, perhaps ironically, that the distinctiveness of English medical law, rooted in common law traditions, should be taken seriously in any account of its development. To do so is a major burden of this book. In realizing that ambition, I draw on traditions of scholarship and teaching associated with Warwick Law School where I spent ten stimulating and productive years. The rhetorical approach I elaborate here seeks to continue Warwick approaches to understanding law in its broader social context. The opportunity to work alongside scholars of and from the global south at Warwick added clarity and critical focus to my view of health law and the health care system in Britain. Periods at Liverpool and now Cardiff Law Schools, both noted centres of scholarship in medical law, have enriched my understanding of the interplay between law and ethics in this field. I have accumulated many debts to supportive colleagues at all of these institutions and beyond in the development of this work. Thanks are due to Daniel Cullen and Patrick McNestry for their excellent help in preparing the manuscript and to Laura Muir and Colin Perrin at Routledge for editorial advice. Chapters draw on papers which have appeared in *Social and Legal Studies*, the *International Journal of Law in Context*, *Legal Studies*, the *Medical Law Review* and the *Northern Ireland Legal Quarterly*. Research for this book was facilitated by a Research Leave Award of the Arts and Humanities Research Council. I am grateful to Central Manchester University Hospitals NHS Foundation Trust for permitting me to use the image of Aneurin Bevan on the cover of this book and to the Press Association for releasing the image to the publisher. I wish to express particular gratitude for their insightful comments and generous advice to Gavin Anderson, Marie Fox, David Gurnham, Gillian Hundt, Jean McHale, Ambreena Manji, Richard Mullender, Sally Sheldon, Michael Thomson, Ralf Rogowski and Kenneth Veitch. I am of course responsible for any errors and infelicities. This book is dedicated to my parents and to my grandfather.

Chapter 1

Rhetoric

This is a critical study which seeks to 'resurface the politics and history presently submerged in the enterprise' of medical law (Hutchinson 2000: 173). The approach taken in this book can be distinguished from the dominant strand in medical law scholarship which posits medical ethics (or bioethics) as a higher instance at which statutory and case law developments can be reviewed. On this model, legal developments are to be evaluated according to whether they adequately reflect ethical principles and advance ethical goals. To do so is the pre-eminent task of the medical law scholar. Moreover ethics is not merely involved at the stage of reviewing the law after it has been developed. It is present from the outset, helping to formulate the problems which the law addresses and seeks to 'solve'. For example, the issues in euthanasia are presented in terms of patient autonomy as understood in different ethical theories.[1] The criminal law on homicide is then called upon instrumentally to ensure that autonomy is accorded appropriate respect. The rules on culpability, as well as specific sentencing decisions, are evaluated in these terms.[2] Of course ethical values and the legal solutions flowing from them vary greatly. Patient autonomy is given diverse and incompatible meanings in different ethical traditions.[3] Notwithstanding these inconsistencies, a model of legal doctrine as subordinate to the higher values of ethics still dominates the mainstream of medical law scholarship. In fact, as Kenneth Veitch has shown, medical ethics was indispensable in the creation of medical law as a distinct academic sub-discipline (2007: 13ff.). Its promise of normative grounding and scholarly rigour beyond what is customary in the common law bolstered the claim of legal academics to jurisdiction over controversies in health care. Even medical lawyers who draw on critical social theory tend to anchor their work in the normative values of liberal bioethics, promoting an expansion of patient autonomy.[4] This congruence affords medical lawyers a common idiom in which to debate the developing law. It also allows them to aspire at least to principled coherence in a discipline which otherwise borrows its doctrinal substance from a variety of more established areas of law, e.g. criminal law, equity and so on.

This book proposes a different mode for analysing medical law, one which is arguably more faithful to the detailed substance of the law and to its reciprocal relation with the broader social setting. It suggests that the standard model of scholarship rests on an oversimplified understanding of the nature of legal argumentation which neglects the pervasive phenomenon of indeterminacy in lawyers' reasoning. It challenges the more or less instrumental notion of law straightforwardly implementing the reasoned dictates of ethics or any other 'master discipline' as being incompatible with legal indeterminacy. It resists what might be called the formalist tendency to treat medical law and ethics as an ideally self-sufficient whole. That goal would to a great extent entail the detachment of doctrine and scholarship from their broader political and economic contexts. Against this, it seeks to show that these contexts need to be accounted for, since they shape the very texture of the law. It argues that such an account is best developed by reading medical law rhetorically.

What does it mean to propose a 'rhetorical' analysis of medical law? An answer to this will be sketched in the following sections of this chapter and elaborated throughout the book. For now we can summarize that it involves studying the arguments of legislators, judges, advocates, legal scholars and interested others as strategic exercises aimed at persuading specific audiences of the truth of certain facts and the desirability of certain courses of conduct (Perelman 1982: 9). Orthodox legal analysis and mainstream ethics cultivate a certain blindness as to the identity of the speaker and as to the constitution and location of her audience. Indeed this is seen as a prerequisite of fair, unbiased deliberation. By contrast a rhetorical approach returns us to the concrete context of any given judicial, parliamentary or academic speech. Who spoke, when, to whom, and for what purposes? Such an analysis requires us to pay close attention to the actual texts of medical law decisions and opinions, to take seriously the forms and idioms, as well as the detailed substance, of the arguments, deployed by speakers to persuade their hearers or readers. As such it counters the tendency in law and ethics towards abstraction, whereby the actual words of the judge or parliamentarian are condensed into a kernel of abstract rules and principles, with much of what was actually said cast off as mere interpretive chaff.

What is rhetoric? Persuasion and cultural sociology

The study of rhetoric dates back to classical Greece, with Aristotle's *Art of Rhetoric* being a key text, and to Roman authors such as Cicero and Quintilian. Classical rhetoric was a staple of education for lawyers and other professionals in Europe until the rise of rationalism in the seventeenth and eighteenth centuries (Dixon 1971: 42). From this period it fell into decay, being increasingly cast as a literary supplement to empiricist and rationalist philosophy. Political and moral theorists from Hobbes and Bentham to John Rawls have defined their work in anti-rhetorical terms (Kronman 1998–9: 684–686). For example, John Locke held that:

> we must allow that all the art of rhetoric ... all the artificial and figurative applications of words eloquence has invented, are for nothing else but to insinuate wrong ideas, move the passions and thereby mislead the judgment, and so are perfect cheats.
>
> (1979: 508)

Modern law and legal theory have also participated in this embrace of rationalism and the repudiation of their rhetorical traditions. As Peter Goodrich has written:

> [the] dominant tendency within [modern] jurisprudence has been that of the formalist project of applying the categories of logical philosophy to the linguistic produce of the law, for the purposes of inserting the newly born norms of legal judgment into the sterility and safety of a systemic normative justificatory framework.
>
> (1987: 88)

The law aspires to 'monologism' to use Mikhail Bakhtin's term: speaking unambivalently and with one voice (1982: 270). In substance it is a system of rules. Its content is pre-given, to be found by the interpreter rather than actively created in the process of argumentation (White 1985: 685). Law cultivates authority and self-sufficiency, seeking to dominate or marginalize non-legal languages (Goodrich 1984: 177). It prefers as external partners, so to speak, disciplines which offer determinate, exclusive answers, e.g. neo-classical economics or orthodox bioethics. It spurns those associated with openness and complexity, e.g. literature or cultural anthropology (Wetlaufer 1990: 1572).

Rhetoric is no longer the substance of law, then, but is rather viewed as the other of scientific legal studies. It is an embarrassing hangover, an excess of language to be purged through the rigorous, formalistic training of students and theoretical endeavours such as the sharp delimitation of the 'province of jurisprudence' (John Austin) or the elaboration of a 'pure theory of law' (Hans Kelsen).[5] As in general contemporary speech, 'rhetoric' in law is a term of abuse, synonymous at best with superfluous embellishment, or at worst with spin and outright lies (Fish 1990: 482; Leval 1996).

This book refuses such a characterization. Rather, it draws on the insights of modern theorists, such as Chaïm Perelman, and of legal scholars, such as Goodrich, James Boyd White and Allan Hutchinson, as well as classical sources, to retrieve a more central role for rhetoric in analysing the substance and significance of arguments in law generally and in medical law in particular. It proceeds on the basis that virtually all speech, beyond perhaps the tautological systems of inference in mathematics and formal logic, concerns things which 'admit of being otherwise' to adopt a phrase from Aristotle.[6] Given this ultimate indeterminacy, argument cannot simply be a matter of straightforward demonstration, capable of convincing a 'universal audience', i.e. anyone and everyone wherever they find themselves, as aspired to by rationalist philosophers and orthodox legal theorists (Perelman 1982: 15). Rather than revealing a body of rules that was already there, law involves persuasion (White 1985: 688). It is concerned with the reasonable, rather than the rational, and that is contingent on the time and place, the specific historical and institutional contexts, within which an argument is made (Burke 1969: 55). Interventions in law, as in economics, politics, science and so on, are inevitably strategic in nature.[7] They draw on more or less concrete and localized common sense and cultural forms, as well as formal and stylistic devices, towards the goal of persuasion. They fall to be studied for their effectiveness in rhetorical terms with reference to the manner in which they select among and deploy these elements. One upshot of this is that, ironically, any bid to claim the mantle of 'reason' by condemning an opposing view as 'mere rhetoric' is itself a thoroughly strategic, or rhetorical, move (Wetlaufer 1990: 1552).

Rhetorical analysis promises considerably more than the identification of apt techniques for moving audiences, however (Aristotle 1991). It also allows us to study speech from the perspective of politics and power. Thus, as Goodrich notes, rhetoric is:

> political criticism in its classical sense of the study of arguments related to the historical situation and immediate needs of the community (*polis*) to which the speech or discourse is addressed.
>
> (1986: 171–172)

This criticism is useful across a number of dimensions. It directs us in the first instance to investigate how the 'historical situation' and the nature of 'the community', as well as its 'needs', are represented. This is not a simple process of reflection. Audiences, social contexts and shared values are not objective phenomena to be variously addressed, alluded to or invoked by the speaker. Rather each is itself actively called into being in the text or speech. The power of rhetoric is obviously manifest in the instrumental sense of the actions it succeeds in recommending. But it is also evident in this constitutive sense of determining the purposes of communities, delimiting their membership and defining their shared history (White 1985: 695).

This political dimension facilitates a critical reading of legal texts that contrasts with the ideals of social unity and harmony sometimes associated with rhetoric's classical pedigree.[8] The essentially conservative evocation of fractureless communities, discovering unproblematically shared values and acting on them, is quite at odds with the approach taken in this book. Deploying rhetorical analysis as a form of 'cultural sociology', it treats the substance of legal speech itself as a 'locus of historical conflict': a site of struggle between rival common-sense notions of the nature of society and its values, and the relationship of both to the law (Barthes 1994: 47). It investigates the range of understandings which have characterized the field of medical law. It also attends to the discursive processes by which certain groups are typically privileged as audiences of medical law – doctors and lawyers – while others are marginalized or excluded – patients, particularly women. It considers some of the strategies by which certain speakers, but not others, are invested with authority and achieve credibility. The rhetorical politics of medical law will be found in the ongoing efforts to sustain the taken-for-granted nature of such limits and in the countervailing attempts to destabilize them and to secure representation and voice for the excluded.

The analysis of medical law as rhetoric showcased in this book is underpinned by two distinctive theoretical orientations to law: namely the ultimately indeterminate nature of legal decision making, and the embedding of law in its broader social and economic contexts. In the next two sections I will outline key elements of these orientations and suggest a means of reconciling them. In order to illustrate the potential of this combined mode of analysis, I then offer a brief rhetorical reading of a prominent English decision on the rationing of medical treatment.

Why is law rhetoric? Legal indeterminacy

In his non-foundationalist theory of adjudication, Allan Hutchinson provides an account of legal indeterminacy which is explicitly linked with a view of law as rhetorical practice. Hutchinson rejects the orthodox position that law is or can be a 'largely grounded, complete, and certain [mode] of human interaction' (2000: 10).[9] He argues that foundationalists, whether positivists (like HLA Hart) or neo-naturalists (like Ronald Dworkin), suppress or marginalize the messiness of legal practice and the endemic instability of meaning in law. Their hope that rules or principles can be (largely) defined in essence and construed harmoniously is misplaced (Hutchinson 2000: c.3). Modern law can no longer be finally grounded in stable principles, whether these are supposed to be immanent to the law itself, or found outside it in objective morality or human nature.

In developing his own position, Hutchinson steers between formalism on the one hand and nihilism on the other. The lack of an enduring foundation for law means that the distinctions drawn by courts and in legal reasoning more generally are provisional only. This does not mean that they are wholly arbitrary, however. A judge, deciding in good faith, cannot ignore the relevant material, e.g. precedents, statutes and constitutional provisions (Hutchinson 2000: 180ff.). Rather, in order to be recognized as performing adjudication *within the law* she has to argue that it is applicable in the resolution of the matter at hand. Though it can never conclusively determine the outcome, engagement with the legal materials is required (Hutchinson 2000: 191). Beyond this good faith commitment to 'go through' the law, what counts in adjudication and in legal reasoning more generally is not the 'philosophical validity or interpretive correctness' of a particular decision, but its 'rhetorical force and political acceptability' (Hutchinson 2000: 193). Hutchinson demonstrates this in a brilliant reading of *Miller v Jackson*,[10] a case where remedies were sought against a cricket club by a neighbouring householder whose enjoyment of their property was continually disturbed by landing cricket balls (2000: 167). He shows how Lord Denning's interpretation of nuisance and negligence law there depended on a thoroughly political categorization of the interests of the club as public, and those of the householder as private. The outcome was indeterminate in that this ranking could as easily have been reversed. Denning's achievement was to render it plausible, not just with reference to extant legal doctrine, but also crucially through portraying cricket as emblematic of an ideal of Englishness which it is the task of the law to protect. His judgment, says Hutchinson, 'draws what appeal and cogency it has from the only source available – not from the logical force of its doctrinal analysis – but from his rhetorical efforts to tap the political sensibilities and sympathies of his intended audience' (2000: 170).

Hutchinson emphasizes the creativity and the personal political vision of judges such as Denning or Cardozo, and the present study would not deny the distinctive contribution of individuals whether judges or, indeed, academics.[11] But it pushes beyond Hutchinson, investigating the extent to which such visions are shared (or at least overlap) as between judges and others, and furthermore how they borrow from and contribute to non-legal imaginings. Returning to Bakhtin, we can suggest that, notwithstanding its 'monologism', its aspiration to speak with one voice, law is inevitably 'dialogic' in form (1982: 292). The meaning of any particular legal 'utterance' is not produced self-sufficiently, but in relation to, or 'in dialogue' with other utterances. The continual linking and reinterpretation of precedents is an obvious example from the common law (West 1997). But law is also 'intertextual' in the broader sense of 'quoting, invoking, alluding to, affirming or denying' non-legal texts (Vargova 2007: 422). Such 'texts' include written and non-written sources, ranging from classical myths, religious stories and philosophical treatises, to novels, dramas and poetry, and political declarations and tracts. Diverse non-legal vocabularies, genres and linguistic conventions are also drawn upon (Frow 2005: 49). This 'larger cultural weave' is an inextricable part of legal argumentation (Abbott 2008: 101). Indeed Lord Denning's judicial oeuvre was intertextual in just this way, articulating a pastoral vision which resonated with long established literary views of England as a garden (Klinck 1994). Rhetorical analysis of medical law, therefore, needs to be done as historically informed cultural criticism, paying close attention to the 'echoes and reverberations' of other texts in judicial and academic interventions (Bakhtin 1986: 91).

Legal rhetoric in context: a materialist perspective

The second broad orientation of this study is towards a contextual and in particular a 'materialist' understanding of law. Inspired by Marx's critique of capital, such approaches have traditionally envisioned an economic base determining a legal superstructure (Collins 1982). That model is useful in prompting us to consider the connections between different spheres and to look for patterns and influences beyond the narrow focus of specialized disciplines (Williams 1977: 75). The need for such a widened focus is particularly great in medical law, which has generally lacked systematic reflection on the social and economic contexts of legal decision making. However, the base–superstructure model becomes an impediment to understanding in so far as it represents law as merely reflecting the prior truth of the economy (Jameson 1981: 18). This is, of course, manifestly inaccurate.[12] The law on informed consent, for example, cannot simply be read off from the concentration of the means of production or the prevalence of wage labour.

Hutchinson agrees that there is no single 'deep logic' to the law – materialist or otherwise. But he extends this insight, claiming that all is flux, since 'capitalism no longer exists as a conceptual unity or a historical entity' (2000: 231). The most that can be expected of critical scholars then is 'detailed' and 'episodic accounts' of external influences on the development of specific legal doctrine (Hutchinson 2000: 233). However, this emphasis on contingency and particularity goes too far in my view. As Paddy Ireland has pointed out, the death of capitalism has been pronounced by scholars precisely in a period when the academic milieu itself is subject to increasing commodification (2002: 135–137), and, it might be added, when health care provision in England and elsewhere is being transferred steadily to the market. Hutchinson's denial pays oblique tribute to the capitalist system, ascendant in the period from the fall of the Berlin Wall, too big to fail during the economic crash of 2008 and restored via austerity programmes thereafter.[13]

The challenge then is to conserve the insights of legal indeterminacy while recognizing the enduring influence of the capitalist economy. A way forward is offered by the idea of 'ecological dominance' developed in the work of Bob Jessop (2000).[14] This refers to the capacity of the economy to exert asymmetric influence over the functioning of other social systems without, however, removing their autonomy or 'operational independence'. Legal and medical decisions cannot be reduced to profit calculations. But capitalism's greater flexibility, complexity and capacity for re-organization mean that other systems are nonetheless forced to deal with the problems thrown up by it and to identify its successful functioning as one of their own goals. It needs to be noted that these are tendencies only, economic domination is often resisted, and that the path of influence, though asymmetrical, runs in both directions, e.g. changes in the law or the practice of medicine affect the development of the economy.

The ecological model suggests that capitalism is never found in a pure state, but is always 'socially embedded' (Polanyi 1944). It depends on the authentic contributions of other systems in its environment for goods which it cannot produce directly itself, e.g. healthy workers, social peace, political legitimacy. Jessop identifies two distinctive patterns of social embedding in post-war Britain which will provide an important frame for the discussion of medical law rhetoric in the rest of this book (1997). The first, so-called Keynesian, phase lasted to the mid-1970s. It was marked by mass production and consumption with an emphasis on secure male employment. The national territory was the primary frame for economic regulation. Welfare was provided on the basis of citizenship and administered paternalistically by professionals exercising considerable discretion. The effect of this combination was to embed the economy deeply in the wider society and, thus, to set considerable limits to the scope of the market. This is a vital context for the early development of medical law. The nationalized form of the NHS was typical of the period. So too was the de-commodification of access to health care and the considerable autonomy exercised by doctors. I will argue throughout this book that medical law contributed to the broader set of Keynesian arrangements and equally that much of its plausibility derived from the common sense of that era.

The second, neo-liberal phase emerged from the crisis of the Keynesian system in the mid-1970s. Industrial unrest, declining productivity and the growing costs of welfare led businesses to escape the constraints of the nation state by globalizing their operations (Glyn 2006). This process of 'disembedding' has seen an increase in the ecological dominance of the economy (Jessop 2001). As well as wholesale privatization, many public services now mimic markets in their organization and engagement with clients. The social supports of the post-war economy have also been weakened by rights-based critiques of welfare provision and the social and economic subordination of women. Again medical law is implicated in these processes. Challenges to professional discretion over access to abortion and fertility treatment, for example, are not reducible to a mere expression of the 'needs of the economy'. But they have contributed to undermining the taken-for-granted status of the Keynesian mode of embedding capitalism and to its replacement with another.

The materialist focus of this book is reflected in a particular concern with medicine and law as forms of work. Contrary to what might be expected, this focus is consistent with a rhetorical approach to medical law. As Raymond Williams argued, culture and, therefore, law itself involve productive activity as much as technology and industry (1977: 94). The judge (and we might add the doctor) can be compared to an industrial craftswoman whose work involves individual creativity applied within a social organization and a broader political context (Hutchinson 2000: 297). In this spirit the book reads the debate over doctors' discretion, which has been central to the development of medical law, as one over the nature and conditions of clinical labour. I will argue that the privileging of professional judgment in law was sustained by images of clinical work which echoed with judges' understanding of their own practice. Moreover the situation of doctors in the early decades of the NHS exhibited in heightened form the more general restrictions on labour markets under the Keynesian regime. This 'partial decommodification of work' was achieved through substantial trade union rights and worker autonomy over the production process (Huws 2003). Equally, as Duncan Wilson has noted, the movement to limit professional autonomy from the late 1970s on coincided with the broader, 'neo-liberal world view' of the then Conservative government which aimed at disciplining workers and 'allowing managers to manage' (2014: 120).

Reading medical law as rhetoric: *R v Cambridge Health Authority, ex parte B*

This introduction has, thus far, been cast in fairly abstract terms. Before going on to outline the structure of the book, I will try in this section to provide a brief concrete example of the power and utility of rhetorical analysis in medical law. Re-reading the 1995 decision of the Court of Appeal in *R v Cambridge Health Authority, ex parte B*,[15] I pick out the key textual strategies, examples of intertextual dialogue and contextual resonances from which the judgment draws its persuasiveness. In *ex parte B* Lord Bingham MR overturned the decision of Laws J to grant judicial review of the Health Authority's refusal to fund chemotherapy and a bone-marrow transplant operation. The patient, a ten-year-old girl, suffered from acute myeloid leukaemia and had not responded to earlier rounds of treatment. Though doctors in the United States and at a private clinic in London were willing to provide the therapy, the Health Authority refused, given that there was only a 10–20 per cent chance of success for each of the two procedures sought and the extreme additional discomfort likely to be caused. The £60,000 needed to pay for the procedures could be more effectively used.

Laws J had ruled that the Health Authority gave insufficient consideration to the wishes of B's father and had misdescribed the treatment as 'experimental'. Most importantly it had merely invoked the general scarcity of health care resources, rather than explaining its financial and clinical priorities in detail. On a traditional, doctrinal view, Lord Bingham's rejection of this ruling reasserted a narrow ultra vires basis for judicial review, deeming the engagement and explanations offered by the Health Authority to be well within then applicable administrative law requirements (Syrett 2000). However there is considerably more to the decision than this in terms of its length and substance. In the absence of any explicit engagement with case law or other authorities, the whole judgement is given over to establishing a 'rhetorical climate' sufficient to justify the very difficult decision to deny life-saving treatment to B.[16]

The plausibility of Lord Bingham's judgment can be traced to its formal and substantive elements, many of which can be labelled using terms from classical rhetoric. It is laid out (*dispositio*) so as to give considerable space to the views of the Health Authority, its doctors and the medical experts elsewhere who agreed with them. The credibility of the latter is indicated through their titles and the naming of the prestigious institutions in which they were employed.[17] It is also secured, more indirectly, through the incorporation of non-legal genres into the text of the judgment. Witnesses' estimation of the likelihood of treatment succeeding is conveyed in 'hard' percentage terms. Extensive extracts from their correspondence about B's treatment are reproduced verbatim. By contrast the evidence supporting B's claim takes up much less space. It is paraphrased rather than quoted directly and is said to contain only 'a certain amount of learned material', provided by unnamed American experts.[18]

In style (*elocutio*) the judgment exhibits the drive to monologism typical of law discussed above. It uses oratorical definitions to delimit sharply the competence of the court and to challenge the belief (*correctio*) that the courts are 'arbiters as to the merits of such cases'.[19] It adopts an axiomatic, coercive mode of expression, rooting its conclusion in 'facts' about which 'no real evidence is required' given what is 'common knowledge'.[20] Lord Bingham mocks (*meiosis*) Laws J's reasoning by suggesting exaggeratedly (*hyperbole*) that it presumed 'a perfect world' (*antithesis* of the 'real world') where 'the Authority had sufficient money to purchase everything … it would wish to'.[21] The self-evident constraints on health authorities are performed textually by a striking repetition of beginnings and endings (*anaphora*).

> They cannot pay their nurses as much as they would like; they cannot provide all the treatments they would like; they cannot build all the hospitals and specialist units they would like.[22]

The air of fatalism or tragedy, thus produced, is an example of *pathos*, an important method of proof in rhetoric. In this mode Laws J held that the Health Authority could not simply 'toll the bell of tight resources' to deny B.[23] The phrase from John Donne connotes not only mortality, but also solidarity, being preceded by the affirmation that 'any man's death diminishes me, because I am involved in mankind' (*Meditation XVII*, verse 4, lines 4–6).[24] Lord Bingham too confirms (and creates) the identity of his audience as a community 'in which a very high value is put on human life'; he expresses 'every possible sympathy' with B and her family (*commiseratio*).[25] But a closer reading of his judgment makes clear that the evocation of her plight goes to show the objectivity and, therefore, the authority (*ethos*) of the judge, as well as those of the Health Authority and its experts, in facing up to a difficult decision.[26] By contrast B's father, straining 'every nerve' and putting 'pressure' on the doctors to save his daughter's life, is cast as an understandably partisan character in the drama of the case.[27]

The judgment in *ex parte B* is also built around a set of topics (*topoi*) or common-sense assumptions concerning the National Health Service, the nature of medical work and the role of the courts in engaging with both. These resonate in dialogic fashion with more general distinctions between the state and the market, utopia and anti-utopia, law and politics, the clinical and the financial. Lord Bingham defines the problems of access to care which the case presents as phenomena specific to the NHS. By contrast with the US, where health care 'does not come free and ... does not come cheap', treatment has been largely removed from the market in Britain.[28] This has led, however, not to the abolition of scarcity, but to its displacement from the realm of commerce to that of public administration. As the very fact of B's case and many others like it make clear, the effect has been to render visible that which the market had made invisible, to politicize that which had seemed to be a matter of fate, to bring within the purview of the law that which had been juridically irrelevant. Struggles over individual rationing and the overall NHS budget had become increasingly intense during the crisis of the 1970s and thereafter. Lord Bingham responds to this threat by mustering considerable rhetorical power to re-naturalize the scarcity of resources, as the appeals to self-evidence discussed above indicate. His language in this regard also has a strongly intertextual quality. In contrasting the 'real world' with a 'perfect world' of plenty he challenges the utopian aspirations of the founders of the NHS to make health care accessible to all citizens. He also echoes more recent neo-liberal critiques which have emphasized the impossibility of realizing that vision and the costs of trying to do so.

Clinical judgment is central to Lord Bingham's depoliticization strategy. As a form of labour it is sheltered from over-exacting scrutiny, consistent with what I have labelled the 'Keynesian' approach. This exemption allows it to function here, as in many other areas of medical law, as a 'place' (*topos*) or 'black box' to which political controversy and legal indeterminacy can be displaced and concealed. Thus, Lord Bingham quotes approvingly the Health Authority's affirmation that the decision to refuse treatment had been 'made taking all clinical ... matters into consideration and not on financial grounds'.[29] Within the 'clinical' a further telling distinction is made between novel or 'experimental' therapy and 'standard therapy', supported by most practitioners.[30] Categorization of the treatment sought here as experimental was warranted by credible expert evidence (as discussed above) and by the relatively long experience of the doctor treating B. The plausibility of these distinctions is supported by their resonance with common-sense understandings of medicine: images of progress driven forward by experimentation; of the profession as composed of majority and minority opinions in competition; and of individual practitioners exercising fine judgment informed by practical experience. Professional judgment is effective in *ex parte B* when taken in tandem with a further key figure of British health policy and medical law: the waiting list. Lord Bingham held that the Health Authority could not be required 'to come to the court with its accounts' in order to explain its priorities in detail. Immediate access to all treatment was 'unrealistic'.[31] There was a notional queue for treatment and the patient's place in it would be determined by medical opinion.

Structure of this book: topics of medical law

This book will draw on the diverse elements of rhetorical analysis exemplified in *R v Cambridge Health Authority, ex parte B*, as well as concepts drawn from more modern cultural and literary criticism. But the topic is the key figure which will enable us to link medical law to its contexts, to suggest a certain unity to the discipline and to track changes within it. I have suggested that topics are positions or common-sense assumptions shared between speaker and audience, from which an argument can begin. As Jack Balkin has argued, particular disciplines are marked out by distinctive topics (1996). Law's topics are heterogeneous in form.[32] They include formal materials, such as precedent cases, statutes, rules of statutory construction and so on, as well as maxims, standards, principles and policies; but also presumptions about the natural world and the society in which the law operates. Topics are not logically coherent. They may compete with or contradict one another. Topics can never compel a unique conclusion. Rather they must be combined, like the 'legs of a table' or the strands of a rope, to make a stronger or weaker case.[33] While blackletter rules may be viewed as valid or invalid, in or out of the law, the status of most other topics depends on the extent to which they are accepted as part of the law's common sense. Certain assumptions may lose their 'taken-for-granted' status (e.g. that patients depend exclusively on their doctors for medical information), with the result that they no longer function as secure places from which to proceed with an argument (e.g. about the doctor's duty of disclosure prior to treatment).[34]

As I noted at the beginning of this chapter, teachers and textbook writers have used bioethics to lend distinctiveness and coherence to medical law. However, the effect of this turn has been to de-contextualize and de-historicize the discipline. At most it posits a gradual process whereby the law works itself pure and comes to embody ethical principles. The present work is intended as a challenge to that model. In the next chapter, I argue that the dynamic of medical law is to be found, not in a smooth process of evolution, but in the rhetorical struggles which are an inevitable feature of legal decision making under conditions of indeterminacy. In subsequent chapters, I take up the promise of rhetorical analysis to return medical law to its social, cultural and historical contexts. Across the book I identify a set of common-sense assumptions which constituted a specifically British medical law in the post-war period and whose decline has marked a crucial shift in the discipline. Many of these topics were picked out in the foregoing review of Lord Bingham's judgment in *R v Cambridge Health Authority, ex parte B*: national space; time and the organization of treatment; the NHS as a utopian project; the idea of medicine as an art and as a progressive science. In each chapter I consider how a given topic has been articulated in case law, legislative debates and academic discussion; investigate the literary and cultural resonances which gave it plausibility; locate it with reference to the broader Keynesian welfare settlement; and track the manner in which its common-sense status has been challenged. In the final chapter, I return to ethics, offering a rhetorical and contextual explanation of its rise as the master discipline for medical law.

Notes

1 See the review of the relevant debate in Lewis (2007: 22–25, 41–42).
2 For examples of each, see respectively Huxtable and Möller (2007) and Freeman (2002).
3 For a fuller discussion, see the essays in Taylor (2005).
4 See, for example, the essays in Sheldon and Thomson (1998).
5 See Goodrich (1984: 185).
6 See Perelman (1982: 15).
7 For example, see Epstein (1996).
8 For a broad critique of rhetorical revivalism in these terms, see Goodrich (1996).
9 See also Frug (1988).
10 [1977] QB 966 (CA).
11 See Hutchinson (2000: 36).
12 Ibid. (218–224).

13 Indeed Hutchinson's privileging of the particular and the episodic exemplifies in itself what Fredric Jameson has called the 'cultural logic of late capitalism' (1991).

14 Jessop's thinking in this regard is strongly influenced by Niklas Luhmann's theory of social systems. I explore the utility of this approach to a theory of medical law in the next chapter.

15 [1995] 1 WLR 898 (CA).

16 See Hutchinson (2000: 170).

17 *R v Cambridge Health Authority, ex p B* [1995] 1 WLR 898 (CA per Lord Bingham at 901).

18 Ibid. (CA per Lord Bingham at 903).

19 Ibid. (CA per Lord Bingham at 905).

20 Ibid. (CA per Lord Bingham at 906).

21 Ibid. (CA per Lord Bingham at 906).

22 Ibid. (CA per Lord Bingham at 906).

23 Quoted by Lord Bingham, see *R v Cambridge Health Authority, ex p B* [1995] 1 WLR 898 (CA at 906).

24 Donne (1987: 73)

25 *R v Cambridge Health Authority, ex p B* [1995] 1 WLR 898 (CA per Lord Bingham at 905, 907).

26 This strategy of producing sympathy for the judge will be considered more fully in Chapter 3.

27 *R v Cambridge Health Authority, ex p B* [1995] 1 WLR 898 (CA per Lord Bingham at 900, 905).

28 Ibid. (CA per Lord Bingham at 901).

29 *R v Cambridge Health Authority, ex p B* [1995] 1 WLR 898 (CA at 902).

30 See the statements of Professor Goldman quoted by Lord Bingham: *R v Cambridge Health Authority, ex p B* [1995] 1 WLR 898 (CA at 902).

31 *R v Cambridge Health Authority, ex p B* [1995] 1 WLR 898 (CA at 906).

32 See Viehweg (1974).

33 Hutchinson (2000: 176), quoting Wisdom (1953: 157).

34 See the discussion in *Montgomery v Lanarkshire Health Board* [2015] UKSC 11, [2015] 2 WLR 768 (per Lords Kerr and Reed at [75]–[76]).

References

Abbott, HP (2008) *The Cambridge Introduction to Narrative*, 2nd edition (Cambridge, Cambridge University Press).

Aristotle (1991) *The Art of Rhetoric* (London, Penguin).

Bakhtin, MM (1982) *Dialogue in the Novel* (Austin, TX, University of Texas Press).

Bakhtin, MM (1986) *Speech Genres and Other Late Essays* (Austin, TX, University of Texas Press).

Balkin, JM (1996) 'A Night in the Topics: The Reason of Legal Rhetoric and the Rhetoric of Legal Reason', in P Brooks and P Gewirtz (eds), *Law's Stories* (New Haven, CT, Yale University Press) 211.

Barthes, R (1994) *The Semiotic Challenge* (Berkeley, CA, University of California Press).

Burke, K (1969) *A Rhetoric of Motives* (Berkeley, CA, University of California Press).

Collins, H (1982) *Law and Marxism* (Oxford, Oxford University Press).

Dixon, P (1971) *Rhetoric* (London, Methuen).

Donne, J (1987) *Devotions upon Emergent Occasions* (Oxford, Oxford University Press).

Epstein, S (1996) *Impure Science. AIDS, Activism and the Politics of Knowledge* (Berkeley, CA, University of California Press).

Fish, S (1990) *Doing What Comes Naturally. Change, Rhetoric, and the Practice of Theory in Literary and Legal Studies* (Durham, NC, Duke University Press).

Freeman, M (2002) 'Denying Death its Dominion: Thoughts of the Dianne Pretty Case', 10 *Medical Law Review* 245.

Frow, J (2005) *Genre* (London, Routledge).

Frug, J (1988) 'Argument as Character', 40 *Stanford Law Review* 869.

Glyn, A (2006) *Capitalism Unleashed* (Oxford, Oxford University Press).

Goodrich, P (1984) 'Law and Language', 11 *Journal of Law and Society* 173.

Goodrich, P (1986) *Reading the Law. A Critical Introduction to Legal Method and Techniques* (Oxford, Blackwell).

Goodrich, P (1987) *Legal Discourse. Studies in Linguistics, Rhetoric and Legal Analysis* (London, Macmillan).

Goodrich, P (1996) 'Antirrhesis: Polemical Structures of Common Law Thought', in A Sarat and T Kearns (eds), *The Rhetoric of Law* (Ann Arbor, MI, University of Michigan Press) 57.

Hutchinson, A (2000) *It's All in the Game. A Non-Foundationalist Account of Law and Adjudication* (Durham, NC, Duke University Press).

Huws, U (2003) *The Making of a Cybertariat. Virtual Work in a Real World* (London, Merlin Press).

Huxtable, R and M Möller (2007) ' "Setting a Principled Boundary"? Euthanasia as a Response to "Life Fatigue" ', 21 *Bioethics* 117.

Ireland, P (2002) 'History, Critical Legal Studies and the Mysterious Disappearance of Capitalism', 65 *Modern Law Review* 120.

Jameson, F (1981) *The Political Unconscious. Narrative as Socially Symbolic Act* (London, Routledge).

Jameson, F (1991) *Postmodernism or the Cultural Logic of Late Capitalism* (London, Verso).

Jessop, B (1997) 'Capitalism and its Future: Remarks on Regulation, Government, and Governance', 4 *Review of International Political Economy* 435.

Jessop, B (2000) 'The Crisis of the National Spatio-Temporal Fix and the Tendential Ecological Dominance of Globalizing Capitalism', 24 *International Journal of Urban and Regional Research* 323.

Jessop, B (2001) 'Regulationist and Autopoieticist Reflections on Polanyi's Account of Market Economies and the Market Society', 6 *New Political Economy* 213.

Klinck, D (1994) ' "This Other Eden": Lord Denning's Pastoral Vision', 14 *Oxford Journal of Legal Studies* 25.

Kronman, A (1998–9) 'Rhetoric', 67 *University of Cinncinnati Law Review* 677.

Leval, PN (1996) 'Judicial Opinions as Literature', in P Brooks and P Gewirtz, *Law's Stories* (New Haven, CT, Yale University Press, 1996) 206.

Lewis, P (2007) *Assisted Dying and Legal Change* (Oxford, Oxford University Press).

Locke, J (1979) *An Essay Concerning Human Understanding* (Oxford, Oxford University Press).

Perelman, C (1982) *The Realm of Rhetoric* (Notre Dame, IN, University of Notre Dame Press).

Polanyi, K (1944) *The Great Transformation. The Political and Economic Origins of Our Time* (Boston, MA, Beacon Press).

Sheldon, S and M Thomson (eds) (1998) *Feminist Perspectives on Health Care Law* (London, Cavendish).

Syrett, K (2000) 'Of Resources, Rationality and Rights: Emerging Trends in the Judicial Review of Allocative Decisions', [Online] 1 *Web Journal of Current Legal Issues.* Available at: www.bailii.org/uk/other/journals/WebJCLI/2000/issue1/syrett1.html [Accessed: 30 September 2015].

Taylor, JS (ed.) (2005) *Personal Autonomy. New Essays on Personal Autonomy and its Role in Contemporary Moral Philosophy* (Cambridge, Cambridge University Press).

Vargova, M (2007) 'Dialogue, Pluralism, Change. The Intertextual Constitution of Bakhtin, Kristeva and Derrida', 13 *Res Publica* 415.

Veitch, K (2007) *The Jurisdiction of Medical Law* (Aldershot, Hampshire, Ashgate).

Viehweg, T (1974) *Topik und Jurisprudenz. Ein Beitrag zur rechtswissenschaftlichen Grundlagenforschung,* 5th edition (Munich, CH Beck).

West, R (1997) 'Bakhtin and Common Law Change', 72 *Washington Law Review* 291.

Wetlaufer, G (1990) 'Rhetoric and its Denial in Legal Discourse', 76 *Virginia Law Review* 1545.

White, JB (1985) 'Law as Rhetoric, Rhetoric as Law. The Arts of Cultural and Communal Life', 52 *University of Chicago Law Review* 684.

Williams, R (1977) *Marxism and Literature* (Oxford, Oxford University Press).

Wilson, D (2014) *The Making of British Bioethics* (Manchester, Manchester University Press).

Wisdom, J (1953) *Philosophy and Psychoanalysis* (New York, Philosophical Library).

Chapter 2

Paradox

What is the dynamic of change in medical law? The dominant liberal view suggests a process of gradual improvement, a movement from vagueness and particularism to clarity and abstraction in law, and from paternalism to patient autonomy in medicine.[1] Progress towards these goals may be slow and faltering due to institutional inertia and backward thinking among doctors and judges. But, with doctrinal change and the enlightenment of practitioners in both disciplines, steady improvement is possible.[2] The law will work itself clear of impediments to reason and liberty. This liberal model has been subjected to sharp criticism in a number of important respects. First, it tends to overlook the chronic failure even of 'reformed' medical law to meet posited standards of conceptual clarity and principled coherence. On the contrary, a review of relatively recent case law suggests that paradoxes and perplexities abound in practice (Miola 2007). Second, it idealizes legal processes in a manner that simplifies the actual reasoning of the courts. Litigants and their lawyers use law for individual or strategic ends, which produces uneven and sometimes contradictory developments in legal doctrine (Montgomery 2006). Third, in assuming that the law inherently embodies values of rationality and freedom, it is blind to the active and strategic role of academics in creating a new discipline of medical law (Veitch 2007). Fourth, it reproduces law's general tendency toward monologism, discussed in Chapter 1. In particular, it assumes that medical law can be kept separate from the contingencies of politics and developments in the economy.

The present chapter draws on these critiques to propose an alternative model of change in medical law, one which gives a central place to rhetorical struggles. It goes further than each, however. First, it argues that the perplexities of medical law are not merely local difficulties, but symptoms of modern law as a whole. Second, given this phenomenon of endemic contingency, and consistent with the discussion of legal indeterminacy in Chapter 1, it affirms that the reasoning of the courts must be studied as an exercise in persuasion, not logical demonstration. Third, it proposes that academics and other commentators involve themselves in medical law not as detached experts, but rather as participants in ongoing struggles over how to manage legal contingency. Their authority to intervene is itself a matter of plausibility, secured by rhetorical means. Fourth, it argues that this unceasing struggle to achieve plausibility means that medical law argumentation is unavoidably political.

The chapter begins by reviewing the pathologies of contemporary medical law diagnosed in the work of José Miola. He reveals a catalogue of inconsistencies, circularities, gaps and blockages in areas of the law supposed to have been brought under the discipline of reasoned moral standards. I will go on to argue that these legal phenomena can be read symptomatically by drawing on the theory of social systems associated with Niklas Luhmann and further developed in the context of law by Gunther Teubner. These writers would agree with critical legal scholars such as Allan Hutchinson, whose work was discussed in Chapter 1, that the problems identified by Miola are not merely local difficulties. Rather, they exhibit the indeterminate nature of modern law as a whole. According to systems theory writers, these paradoxes and perplexities cannot be dissolved or overcome. They can only be 'managed' (or 'deparadoxified') by being displaced to other decision makers (or 'black boxes') outside the legal system or by being made the subject of ever more complex distinctions within it. Either way, as our discussion of Hutchinson's work has already indicated, these management strategies will never be final or conclusive, but at best only persuasive and provisional. To make them plausible is the central rhetorical labour of the judge, or of any other lawyer taking a position on the matter at hand. The same is true of those who oppose the particular position taken. They will succeed in destabilizing (or 'reparadoxifying') the displacements effected and the distinctions drawn to the extent that they can show them to be essentially arbitrary.

This offers a useful model for the analysis of change in medical law which is pursued in subsequent sections. The widely recognized tendency of postwar judges and legislators, encapsulated in McNair J's direction to the jury in *Bolam v Friern Hospital Management Committee*,[3] to defer to clinical judgment can be framed, not as a wild aberration, but as a pragmatic strategy for managing legal contingency. The task of the critic is to illuminate both the rhetorical means by which this move was justified and the counterstrategies which have sought to discredit it. The rest of the chapter traces this process of establishing and undermining plausibility with reference to two specific areas of medical law. First, the Abortion Act 1967 which made access to lawful termination of pregnancy conditional upon the approval of two registered medical practitioners; and, second, the English jurisprudence concerning the sterilization of people with learning disability. In both instances, the original delegation of decision-making power gained vital support from common-sense representations of the nature of medical practice and its privileged role in interpreting and managing the human body. In both instances, academic commentators have sought to contest the delegation of power by revealing its contingent foundations: parliamentary deal-making in the case of abortion; and the socially constructed nature of medical categories, including the body, in the case of learning disability.

Pathologies of medical law

In *Medical Law and Medical Ethics: A Symbiotic Relationship* (2007) Miola examined the influence of biomedical ethics upon the development of English medical law across a range of specific areas. For liberal commentators, ethics is useful as a source of substantive values, such as patient autonomy, which can provide enduring grounds for legal argumentation.[4] Moreover its formal qualities of order and abstraction embody the type of rationality to which the law aspires. However, Miola's broad conclusion is that, with the exception of informed consent, the renaissance has failed to exert the hoped-for influence upon medical law (2007: 209ff.). Whether intentionally or not, much of Miola's study reads like an exercise in legal deconstruction. Evidence is accumulated from the case law that the project of providing a foundation (or 'grounding') for medical law in biomedical ethics has failed. Medical law is in fact beset by a series of what we might call 'pathologies'. These are outlined in the following paragraphs.

Over-determination[5]

Medical ethics, as developed by philosophers and as codified by professional bodies, was aimed at rationalizing and standardizing decision making. However the proliferation of rival standards emanating from different bodies means that ethical controversies are over-determined. No clear answers are available in many cases and the final decision is remitted to the conscience of the individual practitioner (Miola 2007: 213). This problem is not simply due to the multiplication of official and semi-official standard-setting bodies, for example the General Medical Council (GMC) and British Medical Association (BMA). It is also inherent in the academic enterprise of philosophical ethics. For one thing, the variety of theoretical approaches taken by philosophers means that ethical justifications can be offered for diametrically opposite solutions to most problems (Miola 2007: 48). Moreover these justifications are themselves inherently unstable, given the nature of modern ethics as a critical practice. Philosophical ethics gains its authority precisely from its instability and revisability. We are required, in the words of one of the foremost bioethicists John Harris, to assess our beliefs and values by 'testing them to destruction' (1994: 5, quoted in Miola 2007: 57).

Renvoi

In the landmark case of *Gillick v West Norfolk and Wisbech Area Health Author-ity*[6] the House of Lords held that it would be lawful for doctors to prescribe contraception to competent under-16s without their parents' involvement. Once these broad principles were laid down, the majority held that the law should defer to the ethical standards of the medical profession as regards their implementation in clinical practice. This delegation to professional norms is a feature of several areas of medical law.[7] Unfortu-nately, as Miola carefully shows, on examination, existing ethical guidance often simply refers back to the legal authorities (2007: 112). This sets up an oscillation between law and ethics comparable to the problem of renvoi in the conflict of laws (e.g. English choice of law rules say Italian law applies and vice versa). The vicious circle can only be broken by reintro-ducing the conscience of the individual practitioner as a means of 'getting a decision made' on the question of whether treatment is to be provided or not (Miola 2007: 114).

Contradiction

Of even greater embarrassment to the law is the decision of the Court of Appeal in *Re W (A Minor) (Medical Treatment: Court's Jurisdiction)*[8] which fol-lowed on from *Gillick*. It held that the refusal of treatment by a minor could be overridden on the authority of the court exercising its inherent jurisdiction. In so ruling, Lord Donaldson sought to discount the poten-tially 'hair-raising' implications of this view of the law, which seemed to concede massive intrusive power to individual doctors.[9] He trusted, for instance, that professional ethics would block doctors from imposing an abortion on a 16 or 17 year old, even though the court's ruling technically permitted this.[10] This is, of course, blatantly self-contradictory: a given course of conduct is deemed at one and the same time to be acceptable and unacceptable in the eyes of the law.

Under-determination

Legislation intended to break with *Bolam*-influenced law on the medical treatment of incompetent adults by controlling and 'programming' the test of best interests used in clinical decision making ends up doing pre-cisely the opposite. This is due to the under-determined nature of the rele-vant test set out in the Mental Capacity Act 2005, s 4 of which contains a checklist of factors regarding the best interests of an incompetent patient.[11] These need only be 'considered' (ss 4(3), 4(6)) or 'taken into account' (s 4(7)). As Miola points out, the test thus remains open-ended, its specific application ultimately depending on the judgement of the doctor involved. GMC and BMA guidance is equally indeterminate (2007: 145, 146). Consequently the same procedure carried out on the same patient can, with equal justification, be both ethical and unethical, lawful and unlawful (Miola 2007: 215).

Medical ethics, thus, either remits the question to law or it functions merely as fragments of discourse, available for piecemeal quotation by judges. Either way it disappoints the ambitions of reformers by failing to eliminate contingency in medical law decision making; in fact, it increases it. Judges themselves add to the confusion through their inconsistent treatment of sources of ethics (Miola 2007: 217). In many areas the ineffable judgment of the doctor continues to function as a backstop to clinical, ethical and legal decision making.

Paradoxes and plausibility in medical law

It is tempting to think of the indeterminacies and perplexities identified by Miola as problems specific to medical law alone, capable of being conclusively remedied by feats of clearer thinking or institutional reform. However, I will argue in this section that such problems are not a consequence of a failure to reason adequately, but proceed from the inherently contingent or paradoxical form of modern law. The following analysis draws heavily on insights from the theory of social systems associated with the work of Luhmann and in particular its development by Teubner. However, it is not intended as a straightforward or orthodox application of these theories. Rather, it seeks to combine them with perspectives from critical legal scholarship, for example that of Hutchinson, regarding the role of plausibility and rhetoric in the management of legal indeterminacy. While sometimes seen as a 'conservative' theorist in broadly social and political terms, Luhmann's model of self-producing social systems has 'striking similarities' with critical and deconstructive approaches to law and society (Teubner 1997: 766). As Urs Stäheli has noted, these apparently divergent approaches may nonetheless be combined in a productive reading of legal developments (2000: 13, 19).

Law's contingency: generic and local paradoxes

The role of paradox in systems theory accounts can only be understood with reference to their broader understanding of how law functions, which I will sketch briefly in this section.[12] According to Luhmann, law consists of communications applying the code 'lawful/not lawful' in accordance with legislative and other programmes, e.g. the statement that a given disclosure of medical secrets is a breach of confidentiality in accordance with existing tests.[13] Valid legal operations, or communications, such as court judgments, necessarily refer to previous legal operations, such as precedent cases. Law is thus recursive: it continually makes and remakes itself out of its own normative resources. As a result it is 'operationally' closed to its environment, which is composed of other similarly functioning social systems, such as science, politics, medicine and the economy, as well as the natural world, including the human body and the human psyche. It will be seen later that this does not mean that the law cannot take account of and be influenced by its environment. However, it remains true that a valid decision on lawfulness needs to connect with previous legal material in a process that echoes Hutchinson's 'good faith' obligation on decision makers to 'go through the legal material'. Such a decision cannot be replaced by one on truth, profitability or therapeutic benefit and remain a properly legal decision. To this extent, every legal communication reproduces the distinction between the legal system (to which it allocates itself and the material with which it connects) and its environment. Modern law, for Luhmann as for critical legal scholars, is thus fully self-referential: it creates itself out of itself; it defines itself in terms of itself; it bestows validity upon itself. There is no effective ground or justification external to the legal system which provides a 'foundation' for law and which can securely establish the distinction between law and non-law. In the beginning (and ever after) a line must be drawn, creating form out of pre-legal formlessness. The line was and remains contingent, arbitrary, an 'act of violence' (Clam 2006: 84). Herein lies the original paradox of the legal system. Law, esteemed as the negation of violence, in fact proceeds from it (Teubner 1990: 765).[14]

Systems theory recognizes that this arbitrariness, or violence, is not merely present in the basic distinction between the legal system and its environment.[15] Since every legal operation reproduces this distinction, the spectre of contingency is 'pervasive' throughout the law (Teubner 1990: 26). A given application of the code could always have 'gone the other way'. Thus, law is binding, but provisional; normative, but arbitrary. Contrary to the expectations of traditional legal scholarship, then, paradox is not merely a marginal problem, capable of being purged or at least contained in relation to an otherwise complete and coherent legal system. It is a pervasive and definitive feature of law. In this regard it is worth considering the distinction drawn by Oren Perez between 'generic' and 'local' paradoxes (2006: 17–22). The former include, of course, the fundamental entanglement of law and violence discussed above.[16] The latter refer to 'the decisional paradoxes of daily legal practice' which emerge as the law seeks to manage contingency in its specific branches and in response to 'concrete socio-legal dilemmas' (Teubner 2006: 50; Perez 2006: 17). It is important to note that Perez's understanding of 'local paradoxes' extends more broadly than the strict category of paradoxes in logic. It also includes 'doctrinal weaknesses and inconsistencies', such as the pathologies of medical law revealed in Miola's work: over-determination, renvoi, contradiction and under-determination (Perez 2006: 22).[17]

Paradoxes are a source of persistent embarrassment for theories which ideally equate law with logic and which take consistency as the legal system's overarching value.[18] But legal decision making 'goes on' notwithstanding. How is this possible? Recall that, for systems theorists, as for the rhetorical critics discussed in Chapter 1, law is an activity – in the first instance, an ongoing sequence of communications – not a body of rules (Clam 2006: 90; Suber 1990: 11). Paradox is integral to these operations and to the law's distinctive identity and independence. Without the distinction of law from non-law, the legal system would lose its autonomy and cease to exist as such. It is not open to lawyers simply to purify the law of its logical flaws once and for all. In practice the foundational paradox of law and violence, as well as the local paradoxes of legal practice, are 'managed' operationally on an ongoing basis without ever being finally removed from the legal system. Indeed, as Clam argues in general terms, and as I will suggest for the case of medical law, it is this dynamic process of 'unfolding the paradox' and managing contingency that generates the very substance of law (2006: 86).

Managing contingency: deparadoxification and plausibility

Recognition of the law's basic entanglement with violence and arbitrariness, as discussed above, would paralyze legal decision making. The legal system manages this generic paradox and the more localized paradoxes identified by Perez by hiding them on an ongoing basis.[19] This process of concealment (or 'deparadoxification') takes a number of forms. Most importantly, the law develops 'programmes' which specify how the otherwise contingent code lawful/unlawful 'is to be applied correctly' in specific cases (Luhmann 1993: 190). These include constitutional provisions, legislation and the principles of the common law which make application of the code depend on specific criteria, as opposed to the bare will of the immediate decision maker. The elements of the programme will commonly be a mix of distinctions within the law and displacements to other decision makers. For example, the law on the capacity of minors to consent to contraceptive treatment, referred to already in *Gillick*, is a composite of common law and statute, and can thus be said to include both of these elements.[20] A distinction is drawn between over-16s and under-16s: the former are presumed competent, the latter must prove that they are. But, as was noted above, the actual decision on competence in the case of under-16s is deferred to the clinical judgment of the doctor. The underlying contingency of legal decision making in this field will be effectively concealed for as long as this regime of distinction and displacement holds good. *Gillick* also illustrates the opportunity that programming affords the legal system to use, or more precisely to recreate, information about its social and natural environment – in the form of distinctions – as a means of deparadoxifying its own operations (King and Thornhill 2003: 60). For example, changed understandings of child development were put forward by the House of Lords in *Gillick*, as a basis for recognizing the possibility that some under-16s could have the capacity to consent to treatment.[21]

Law is, thus, 'cognitively open': its communications depend on reconstructions of the world around it. But it remains operatively closed, in so far as legal validity depends on connection to previous *legal* material. A change in medical opinion regarding the need for teenage contraception could not of itself have changed the corresponding legal regime. Only the law decides on this. Programmes, even those most deferential to outside opinion, are themselves the result of operations of the legal system. As such they are always susceptible to repeal and amendment in the case of legislation, overruling and distinguishing in the case of common law. On the one hand, this bestows great flexibility on law, allowing it to continually modify how it represents its environment and thus adapt to changes therein (Perez 2006: 19).[22] In his judgment in *Gillick*, Lord Scarman laid great emphasis on just this capacity of the common law.[23] On the other hand, it also means that the law's programmes are themselves fully contingent. A change in legislation may render unlawful today what was lawful yesterday. Statutes and precedents, often incompatible in their detail, proliferate. Inconsistent representations of the law's social environment can be found in quite proximate areas of doctrine. For systems theory writers, a measure of provisional stability is restored by legal argumentation as developed by academics, but also by judges and advocates in the course of their reasoning (Luhmann 1993: 338ff.). Primary applications of the code lawful/unlawful, informed by its programmes, are considered and an attempt made to organize and rationalize them, accounting for rules and exceptions, drawing distinctions and seeking justifications in terms of the broader principles and policies. The rationalizing project of academic medical lawyers can be characterized in functional terms as just such a deparadoxification strategy. The relative failure of the project, diagnosed by Miola, can equally be rendered as an inability fully to discharge that function. Problems of this sort are in no way confined to medical law. The stability bestowed on any given field by doctrinal argumentation is always only provisional. Rival interpretations of the primary materials may gain the ascendancy or, more likely, new legislation and new precedents will make the previous doctrinal orthodoxy untenable.

The management of contingency then is never conclusive. The distinctions and displacements by which deparadoxification is achieved may give the law 'an aura of endowing its operations with a rational validation, but no more' (King and Thornhill 2003: 48). The key question, as Teubner notes, is whether the proposed distinctions are sufficiently plausible within the web of other legal distinctions (2006: 51). This suggests that every move to deparadoxify legal operations is itself an exercise in contingent persuasion. As such it may be profitably studied, having regard to its construction and effects, as a species of rhetoric. Morten Knudsen has accurately captured this productive, though unexpected, convergence between systems theory and the broader approach taken in this book:[24]

> Classical rhetoric had a well developed teaching of 'places' … [or topics] where arguments are found (and thus where contingency can be displaced to).… Especially when this reservoir of arguments belongs to tradition its contingency is hidden and thus efficient for deparadoxification.
>
> (Knudsen 2007: 117)

Topics were introduced in Chapter 1 as a key focus for the rhetorical analysis developed in this book. As I noted there, they can be defined as common-sense assumptions or 'self-evident premises' shared by speaker and audience (Fischer-Lescano and Christensen 2012: 109). They include the familiar material of legal argumentation (e.g. statutes, precedents, maxims and principles), but also stereotyped representations of the law's environment, the social and natural world upon which it acts (e.g. the ideal of women as mothers and homemakers, or the public interest in restricting doctors' liability for malpractice). Topics are central to the rhetorical management of law's contingency. Both forms of deparadoxification discussed above – distinctions and displacements – are captured by the spatial character of the topic. Thus, topics can either be arranged as a grid or storehouse of arguments or defined as places where the oscillation of thought associated with paradoxes can come to rest.

The rhetorical nature of legal argumentation in this systems theory model is by no means confined to the elaboration of topics. Like paradoxes, the demand for plausibility is pervasive in the law. Distinctions and displacements will themselves need to be justified, for instance. Consequently, as we saw in the case of *R v Cambridge Health Authority, ex parte B*,[25] discussed in Chapter 1, the whole of a judgment or an academic intervention needs to be studied as an integrated and multi-faceted rhetorical performance. Its effectiveness falls to be examined from the point of view of formal style, the audience addressed, the persona which the speaker creates for herself and so on.[26] The aesthetic, as well as the substantive, qualities of the opinion delivered will add to its rhetorical force and thus contribute to the functional goal of concealing the contingency of legal decision making.[27] This rhetorical turn also suggests that deparadoxification is not merely an objective by-product of the workings of the system. It is itself contingent and has to be actively and continually achieved by those engaging in legal argumentation.

The audience for legal arguments is composed in the first instance of other lawyers, including judges. Their plausibility may be inferred from the extent to which the recommended distinctions and displacements are taken up by future legal decision makers. But the audience cannot be neatly limited to such practitioners. Academics and other commentators can also be said to be addressed by legal argumentation. While it is true that 'implausible' legal decisions remain technically valid, scholarly and other critiques may function as 'irritations' provoking the legal system to reconsider and abandon specific deparadoxifications. The next section considers in more detail the different forms which these critical irritations take and the manner in which they impel the development of the law.

Undermining plausibility: reparadoxification and estrangement

The management of contingency is provisional only. Deparadoxification strategies defer and hide law's indeterminacy, but they cannot remove it completely or finally (Teubner 1990: 25). The paradoxes of law are liable to come to the fore when 'the ways of concealing them lose their plausibility' in changed circumstances (Teubner 1997: 771). This process of 'reparadoxification' happens in three main ways: as an effect of doctrinal criticism, radical challenge to legal categories or social and economic change. It will be argued here that in each case reparadoxification takes the form of a 'critique of representation' (Jameson 1998: 38). As discussed above, all systems are operationally closed to their environments. They take in information, but this is always refracted through their own procedures. To return to the example used in the last section, popular opinion and medical knowledge concerning child development are vital to the plausible legal decision making in the area.[28] But that information is always reconstructed, or 're-presented', within the system. Consequently, as Kirsty Keywood has shown, the law's portrayal of other systems, such as medicine, will inevitably be different from their own understandings of themselves, often appearing as skewed and simplistic (2001a, 2003). Distinctions significant in medicine may be overlooked or given little weight.[29] The reason for this is that the legal representation is oriented toward a persuasive decision on lawfulness, whereas, for instance, the medical understanding is oriented toward acceptable diagnosis and therapeutic intervention. Law reduces the complexity of its environment to a form, or topic, useable in its own operations. It is, in Maureen Cain's words, 'necessarily out of touch' with the world around it (1976: 226). These representational shortcomings form the target of the different critical or reparadoxification strategies in law.

Doctrinal arguments commonly start by challenging rival interpretations of the extant legal materials. Their purpose in this is to show that the pattern of distinctions put forward by a court or other commentators is unpersuasive. A number of examples are offered by the case law on the withdrawal of tube feeding from patients in permanent vegetative state (PVS).[30] In *Airedale NHS Trust v Bland*,[31] the House of Lords predicated the lawfulness of this procedure on the combined application of the following distinctions, or 'topic grid': the patient is diagnosed as being in PVS, not some lesser state; tube feeding is treatment, not basic care; withdrawal of treatment is an omission not an act; and omissions are not culpable if continued treatment is futile rather than being of any benefit to the patient.[32] Each of these has been criticized by various commentators for being, in effect, a distinction that does not make a difference.[33] In other words, their use in legal reasoning fails to guide the judge, or doctor, in any significant way. Decisions made on the basis of these criteria are to that extent arbitrary, contingent on the preferences of the decision maker. Put differently, it can be said that these distinctions fail to represent the most serious moral issues at stake in PVS cases. It should be noted in this connection that, although medical ethics has failed to discipline the whole of medical law in a 'positive' sense, it is a fertile source of such 'negative' criticism. Recalling Harris's remarks, quoted above, we can say that legal categories, as well as moral beliefs, are 'tested to destruction' in the process of critique or reparadoxification.

Doctrinal arguments of this sort generally aim at refining, but not overthrowing the specific legal regime in place. They can be contrasted with what Jiří Přibáň has termed radical strategies of 'dissent'. Rather than seeking 'the improvement and stabilization of the system' the latter often proceed from the notion that the system of law, understood as a practice of misrepresentation, may itself be the source of injustice (1999: 171). Reparadoxification by dissent has been a particularly common feature of medical law scholarship inspired by feminist and queer theory.[34] The rhetorical nature of the dissenting mode can be clarified by drawing on the idea of 'estrangement', developed in the theatrical practice of Bertolt Brecht. Put simply, Brecht sought to discredit traditional drama and its overriding concern with inducing feelings of empathy and identification between actors, characters and spectators on the basis of their 'common humanity' (Willett 1964: 60). The latter 'mode of representation' had the effect of making real social problems appear to be a matter of fate. By contrast the theatre of estrangement would show these problems to be historical artefacts, constructed and thus capable of being changed or replaced altogether (Jameson 1998: 40).

Like Brecht, dissident critics seek not to stabilize the system through incremental modification, but radically to disrupt the unity of speaker and audience around the shared common places of topical reasoning, to reveal 'the latent presence of violence' in legal institutions (Benjamin 2007: 288). Moreover they seek not only to challenge specific portrayals of the law's environment, but also to transform the means of representation themselves.[35] They commonly deploy statistical, historical, literary and cultural as well as orthodox legal sources in a bid to destabilize the assumption that law is a solid, unitary and hierarchical discourse (Goodrich 1996: 112–113). Michael Thomson's critique of medical law provides a good example of such strategies (2008).

The strategy of estrangement is not merely an intellectual game. The law's common sense categories are most often constituted negatively, through exclusion and denial. To take one example: the class of persons eligible for state-funded health care is defined through the category of citizen which itself depends on a more or less arbitrary exclusion of non-citizens.[36] We can call that which lies beyond the line of distinction and exclusion the 'political unconscious' of the medical law text (Jameson 1981: 34). Dissenting commentators and patient activists have set themselves the task of recovering what has been made unconscious, to confront the law's representational shortcomings with a richer account of its environment. Beyond that, they also seek procedural reform to allow excluded groups or individuals to influence directly the law's construction of their situations, needs and wishes.[37] In sum, the dissenting strategy attributes normative value to contingency itself.[38] While accepting the fact that legal deparadoxification is inevitable and that it depends on simplifications of some sort, commentators argue that these should be achieved in 'as open, accountable and revisable a manner as possible' (Fitzpatrick 2001: 105).

The final impetus for reparadoxification comes from what Teubner has called developments in 'hard core social reality' which undermine the descriptive adequacy of existing legal distinctions and confront the law with its own underlying paradoxes (1997: 771). The effect of European Union and international human rights law on questions of access to therapy provides a good example. These legal and political developments function as external irritations, triggering the 'self-deconstruction of the law' (Teubner 1990: 769). As will be discussed in Chapter 3, they have the rhetorical effect of de-naturalizing the national spatial frame on which the older case law on allocation was predicated. The distinction between nationals and European non-nationals no longer makes (such) a difference in this area of the law. A similar process is observable in relation to professional judgement which, as will be seen in Chapter 6, traditionally functioned as a 'black box' absorbing the contingency of decision making in medical law. Latterly the plausibility of this displacement has been threatened by the rise in health care organizations of explicit clinical guidelines and evidence-based medicine (Vogd 2002). Of course it needs to be recalled that this new 'hard core reality' is not simply presented to the law in a mechanical fashion.[39] Rather, it is effective only through rhetorical strategies of reparadoxification and renewed deparadoxification through the development of new distinctions and displacements.[40]

Managing and revealing contingency in medical law

Having set out a theoretical frame for the dynamic of change in medical law, I want in this section to consider two concrete examples of these processes. I consider two of the most important 'places' to which the contingency of medical law has been traditionally been displaced: the clinical judgment of the medical practitioner and the human body itself. Each has functioned as a topic of medical law reasoning reducing complexity, thus deparadoxifying legal decision making and allowing it to proceed. Each has been subject to diverse forms of undermining or estrangement accompanied by proposals for improved representation of the law's environment. Each nonetheless continues to function as a topic in medical law reasoning, albeit of diminished plausibility. The following discussion does not pretend to be comprehensive. It concentrates chiefly on two substantive areas of medical law within which these topics have been elaborated: the Abortion Act 1967 and the common law concerning the sterilization of incompetent persons. Moreover, it focuses on a representative sample of academic authors, whose work both describes and participates in the dynamics of deparadoxification and reparadoxification.

Abortion Act 1967

Under the Abortion Act 1967, s 1(1) access to lawful termination of pregnancy in Great Britain is dependent on the judgement of two registered medical practitioners that certain enumerated grounds have been complied with. Each of these grounds is defined in medical terms: threats to the woman's life or health (s 1(1)(a), (b), (c)) or a substantial risk of serious handicap to the child if born (s 1(1)(d)). There is limited provision for the woman's social circumstances to be taken into account (s 1(2)), but this is merely a factor in the doctor's overall decision. The Act provides, furthermore, that abortions may only be carried out by registered medical practitioners or by health care workers under their direct supervision (s 1(1)).[41] In essence, the Act effects a deparadoxification by displacement: legal contingency in this sensitive area is absorbed by the 'black box' of professional opinion. The precise form of this deferral has been upheld and enforced in the relevant case law. While courts are reluctant to investigate the specific content of the medical decision, they have stipulated that an authentic clinical evaluation must be made in every case. Abortion may not be carried out solely at the request of the woman.[42]

In a critical review, Anna Grear (2004) seeks to reparadoxify this legal regime in two ways. First she argues that the Act fails to represent the relevant environment of the legal system adequately. This is what she terms the 'reductive' nature of the legislation which foregrounds only one aspect, namely medical, of a multi-faceted social phenomenon (Grear 2004: 4). 'Simple medicalization' is substituted for 'the complexity of rights talk'[43] characteristic of the abortion debate in other jurisdictions (Grear 2004: 8). Taking an ecumenical view of that debate, she emphasizes that both the rights of women and the potential rights of the foetus are wholly overlooked in the Act (Grear 2004: 9). While this may have been plausible given 'the absence of any developed rights-aware culture' at the time the Act was passed, it appears wholly arbitrary now (Grear 2004: 11). Grear develops this estrangement effect by stressing the contradictory nature of the Act's approach to clinical judgement. As the courts have affirmed, it places 'a great social responsibility' on the shoulders of the doctor.[44] But this non-medical dimension is hardly compatible with the authentically clinical decision which she is required to make in such cases and for which she is primarily trained (Grear 2004: 9). This strategy is pressed still further by Sally Sheldon. Drawing on the work of feminist social scientists, she highlights the gendered nature of even routine medical decision making (Sheldon 1997: 49–50). Clinical judgement, which was intended to absorb the law's contingency by taking the social controversy out of abortion, is itself inherently social and contestable. As such, it cannot function as a plausible topic of legal argumentation in this area.

Grear's second reparadoxification strategy is directed at the political contingency of the Act's origins. She carefully examines the parliamentary debates which preceded its passing, finding in them clear evidence of 'intense lobbying' by bodies such as the BMA and the Royal College of Obstetricians and Gynaecologists, all seeking to protect the doctor from unwarranted and unpredictable criminal liability (Grear 2004: 4). In fact the latter concern was 'somewhat synthetic' (Grear 2004: 5). As John Keown's historical study revealed, doctors were not significantly restricted by the existing common law regime, nor was there a great deal of uncertainty regarding it (1988: 78, quoted in Grear 2004: 5). In reality the statutory scheme has its origins in the occupational self-interest of the medical profession, which sought to reinforce its domination of health care provision in post-war Britain. The implication of Grear's review is that these merely strategic motives are an unworthy source for morally significant legislation. Again this critique is extended in Sheldon's work. She shows that the parliamentary debates were not framed in the neutral language of public health and social policy. Instead both proponents and opponents of law reform built their arguments upon commonplace images of women as either 'tarts' or 'tired housewives' needing guidance from benevolent doctors (Sheldon 1997: 32ff.). Deference to clinical judgment, as discussed in Chapter 6, had to be actively justified by the invocation of a range of other topics. It is precisely by pointing out the contingent and non-technical nature of these topics that Sheldon seeks to destabilize the core displacement effected by the Abortion Act 1967.

In unpicking the relevant parliamentary debates, both Grear and Sheldon can be said to estrange their readers from the fiction of 'legislative intention'. The latter functions as a topic of legal discourse absorbing the contingency of the law-making process by representing it as a single moment when Parliament speaks unambiguously and with one voice (Goodrich 1986: 122). By way of this representation, the law reduces the complexity of its political environment, allowing decision making to proceed without the need for an endless reconsideration of parliamentary motives (Luhmann 1993: 420). Its role in deparadoxifying legal decision making is structurally similar to that of clinical judgement. Each bars access to the political unconscious of the law. Each may be estranged by opening the 'black box' and showing the complexity and arbitrariness of what is usually taken to be simple and inevitable. The sustained use of non-standard sources, such as the record of parliamentary debates or the findings of social scientists, serves to break the normal frame of legal analysis. It interrupts what would otherwise appear as an inevitable flow from fictitious parliamentary will to valid law.[45]

The authority of academic commentators in this area is achieved in and through the rhetorical form of their engagement with the issues. Thus, Grear's discussion of the contingencies of the Abortion Act and of the preceding parliamentary debates is realized through a metaphorics of visibility. The effect of the Act is to 'submerge', 'sublimate', 'suppress', 'mask' and 'eclipse' the significant social and moral issues in this area (Grear 2004: 6, 6, 7, 7, 9). By implication, the role of the scholar is to reveal, to illuminate, to clarify. Like Brecht's theatre of estrangement, there is an inherently didactic purpose to academic reparadoxification. The commentator is 'produced' by her own text as a fearless teacher and dispeller of illusions.[46] The importance of this role is sustained by the generic priority given to truth over falsehood and by the embodied preference for light over darkness.[47]

Grear concludes by proposing an alternative mode of deparadoxification, one which she claims is a 'thoughtful and multi-faceted response to the complex issues' currently hidden 'beneath a medical short cut' (2004: 7). The law should be opened up to the different moral positions on abortion. This promotes the formal objective of giving a say to formerly silenced groups. But, more than that, it values complexity and contingency for their own sakes. Warning against 'inappropriate closure', Grear argues that 'the integrity of the abortion debate' should itself be respected by the law (2004: 11, 9). She recognizes the functional cost of adopting this approach, noting the deadlocked and 'interminably polarized' nature of the abortion debate in the United States and elsewhere (2004: 13). Moreover, as she notes, rights-talk itself tends to simplify the complexities of social life, reducing the issues in abortion to a binary contest of abstract principles (2004: 11).

The foregoing difficulties are addressed by the second component of her reform proposal. This takes the form of a political supplement to the law: a broad strategy to promote welfare and economic rights, responsible sexual behaviour among men and the empowerment of women (Grear 2004: 14). Such a 'transformative' widening of responses to abortion would allow the law to meet the normative challenges of the moral debate while minimizing the practical consequences of its doing so (Grear 2004: 14). Though not concealing the law's contingency, Grear's proposal aims to defuse its impact by substituting administrative bodies for the legal system as the effective locus of decision making. The problems with this segmented division of labour are fairly clear. For one thing, the expectation that social policy concerning abortion can be insulated from the instability of ethical debate is likely to be disappointed. Pro-choice and pro-life campaigners are likely to monitor closely and, where appropriate, to challenge wider health policy relevant to abortion. Moreover, the reform would reduce the law to a debating forum with little significant social effect. This too is likely to founder on the inherently practical orientation of the law which justifies itself to itself as an effective mode of governance, the embodiment of justice and an instrument in society (Murphy 1997: 88). If the values at stake are as important as Grear asserts, and if they are explicitly to inform the law's programmes, valid grounds will be available, allowing courts to review administrative measures of state policy in relation to abortion. The moral debate, as hosted by law, will necessarily have a significant, albeit not wholly predictable, effect on access to termination of pregnancy in the 'real world'.

Sterilization of learning disabled patients

The law concerning the sterilization of incompetent patients in England has been marked by a similar pattern of deparadoxification and reparadoxification focused on the topics of both clinical judgement and the human body.[48] In its 1987 decision in *Re B (A Minor) (Wardship: Sterilisation)*,[49] the House of Lords opted to 'Bolamize' the question of lawfulness rather than framing it in terms of human rights.[50] Their Lordships also dismissed as 'meaningless' a proposed distinction between therapeutic and non-therapeutic sterilizations, seeing no need for a higher level of scrutiny in the latter category of case.[51] As long as the procedure was acceptable to a responsible body of medical practitioners, it would be deemed to be in the best interests of the patient. Where a diverse range of such options was thrown up, any of them would be lawful.[52] In other words legal contingency would be wholly absorbed by clinical opinion. As has been seen in relation to abortion, the reparadoxification strategies of academic commentators concentrated on the representational short-comings of the developing legal regime. Thus, for Lee and Morgan, medicalization obscured the social factors contributing to the vulnerability of people with learning disability: inadequate resources, as well as poor training and supervision of staff (1988: 239). Moreover their Lordships had assessed the capacities, needs and desires of the patient with reference to the criterion of mental age, even though this was widely rejected by developmental experts themselves as a gross oversimplification (Lee and Morgan 1988: 238). Critics also sought to estrange clinical judgement in this context by recalling the controversial twentieth-century history of sterilization.[53] The notorious decision of the US Supreme court in *Buck v Bell*,[54] upholding the constitutionality of state-sponsored sterilization of people with learning disability, functioned as a counter-topic in these arguments. The legislation challenged in that case had harnessed clinical judgement to a philosophy of eugenics, itself informed by racist and misogynistic values.[55] As a negative exemplar, *Buck v Bell* served to disrupt the assumption that the doctor's decision in these cases was purely a matter of medical opinion.

This critique of representation was taken up by the Court of Appeal in the later cases of *Re A (Mental Patient: Sterilisation)*[56] and *Re S (Adult Patient: Sterilisation)*.[57] Moving away from the single test of *Re B*, the Court introduced a distinction between the clinical acceptability of sterilization and its appropriateness in the light of the 'broader ethical, social, moral and welfare considerations' raised in the case of the particular patient.[58] In so far as a range of options passed scrutiny under the Bolam test, the court itself was tasked with making an affirmative choice between them.[59] A mix of clinical and judicial judgement would now absorb the contingency of the decision on lawfulness. However, the retreat from simple medicalization has failed to produce a wholly plausible and stable legal regime. As was seen in the discussion of Miola's work *supra*, the new test of best interests is open-ended and thus inherently indeterminate. Kirsty Keywood has argued that, in coping with this indeterminacy, the courts have adopted a more or less corporeal understanding of learning disability (2001a, 2001b). On this view, the patient's body is represented as the original source of the 'social, emotional and other' problems to be addressed by the court at the second stage of the current test (Keywood 2001b: 192). In essence, the body functions as a proxy for the social. As will be seen in our discussion of the role of 'time' in medical law in Chapter 4, it is itself a topic of reasoning in this area of medical law, its plausibility deriving from its status as a 'natural' entity located in the environment of the legal system (Keywood 2001a: 31).[60]

The deparadoxifying move adopted in *Re S* and *Re A* has been subject to reparadoxification in at least three ways. First, given the central role of medical knowledge in representing the human body, clinical judgement inevitably re-appears at the second stage of the test developed by the Court of Appeal. Doctrinal criticism argues that the distinction drawn between medical and non-medical interests makes no difference, leaving the Bolam test, as detailed in Chapter 1, effectively still dominant (Keywood 2001b: 190). Second, technological advances in areas such as surgery, genetics and reproductive therapies mean that the processes and constitution of the body are now subject to active manipulation. Medicine no longer seeks merely to divine and follow the objective and unalterable laws of nature, it also rewrites them (Bauch 1996: 58). The result of this development in 'hard core social reality', to draw on Teubner again, is that the body has now been brought within the realm of the social (Bauch 1996: 61). The instability in clinical and legal reasoning produced by this qualitative change is evident, not just in connection with sterilization, but across the breadth of medical law. For example, with advances in care at the end of life, the legal fact of death can no longer simply be predicated upon observable, natural processes (Bauch 1996: 113).[61] It is a matter of social and political contestation and, therefore, endemically unsettled.[62] The estranging effect of these developments is illustrated *a contrario* by the rhetorical exertions of conservative commentators who reassert nostalgic ideas of the 'natural' in a bid to shield the body against manipulation.[63]

The third challenge to the newer case law on sterilization takes the form of 'radical dissent' and proceeds by revealing that the idea of the natural body in law (and medicine) itself rests on a paradox (Buckel 2007: 35). Operational closure, discussed above, means that the physical environment, including the sickness or health of individuals, is knowable to social systems only through their own observations (Kopfsguter 2006: 105). Hence the paradox: the 'natural' status of the body is in fact a cultural product, a 'semantic artifact' produced by communications of the legal, medical and other systems (Keywood 2001a: 31). This insight is consonant with critical social theory, which stresses the thoroughly conventional status of the body (Buckel 2007: 37). As Judith Butler shows, in orthodox thought the body is taken to be the natural source of appropriate gender roles and 'normal' heterosexual desire (1990: 35). She argues, however, that in reality there exists a circular relationship between these elements. Instead of a biological determinism originating in a natural body, both sex and gender are themselves produced by the prevailing norms as to appropriate, heterosexual desire (Butler 1990: 31). The contingent nature of sex and gender is made evident by disruptive practices, such as drag and cross-dressing. Consistent with the analysis developed in this chapter, Butler characterizes such practices as thoroughly rhetorical, involving as they do 'parody', 'hyperbole', 'dissonance' and 'internal confusion' (1990: 187, 43). Each estranges and undermines the common sense of sex and gender, exposing the provisional nature of the binary oppositions upon which they are based (Butler 1990: 192).

Butler's work has been incisively deployed by Keywood in her critique of *Re S* and *Re A*. She argues that the orthodox (hetero-)sexing of the body as male and female with reference to reproductive function serves to marginalize learning disabled people. The latter are assumed in the case law to be reproductive failures and, thus, beyond sex (Keywood 2001b: 193). More than this, their bodies cause them to be 'naturally' vulnerable or sexually voracious (Keywood 2001b: 191). This crude reduction of learning disabled people to a set of embodied traits means that their emotional and sexual interests go unrepresented in the law (Keywood 2001a: 29). Still less are they considered worthy of representing these interests themselves. As was noted above, clinical opinion remains the privileged source of knowledge about the bodies and, therefore, the best interests of learning disabled people. This systemic misrepresentation also has the practical consequence of facilitating, if not positively mandating, intrusive and risky surgical procedures upon them, such as sterilization and contraceptive implantation.

Keywood's work has notable rhetorical and pragmatic affinities with that of Grear, discussed above. She too frames the problems of the law and the tasks of the critic in terms of visibility: the courts are guilty of 'obfuscation' in this area, relying as they do on a medicalized 'picture' of human bodies (2001b: 185, 193); pressing social and ethical questions are 'obscured' from consideration (2001a: 28); the processes whereby legal subjects are sexed need to be 'unmasked' (2001a: 34). She too proposes an institutional shift in order to compensate for the law's representational inadequacies. Decision making in this area could be displaced from the formal legal system to dedicated tribunals, specifically composed of health care professionals and patient advocates, as well as lawyers (Keywood 2001a: 33).[64] Experience with such tribunals in other jurisdictions suggests that they have the potential to ensure that the individual 'remains at the heart of the decision-making process and is not excluded from it because of mental incapacity' (Keywood 2000: 508). This would accommodate the 'plurality of accounts of disability', allowing the law to produce a more plausible and detailed image of its complex social environment (Keywood 2000: 508).

Conclusion

The pattern of developments in the law on abortion and on the sterilization of incompetent adults identified in the foregoing discussion indicates that paradoxes are far from being simply technical problems, quietly impelling legal evolution (Stäheli 2000: 273). Rather, they constitute points of entry for political struggle in law and, thus, a focus for multiple strategies 'to establish and re-establish the terms and arrangements of social life' (Buckel 2007: 45–46; Hutchinson 2000: 173). Radical dissent and broader societal change clearly represent moments in these struggles. However, as critical legal scholars have argued, even routine doctrinal debates are unavoidably a matter of political contestation.[65] The persuasiveness of these interventions and of the distinctions and displacements which they propose commonly depends on their resonance with broader social arrangements. Thus, the deferral to clinical judgement established by the Abortion Act 1967 was consistent with a broader pattern of professional autonomy within the post-war welfare state. It would be wrong, however, to see these specific legal developments as simple reflexes of a fixed, underlying social structure. For one thing, the social context is itself composed of the multiple deparadoxifications and reparadoxifications of other social systems (e.g. medicine, the economy, science), themselves equally contingent and equally rhetorical.[66] For another, as I argued in Chapter 1, legal developments and arguments around them actively contribute to the rise and decline of specific contexts. Feminist critiques which emphasized choice and contingency in abortion law can be seen as 'provocatively doubting the plausibilities' of the Keynesian settlement.[67] They have, as I suggested, made a contribution, however unintended, to the plausibilities of the current neo-liberal dispensation.[68]

Change in medical law needs to be understood as both limited by and contributing to the ecological dominance of the capitalist economy. However, it must also be recognized that it is the venue for a diverse range of social conflicts over exclusions based on gender, sexuality, nationality and capacity, for example, as well as class. The politics of medical law are plural. They cannot be read off from some master-script.[69] They can only be observed in the ceaseless and varied practice of legal argumentation itself. Developing a rhetoric of medical law will depend on the ability to apprehend these doctrinal and representational struggles in their specificity. What is required is a combined mode of social and cultural criticism which is sensitive to the varied contexts of medical law, but which does not lose sight of broader patterns of change. In the next chapter, I will elaborate and refine the model of rhetorical analysis set out thus far through investigating the rise and fall of the national space of the United Kingdom as a topic of medical law.

Notes

1 See the sources discussed in Montgomery (2000, 2006).
2 See Kennedy (1988: 385–413).
3 [1957] 1 WLR 582 (at 587).
4 See, for example, Kennedy (1983: 125) and McLean (1999: 20).
5 These labels are mine.
6 [1986] 1 AC 112 (CA & HL). The *Gillick* case is discussed in more detail in Chapter 4.
7 For examples, see Miola (2007: 79, 185).

8   [1993] Fam 64 (CA).

9   Ibid. (CA at 79).

10 Ibid. (CA at 79).

11 For example, the likelihood of patient regaining capacity (s 4(3)); their past and present wishes (s 4(6)(a)); their beliefs and values (s 4(6)(b)); the views of caretakers (s 4(7)(a)).

12 See further, Philippopoulos-Mihalopoulos (2010: 59–65).

13 See generally, Luhmann (1993: 165ff.); for an introduction, see King and Thornhill (2003).

14 This position is memorably argued in Walter Benjamin's 'Critique of Violence' (in 2007: 277–300); see also Rogowski (1994).

15 On legal deconstruction, see Davies (1996). On the similarities and differences between the two approaches, see Teubner (2006).

16 For other examples, see Perez (2006: 20–22); Suber (1990: 12–14, 197–199).

17 See further Suber (1990: 241ff.).

18 See Fletcher (1985).

19 See further Philippopoulos-Mihalopoulos (2010: 65).

20 The chief sources are, respectively, *Gillick v West Norfolk and Wisbech Area Health Authority* [1986] 1 AC 112 (CA & HL) and the Family Law Reform Act 1969, s 8.

21 *Gillick v West Norfolk and Wisbech Area Health Authority* [1986] 1 AC 112 (CA & HL per Lord Fraser at 171; Lord Scarman at 182).

22 The idea of progress in law is discussed in more detail in Chapter 7.

23 *Gillick v West Norfolk and Wisbech Area Health Authority* [1986] 1 AC 112 (CA & HL at 183). This aspect of Lord Scarman's judgment is explored more fully in Chapter 4.

24 As Stäheli points out, the 'rhetoricity' of language is relatively neglected in Luhmann's work on the legal system (2000: 150).

25 [1995] 1 WLR 898 (CA).

26 See Goodrich (1999: 212).

27 On this function of style, see Jameson (1981: 29).

28 This theoretical framework is laid out and applied convincingly to the law on 'parental alienation syndrome' in King (2002).

29 For example, the 'clinical truths' adopted by the English legal system find no exact parallel in the clinical literature on anorexia nervosa (Keywood 2003: 612).

30 See Chapter 4 for more substantial discussion of PVS cases.

31 [1993] AC 789 (FamD, CA & HL).

32 For a review of *Bland* and subsequent cases, as well as the relevant secondary literature, see Pattinson (2009: 536–543).

33 See, respectively, Mason and Laurie (2006: 594–596); Finnis (1993); Pattinson (2009: 557); and Keown (1997).

34 For example, see the essays collected in Sheldon and Thomson (1998).

35 See Benjamin (2007: 233).

36 This is further discussed in Chapter 3.

37 The Mental Capacity Act 2005 offers a good example of such innovation. It provides inter alia that incompetent persons be encouraged and enabled to participate in any treatment decision concerning them (s 4(4)) and that their past and present wishes and feelings be ascertained and considered (s 4(6)).

38 See Fischer-Lescano and Christensen (2012: 110).

39 For a criticism of Teubner's approach in this respect, see Goodrich (1999: 203).

40 See Stäheli (2000: 221).

41 See *Royal College of Nursing v Department of Health and Social Security* [1981] AC 800 (HL).

42 *R v Smith* [1974] 1 All ER 376 (CA).

43 'Rights talk' here refers to the pervasive presentation of the issues in abortion in terms of a conflict between the rights of the mother and those imputed to the foetus, as well as the tendency to frame the interests of the father in a similar manner.

44 *R v Smith* [1974] 1 All ER 376 (CA per Scarman LJ at 381); *Paton v British Pregnancy Advisory Service Trustees* [1979] QB 276 (QB per Sir George Baker P at 281).

45 See Benjamin (2007: 234).

46 On the 'author' as rhetorical effect, see Booth (1983: 71).

47 See Lakoff and Johnson (1980: 48).

48 The term 'patient' as used here refers to such individuals in the context of the proposed sterilization procedure, rather than to the fact of their disability itself.

49 [1988] AC 199 (HL). *Re B* concerned a 17-year-old woman. The approach to sterilization taken there was extended to adult patients in *F v West Berkshire Health Authority* [1990] 2 AC 1 (HL). For a critical consideration of *F*, see Shaw (1990).

50 This contrasted sharply with the principled approach of the Canadian Supreme Court in *Re Eve* (1987) 31 DLR (4d) 1 (SCC).

51 *Re B (A Minor) (Wardship: Sterilisation)* [1988] AC 199 (HL per Lord Hailsham at 204).

52 *Re W (Mental Patient) (Sterilisation)* [1993] 1 FLR 381 (Hollis J).

53 See Lee and Morgan (1988: 231–232) and Freeman (1988).

54 274 US 200 (1927).

55 This purpose is expressed in Wendell Holmes CJ's frequently cited comment that 'Three generations of imbeciles are enough': *Buck v Bell*, 274 US 200, 207 (1927). On the historical background to the case, see Lombardo (1986).

56 [2000] 1 FLR 549 (CA).

57 [2001] Fam 15 (CA).

58 This formulation is taken from *Re S (Adult Patient: Sterilisation)* [2001] Fam 15 (CA per Butler-Sloss LJ at 28).

59 These decisions pre-date the coming into force of the Mental Capacity Act 2005. Their extension of 'best interests' beyond the purely medical is reflected in the terms of s 4 of the Act. This sets out the factors to be considered when decisions are made on behalf of persons who lack capacity.

60 See further Fletcher, Fox and McCandless (2008).

61 The relevant English law is reviewed in Pattinson (2009: 454–460). This point is discussed further in Chapter 4.

62 For a review of the interaction between the law and medicine of end of life, informed by systems theory, see Lavi (2006).

63 See Gurnham (2009: 157ff.).

64 The implications of this proposal are more fully developed by Keywood (2000) in the related context of anorexia nervosa.

65 For example, see Hutchinson (2000: 167–178).

66 See Jessop (1990: 320–335).

67 See Teubner (2006: 53).

68 See generally Jameson (1997) and Jessop (2000).

69 See Fischer-Lescano and Christensen (2012: 110).

References

Bauch, J (1996) *Gesundheit als sozialer Code. Von der Vergesellschaftung des Gesundheits-wesens zur Medikalisierung der Gesellschaft* (Weinheim, Juventa).

Benjamin, W (2007) *Reflections* (New York, Schocken).

Booth, WC (1983) *The Rhetoric of Fiction*, 2nd edition (Chicago, Chicago University Press).

Buckel, S (2007) *Subjektivierung und Kohäsion. Zur Rekonstruktion einer materialistischen Theorie des Rechts* (Weilerswist, Velbrück).

Butler, J (1990) *Gender Trouble. Feminism and the Subversion of Identity* (New York, Routledge).

Cain, M (1976) 'Necessarily Out of Touch: Thoughts on the Social Organization of the Bar', 23 *Sociological Review Monograph* 226.

Clam, J (2006) 'The Reference of Paradox: Missing Paradoxity as Real Perplexity in Both Systems Theory and Deconstruction', in O Perez and G Teubner (eds), *Paradoxes and Inconsistencies in the Law* (Oxford, Hart) 77.

Davies, M (1996) *Delimiting the Law. 'Postmodernism' and the Politics of Law* (London, Pluto).

Finnis, J (1993) '*Bland*: Crossing the Rubicon?', 109 *Law Quarterly Review* 329.

Fischer-Lescano, A and R Christensen (2012) '*Auctoritatis Interpretatio*: How Systems Theory Deconstructs Decisionism', 21 *Social and Legal Studies* 93.

Fitzpatrick, P (2001) *Modernism and the Grounds of Law* (Cambridge, Cambridge University Press).

Fletcher, GP (1985) 'Paradoxes in Legal Thought', 85 *Columbia Law Review* 1263.

Fletcher, R, M Fox and J McCandless (2008) 'Legal Embodiment: Analysing the Body of Healthcare Law', 16 *Medical Law Review* 321.

Freeman, MDA (1988) 'Sterilising the Mentally Handicapped', in MDA Freeman (ed.), *Medicine, Ethics and the Law* (London, Stevens) 55.

Goodrich, P (1986) *Reading the Law. A Critical Introduction to Legal Method and Techniques* (Oxford, Blackwell).

Goodrich, P (1996) *Law in the Courts of Love* (London, Routledge).

Goodrich, P (1999) 'Anti-Teubner: Autopoiesis, Paradox and the Theory of Law', 13 *Social Epistemology* 197.

Grear, A (2004) 'The Curate, A Cleft Palate and Ideological Closure in the Abortion Act 1967: Time to Reconsider the Relationship between Doctors and the Abortion Decision', [Online] 4 *Web Journal of Current Legal Issues*. Available at: www.bailii.org/uk/other/journals/WebJCLI/2004/issue4/grear4.html [Accessed: 30 September 2015].

Gurnham, D (2009) *Memory, Imagination, Justice. Intersections of Law and Literature* (Aldershot, Hampshire, Ashgate).

Harris, J (1994) *The Value of Life: An Introduction to Medical Ethics* (London, Routledge).

Hutchinson, AC (2000) *It's All in the Game. A Non-Foundationalist Account of Law and Adjudication* (Durham, NC, Duke University Press).

Jameson, F (1981) *The Political Unconscious. Narrative as Socially Symbolic Act* (London, Routledge).

Jameson, F (1997) 'Culture and Finance Capitalism', 24 *Critical Inquiry* 246.

Jameson, F (1998) *Brecht and Method* (London, Verso).

Jessop, B (1990) *State Theory. Putting the Capitalist State in its Place* (Cambridge, Polity).

Jessop, B (2000) 'The Crisis of the National Spatio-Temporal Fix and the Tendential Ecological Dominance of Globalizing Capitalism', 24 *International Journal of Urban and Regional Research* 323.

Kennedy, I (1983) *The Unmasking of Medicine* (London, Granada).

Kennedy, I (1988) *Treat Me Right. Essays in Medical Law and Ethics* (Oxford, Clarendon).

Keown, J (1988) *Abortion, Doctors and the Law* (Cambridge, Cambridge University Press).

Keown, J (1997) 'Restoring Moral and Intellectual Shape to the Law after Bland', 113 *Law Quarterly Review* 482.

Keywood, K (2000) 'My Body and Other Stories: Anorexia Nervosa and the Legal Politics of Embodiment', 9 *Social and Legal Studies* 495.

Keywood, K (2001a) 'Disabling Sex: Some Legal Thinking about Sterilization, Learning Disability and Embodiment', in A Morris and S Nott (eds), *Well Women. The Gendered Nature of Health Care Provision* (Aldershot, Hampshire, Ashgate) 21.

Keywood, K (2001b) ' "I'd Rather Keep Him Chaste": Retelling the Story of Sterilisation, Learning Disability and (Non)-Sexed Embodiment', 9 *Feminist Legal Studies* 185.

Keywood, K (2003) 'Rethinking the Anorexic Body: How English Law and Psychiatry "Think" ', 26 *International Journal of Law and Psychiatry* 599.

King, M (2002) 'An Autopoietic Approach to the Problems Presented by "Parental Alienation Syndrome" ', 13 *Journal of Forensic Psychiatry* 609.

King, M and C Thornhill (2003) *Niklas Luhmann's Theory of Politics and Law* (London, Palgrave).

Knudsen, M (2007) 'Structural Couplings between Organizations and Function Systems: Looking at Standards in Health Care', 14 *Cybernetics and Human Knowing* 111.

Kopfsguter, K (2006) 'Gesundheit in der Weltgesellschaft. Von der Globalisierung eines Funktionssytems', in J Bauch (ed.), *Gesundheit als System. Systemtheoretische Beobachtungen des Gesundheitswesens* (Konstanz, Hartung-Gorre Verlag) 101.

Lakoff, G and M Johnson (1980) *Metaphors We Live By* (Chicago, University of Chicago Press).

Lavi, S (2006) 'Autopoiesis, Nihilism and Technique: On Death and the Origins of Legal Paradoxes', in O Perez and G Teubner (eds), *Paradoxes and Inconsistencies in the Law* (Oxford, Hart) 247.

Lee, R and D Morgan (1988) 'Sterilisation and Mental Handicap: Sapping the Strength of the State?', 15 *Journal of Law and Society* 229.

Lombardo, P (1986) 'Three Generations, No Imbeciles. New Light on *Buck v Bell*', 60 *New York University Law Review* 30.

Luhmann, N (1993) *Das Recht der Gesellschaft* (Frankfurt-am-Main, Suhrkamp).

McLean, S (1999) *Old Law, New Medicine. Medical Ethics and Human Rights* (London, Pandora).

Mason, JK and GT Laurie (2006) *Mason and McCall Smith's Law and Medical Ethics*, 7th edition (Oxford, Oxford University Press).

Miola, J (2007) *Medical Law and Medical Ethics. A Symbiotic Relationship* (Oxford, Hart).

Montgomery, J (2000) 'Time for a Paradigm Shift? Medical Law in Transition', 53 *Current Legal Problems* 363.

Montgomery, J (2006) 'Law and the Demoralisation of Medicine', 26 *Legal Studies* 185.

Murphy, WT (1997) *The Oldest Social Science? Configurations of Law and Modernity* (Oxford, Clarendon Press).

Pattinson, S (2009) *Medical Law and Ethics*, 2nd edition (London, Sweet & Maxwell).

Perez, O (2006) 'Law in the Air: A Prologue to the World of Legal Paradoxes', in O Perez and G Teubner (eds), *Paradoxes and Inconsistencies in the Law* (Oxford, Hart) 3.

Philippopoulos-Mihalopoulos, A (2010) *Niklas Luhmann. Law, Justice, Society* (London, Routledge).

Přibáň, J (1999) *Dissidents of Law. On the 1989 Velvet Revolutions, Legitimations, Fictions of Legality and Contemporary Version of the Social Contract* (Aldershot, Hampshire, Ashgate).

Rogowski, R (1994) 'The Paradox of Law and Violence: Modern and Postmodern Readings of Benjamin's "Critique of Violence"', 18 *New Comparison* 131.

Shaw, J (1990) 'Sterilisation of Mentally Handicapped People: Judges Rule OK?', 53 *Modern Law Review* 91.

Sheldon, S (1997) *Beyond Control: Medical Power and Abortion Law* (London, Pluto).

Sheldon S and M Thomson (eds) (1998) *Feminist Perspectives on Health Care Law* (London, Cavendish).

Stäheli, U (2000) *Sinnzusammenbrüche. Eine dekonstruktive Lektüre von Niklas Luhmanns Systemtheorie* (Weilerswist, Velbrück).

Suber, P (1990) *The Paradox of Self-Amendment. A Study of Logic, Law, Omnipotence and Change* (New York, Peter Lang).

Teubner, G (1990) '"And God Laughed": Indeterminacy, Self-Reference and Paradox in Law', 7 *Stanford Literature Review* 15.

Teubner, G (1997) 'The King's Many Bodies: The Self-Deconstruction of Law's Hierarchy', 31 *Law and Society Review* 763.

Teubner, G (2006) 'Dealing with Paradoxes of Law: Derrida, Luhmann, Wiethölter', in O Perez and G Teubner (eds), *Paradoxes and Inconsistencies in the Law* (Oxford, Hart) 41.

Thomson, M (2008) *Endowed. Regulating the Male Sexed Body* (New York, Routledge).

Veitch, K (2007) *The Jurisdiction of Medical Law* (Aldershot, Hampshire, Ashgate).

Vogd, W (2002) 'Professionalisierungsschub oder Auflösung ärztlicher Autonomie: die Bedeutung von Evidence-Based Medicine unter der neuen funktionalen Eliten in der Medizin aus system- und interaktionstheoretischer Perspektive', 31 *Zeitschrift für Soziologie* 294.

Willett, J (ed.) (1964) *Brecht on Theatre. The Development of an Aesthetic* (New York, Hill and Wang).

Chapter 3

Space

Introduction

The National Health Service held out the promise of a uniform entitlement to health care in case of need across the United Kingdom. In its two dimensions, of national scope and of removing the market from medicine, the Service made a significant contribution to the broader post-war Keynesian settlement. To varying degrees these were also features of health care delivery in many other western countries and, indeed, in newly independent states of the global south (Jessop 2000: 238). As I discussed in Chapter 1, that settlement has been dislodged and replaced by a neo-liberal order. The latter has seen the commodification of health care services across the world under the influence of international economic law and the reforming drive of national elites. This commodification of medicine is manifested in two contradictory tendencies, each of which tends to erode the formerly predominant national dimension of welfare. On the one hand, access is expanded through the creation of cross-border markets benefiting well-resourced patients (Chanda 2002). On the other hand, access is restricted through the global strengthening of monopoly patent rights over essential drugs ('t Hoen 2002). Both tendencies generate pressure for mobility, though this is differentially realized in practice. 'Health tourism' from rich to poor countries, or as between rich countries, is encouraged as a means of reducing the burden on domestic systems and as an invisible export for the receiving nation. World trade law is devoted to assisting this sort of population movement (Arnold 2005). The health catastrophe unfolding among the majority of the world's population equally encourages migration in search of treatment from poor to rich countries (Aginam 2000). However, this movement is resisted by an extensive legal and security apparatus at the frontiers of the developed world.

These developments in health care have been reflected in the changing caseload of national courts. In Britain, as I discussed in Chapter 1, legal challenges to the allocation of resources within the NHS were common from the mid-1970s on (Newdick 2005: 98–100). The decisions in these cases presumed a territorially bounded health system over which Parliament was sovereign. By contrast, the last 15 years or so have seen an increase in patients seeking to travel abroad for health care which is either not funded or prohibited by law in the United Kingdom (Newdick 2006). Equally incomers to Britain have challenged adverse immigration and asylum decisions on the basis that their most basic health needs would otherwise go unmet (Boseley 2008). The courts have strained to apply common law and statute, as well as the relevant provisions of European Union and European human rights law, in the resolution of these cases.

While an explication of these decisions in terms of legal doctrine is of great practical importance to lawyers, litigants and policy makers, my objective here is somewhat different. I wish to refine and apply the rhetorical pattern of analysis set out in the previous chapters to examine the manner in which these struggles over access to care have been conducted and to link them to their broader political and economic context. In particular, I am concerned to investigate judicial representations of the changing global geography of health care. Put briefly I will propose that the territory of the United Kingdom itself has functioned as an implicit assumption or topic of medical law in the manner set out in Chapter 1 and defended in Chapter 2. It operated to deparadoxify the law's decision making by bestowing an air of naturalness on the distinctions drawn in, and deferrals characteristic of, this field. But I will go on to argue that that topic has lost much of its plausibility as a result of 'hard core' processes of globalization set out above, as well as 'dissenting' or humanitarian criticism of migration policy. These have tended to undermine the plausibility of the nation state and to reparadoxify medical law to this extent.

In seeking to clarify the tensions and shifts in judicial reasoning manifest in more recent 'mobility' cases, I will elaborate more fully some of the elements of rhetoric set out in Chapter 1 and defended as a mode of reading medical law there and in Chapter 2. As I noted, these offer tools for analysing the strategic dimensions of judicial speech and linking it to its changing social and economic contexts. My investigation takes as its focus the 2005 decision of the House of Lords in *N v Secretary of State for the Home Department.*[1] Their Lordships ruled in that case that a failed asylum seeker infected with HIV could not challenge her deportation, even though this would result in the effective cessation of life-sustaining treatment. Given its pedigree, this decision is of great formal importance within the British legal system. But, as is clear, it also influences the prospects and behaviour of individuals and institutions in the rest of the world. The House of Lords can, thus, be seen as a 'node' within an emerging network of global health governance, which includes courts, governments, companies, international bodies and non-governmental organizations in different locations (Burris *et al.* 2004; Dodgson *et al.*

2002). The power of such nodes lies not only in their capacity to compel certain behaviours, but also in the development of more or less legitimate rhetorics as regards global health problems (Braithwaite and Drahos 2000).

The chapter is arranged as follows. In the next section I consider in detail the facts and reasoning of the House of Lords in *N*, which were subsequently confirmed by the European Court of Human Rights. The following sections focus on the modes of proof or what might be called the 'means of persuasion' in rhetoric elaborated by Aristotle and others. As well as the substance of the argument, these include the emotions evoked in the audience by the speaker, and the positive character traits of the speaker which might sway an audience. The rhetorical force of each of these modes of proof, individually and in combination, depends on the local and historical context within which they are deployed. In order to set the context for the manner in which the different modes of proof were deployed in *N*, I draw on work in human geography to show the importance of state policies and institutions in 'producing' national space, materially and culturally. I note in particular how the NHS made a profound contribution to the achievement of a British space and the creation of a nationally defined, Keynesian common sense regarding health care entitlements from the late 1940s. I will then argue that more recent, neoliberal reforms, as well as the broader trends already mentioned, mean that the national scale is no longer wholly predominant in the organization and representation of health care delivery in Britain. The judgments in *N* are then considered from this perspective. It will be seen that the national scale of health-care entitlement was deployed to check *N*'s cross-border quest for therapy. However, what was previously implicit now had to be openly asserted by judges, under scrutiny, not just from the rest of the legal community, but also from activists, the media and the general public. Moreover, as with Lord Bingham in *R v Cambridge Health Authority, ex parte B*,[2] the House was concerned to contain and displace the emotions raised by the facts of the case in order to secure their own authority and the plausibility of their judgments. I will interpret this rhetorical strategy with reference to Hannah Arendt's distinction between compassion and pity. I argue that their Lordships sought to display an uncontroversial, personal compassion for *N* as an individual, instead of a rather more risky 'politics of pity' directed towards the large group of which *N* was a representative.

Treatment mobility: the decision in *N v Secretary of State for the Home Department*[3]

N concerned a Ugandan national who had sought asylum in Britain in 1998. Ms N had been kidnapped by the insurgent Lord's Resistance Army and held for two years.[4] On being captured by the Ugandan army, she was subjected to rape and further ill treatment. Soon after her arrival in Britain, Ms *N* was diagnosed as HIV positive, having a CD4 cell count of ten; the normal count is 500. She was successfully treated with anti-retroviral drugs, which restored her CD4 cell count to 414. With the therapy, she would remain well for decades; without it she would die in great pain inside two years. Her application for asylum was refused by the Home Secretary. She claimed before an Immigration Appeal Tribunal that deportation would violate her right to freedom from torture and inhuman and degrading treatment under Article 3 of the European Convention on Human Rights (ECHR). In Uganda anti-retroviral therapy was more expensive than she could afford. A terrible death would be the inevitable consequence of her forced return.

The Immigration Appeal Tribunal, Court of Appeal and House of Lords all rejected this claim. Under the Human Rights Act 1998, s 2(1) they were required to take into account the jurisprudence of the European Court of Human Rights in Strasbourg, and in particular its 1997 decision in *D v UK*.[5] There, D successfully invoked Article 3 of the Convention to resist his deportation from Britain to St Kitts. He had entered the final stages of AIDS-related illness. Given the lack of medical facilities in St Kitts, the absence of any family support there, and his residence in a UK hospice, it would amount to inhuman and degrading treatment to return him. The difficult task of distinguishing the facts of *D* from *N*'s case was achieved through a close study of the subsequent Strasbourg jurisprudence.[6] In all except two out of nine cases, an appeal to remain in a Convention state on grounds of mortal medical need under Article 3 had been rejected.[7] The European Court of Human Rights had confined the ratio decidendi of *D v UK* to cover only cases in which the applicant was already terminally ill.[8] By contrast those benefiting from anti-retroviral therapy were invariably in good health at the time of the trial. Though their deportation to a developing country would mean the end of therapy and certain death, they fell outside the facts of *D* and thus also outside the protection of Article 3. These decisions were clearly influenced by the development of (costly) anti-retroviral therapies in the years after *D* was decided (Palmer 2005: 537).

As Laws LJ had held in the Court of Appeal in *N*, the protection afforded in *D v UK* was an 'extension of an extension' of the core meaning of Article 3.[9] The Convention aimed to protect individuals from inhuman and degrading treatment by signatory states. In *Chahal v UK*[10] this had been extended to cover the direct actions of non-signatory states. There a Sikh militant could not be deported from Britain for fear of being tortured on arrival by agents of the Indian state. Article 3 was further extended in *D* to include circumstances of extreme human need caused by no direct state action at either end. In the present case Laws LJ, and a unanimous House of Lords, held that the scope of Article 3 should be confined to this extent. Beyond *D*, there might be 'other exceptional cases, with other extreme facts where the humanitarian considerations are equally compelling'.[11] But the facts in *N* were not of this order. Thousands in a similar position arrive in the UK every year.[12] The reasoning of the House of Lords was subsequently endorsed by a majority of the European Court of Human Rights (ECtHR) which confirmed that there would be no violation of Article 3 by the deportation proposed in *N*'s case.[13]

It is clear that the decision in *N* did not simply unfold from fundamental principles. Rather the conclusion of the House of Lords was arrived at by way of disanalogy. The facts of *N* were held to be insufficiently similar to those in *D* to allow the same rule to be applied in the later case. As I will discuss further in Chapter 6, analogy and disanalogy are familiar forms of legal reasoning (Stone 1965: 478). But they are never logically compelling in and of themselves.[14] This is borne out by the opinion of the ECtHR minority in *N*. For the dissenting judges, the 'practical realities' of the case were that *N* would endure great suffering soon after returning to Uganda.[15] By contrast with the ECtHR majority and the unanimous House of Lords, they held that any difference with *D*'s case was merely superficial.[16] According to Allan Hutchinson's non-foundationalist theory, considered in Chapter 1, a precedent cannot in and of itself determine the outcome to a subsequent case. Nonetheless, the good faith practice of law requires judges and lawyers to 'go through the law' and to make a specific effort to show that their conclusion is plausible with reference to previous decisions and other legal materials (Hutchinson 2000: 170). In doing so, as we saw, they deploy a variety of persuasive strategies historically comprehended within the study of rhetoric.

Modes of proof in rhetoric

Classical writers elaborated a range of persuasive strategies, focusing on the style of delivery, as well as the content and organization of speeches.[17] Many of these were picked out in the review of Lord Bingham MR's decision in *R v Cambridge Health Authority, ex parte B*[18] in Chapter 1. In the present discussion I wish to narrow and deepen my focus, examining in particular the classical 'modes of proof' in rhetoric. Each is deployed as a means of getting the audience to identify with the speaker and her purposes, creating what Kenneth Burke called a relationship of consubstantiality between them (1969: 55). For Aristotle, there were three such forms of persuasion: *logos* (the substance of what is said); *pathos* (the audience's feelings); and *ethos* (the speaker's character) (Aristotle 1991: 75). Their deployment requires an exercise of skill and judgement on the part of the individual speaker. But, as will be seen in this chapter, the means of persuasion available at any given time and place are socially produced. What we are concerned with are shared common sense, shared feelings and shared understandings of authoritative speech. In this section, I will examine briefly each form of proof, considering its specific relevance to medical law reasoning and, more specifically, the decision of the House of Lords in *N*.

In the theory of rhetoric, *logos* refers to the truth, consistency and plausibility of the argument itself (Aristotle 1991: 75; Hollander 1996: 179). Its most important feature, for present purposes, is the topic or commonplace. This has already been put forward in Chapters 1 and 2 as a central element of the rhetorical approach to medical law developed in this book. At this point I will only recall a number of key features relevant to the present discussion. As I noted, the persuasive strength of a given topic depends on its timeliness, its relevance to the matter under discussion and the extent to which the audience addressed identifies with it. These aspects of the topic are influenced by the ecological dominance of the capitalist economy over other social systems. To be more precise, what is 'timely' and 'relevant' in medical law is significantly connected to the manner and extent to which the market is embedded in the wider society. Thus, the strategies for plausibly concealing the law's indeterminacy (i.e. for deparadoxifying its operations) will vary as between Keynesian and neo-liberal phases. Alongside this, however, it is worth noting that the content of a given topic and its resonance are not simply effects of capitalism in its generic form. These are also shaped by its 'dialogic' or intertextual relationship with a much wider range of other legal, literary and cultural sources. The economy exercises ecological dominance only, not the simple determinism proposed by the base–superstructure model. Thus, while a topic such as that of the nation state will be more or less prominent in the rhetoric of a given period, much of its purchase will come precisely from its capacity to evoke pre- or non-capitalist forms e.g. Britain's island nature or its Protestant heritage.

A speaker will use *pathos* in order to evoke emotions, such as pity, envy and rage, in order to gain the approval of the audience (Aristotle 1991: 75). Pity is the most important of these emotions in the present context. According to Aristotle, it is apt to be felt by those who think they might suffer or who have suffered themselves; it responds to the 'great evils for which chance is responsible', such as death and disease (1991: 163). It may be directed towards the speaker herself or a third party referred to in the speech. In either case, its successful evocation depends on there being sufficient proximity and identification as between the audience and the object of its pity. *Pathos* must not be confused with purely subjective emotion. Just as the rhetorical *logos* is made up of shared common sense assumptions, so *pathos* draws upon public emotions and stock responses to specific situations (Barthes 1994: 75). These responses are themselves 'nourished' by a common culture which produces and disseminates images of suffering and appropriate responses to it (Piper 1991: 738–739).

Pathos is not common in judicial rhetoric, which cultivates an air of neutrality and objectivity.[19] However, as was noted in Chapter 1, this is less true of medical law cases, given the pressing questions of life and death which they often raise. In such instances, the court becomes a kind of theatre of human suffering (Marshall 1984). The visible presence of patient litigants helps to furnish the necessary element of immediacy between them and the audience. Indeed, owing to extensive media coverage, the audience for such decisions is unusually wide. Judges are increasingly aware that activists, religious bodies and the general public are listening in on their decisions, so to speak. Moreover, the public emotions likely to be called forth are both particularly intense and well nourished by media representations and interest group publicity. Given this context, judges often develop compensatory rhetorical strategies to contain the *pathos* aroused by the facts of the case at hand. It will be seen that this was an important feature of the reasoning in *N*.

Ethos emphasizes the speaker's status and authority in order to gain the confidence of their audience (Meyer 1999: 10). It is implicit in the distinctive decoration of courtrooms and in the costuming of judges and barristers. It is also produced within the texts of decisions, as a connotation of the phrasing and the figures of speech used (Barthes 2000: 58). Peter Goodrich has demonstrated how many ostensibly redundant usages in legal speech tend to bolster the authority of the court in reaching a particular verdict (1986: 192). Thus, controversial decisions on the withdrawal of medical treatment are often prefaced by 'oratorical definitions' in which the judge states what are fairly obvious limits to her competence, e.g. 'this court is a court of law, not of morals'.[20] Such statements evoke a distinctive judicial character, one associated with careful deliberation and frankness, a sympathetic persona (Cicero 2001: 171). As Barthes puts it, while she speaks the orator must also keep saying, 'follow me … esteem me … and love me' (1994: 74). The specific characteristics (or virtues) valued in a speaker are not always and everywhere the same. As with commonplaces, their persuasive force varies with the form of speech used (e.g. judicial or political), but also as between different historical periods and geographical locations.

In practice, any given argument will involve a 'complex articulation' of all three modes of persuasion (Meyer 1999: 51). Each is prominent in the reasoning of appellate courts. Judges at this level are typically faced with problematic cases, in which a novel interpretation of the common law or statute is sought, or a ruling one way or the other will have significant social and economic consequences. The overall rhetorical effort will have to be commensurate with the novelty of the question. As well as showing mastery of formal legal sources, a judge will deploy imagery, figures of speech and common sense assumptions to reinforce her argument. However, the problematic nature of such cases often reveals that formerly well-established topics are no longer adequate to the task of persuasion. Frank assertions of judicial authority may be used to compensate for this decline in plausibility.[21] A new or alternative common sense may be articulated. Judicial innovation of this sort can also be understood as a form of political deliberation, often involving an appeal to the audience's passions and sense of reasonableness. Medical law cases are particularly prominent in this regard, as they often involve distressing facts and morally controversial issues thrown up by scientific progress and attracting the attention of the general public. *N* was a clear example. Their Lordships deployed elements of *pathos* and *ethos* with some care in order to support their re-assertion of the national frame for health entitlements. In the following section, I consider the social and political origins of this territorially defined common sense and the important role of the NHS in producing it.

The NHS and the production of national space

It was argued above that national territory is an important topic of health care law in Britain. The present section seeks to explain how it achieved this status. The explanation rests on a fundamental insight from human geography, namely that space is socially produced. The arbitrariness of this production is generally naturalized and hidden (Bourdieu 1977). Specific spatial frames are widely shared and acted on, for example, by the population of a given territory. They are taken for granted, offering a common starting point for political and legal argument. However, this obviousness may be lost in times of economic crisis and political conflict. As a result of these struggles, new spaces and new scales are often created, rivalling or replacing existing ones and functioning as topics of a new rhetoric.

Social theorists traditionally assumed that space was a neutral and transparent medium, innocent of politics and history.[22] However, the 'lived-in' space of individuals and human societies cannot be reduced to the timeless, abstract space of mathematics and geometry.[23] As Henri Lefebvre argued, space is actively and continually produced by human intervention (1991: 33). He identified three 'modes of spatialization' (1991: 33). First was the material construction of space in the form of fences, houses, railways, factories and hospitals. This is the world as experienced every day through tactile, sensual interaction with matter. Second was representations of space in maps, plans and statistical tables. This is the world as conceived of or 'read' by engineers, planners and public health specialists. Third was idealizations of space in myths, utopias and arcadias.[24] These are rooted in the emotional history of individuals and peoples. They 'overlay physical space, making symbolic use of its objects' (Lefebvre 1991: 39). These three modes must not be seen as hierarchical. Each interacts with the others (Harvey 2006: 131). Maps and plans decisively shape the built environment. Construction projects can destroy mythic landscapes or create new ones.[25]

In contemporary society, the state plays a central role in each mode of spatialization. State institutions penetrate everyday life, creating the material, cultural and human infrastructure of the capitalist economy, as well as mapping the spaces thus created. The state seizes upon territorial myths and legends, reproducing them as its own (Elden 2004). The figure of the nation is at the heart of this spatialization. As Nicos Poulantzas put it:

> The modern nation ... tends to coincide with the State and acquires flesh and blood in state apparatuses; it becomes the anchorage of state power in society and maps out its contours.
>
> (1978: 99)

The state produces the nation by producing the national territory, not just at the borders, but also within. The school system, transport authorities, the army and the broadcast media are good examples of these 'state apparatuses', which should be understood broadly to include not just public bodies, but commercial and charitable institutions whose work is orchestrated by the state (Poulantzas 1978: 133). National curricula in history and literature, a uniform system of road signage, frontier posts and television weather maps all secure the common sense nature of the national territory (Bourdieu 2000: 97–98). In the rest of this section I will argue that the NHS has also functioned as a state apparatus of this sort, actively producing British national space in the post-war period.

The NHS was created through the merger of innumerable smaller concerns, e.g. voluntary, charitable and local authority hospitals.[26] Local fragmentation was to be replaced by national ownership and regional organization. For example, a 1937 survey of South Wales revealed that 93 municipal hospitals were controlled by 46 local authorities, alongside 48 voluntary hospitals (Webster 2002: 5). Direct lines of accountability would link clinical practice with the Secretary of State himself. In the words of the Service's founder Aneurin Bevan, 'every time a maid kicks over a bucket of slops in a ward an agonised wail will go through Whitehall' (quoted in Foot 1962: 195). Moreover, as I noted at the outset of this chapter, the NHS defined and sought to meet a uniform entitlement to health care across the territory. Under the old system the best hospital facilities were available where they were least needed.[27] Access to care often depended on the location of the patient or their ability to pay (Bevan 1978: 104). Henceforth care would be funded out of general taxation and free at the point of use to all UK residents.

The NHS contributed to the production of the national scale in each of the three modes elaborated by Lefebvre. It created space materially through its standardized infrastructure of hospitals and clinics. It also represented space, in the (only apparently) mundane form of health statistics. These allowed the measurement of health inequality and health improvement across the nation. Public health in Britain long predates 1948. But the creation of the NHS can be seen as a radical extension of the work done by nineteenth-century sanitarians such as Edwin Chadwick (Porter 1997: c.7). Beyond this, in linking solidarity with citizenship, the Service contributed to an idealization of national space. By putting care of the ill ahead of commerce, Britain was at the forefront of civilized nations. As Charles Webster put it, Health Service staff:

> achieved a sense of corporate unity [believing] they were part of a prestigious national service, capable of achieving in peacetime something like the feats of collective action and patriotic sacrifice recently witnessed in the special circumstances of total warfare.
>
> (2002: 29)

This utopian dimension of the NHS will be considered more fully in Chapter 5.

Of course the actual contribution of the NHS to homogenizing national space failed to match the ideal in each of three modes outlined above. Up to 1974, NHS resource allocation tracked the distribution of existing facilities rather than current need (Timmins 2001: 339–341). Health inequalities, closely associated with class and occupation, persisted (Webster 2002: 221). Individual clinical judgment was privileged over more rational forms of resource use, leading to presumed, though often unmeasurable, divergences in health care provision (Newdick 2005: 52–55). The Service was heavily dependent on staff directly recruited from former colonial territories, particularly the Caribbean and South Asia (Doyal 1979: 205–207).

Notwithstanding the shortcomings just discussed, the national scale remained pre-eminent in this period. Uneven and unequal access could only appear as objects of concern against the ideal of a truly 'national' health service. This is evident in the response of English courts to patients seeking judicial review of health care rationing. As discussed in Chapter 1, courts uniformly rejected these applications on grounds of justiciability (Newdick 2005: c.5). They held that allocation of resources at the macro-level was solely a matter for government. At the clinical level, doctors had to decide. The finitude of resources that produced these cases was defined nationally. Thus Stephen Brown LJ, rejecting an attempt to compel the provision of more specialist nurses in a Birmingham hospital, held that:

> This is not the forum in which a court can properly express opinions upon the way in which national resources are allocated or distributed.... The courts of this country cannot arrange the lists in the hospital.[28]

Government and NHS planners were best equipped to decide on general allocation, not courts adjudicating on individual disputes.

The NHS and the crisis of national space

The crisis of the Keynesian system in Britain and through the West, discussed in Chapter 1, was expressed and provisionally resolved through an extended process of rescaling (Harvey 2006). This process is generally comprehended under the label 'globalization'.[29] The neo-liberal order which has replaced the post-war settlement is characterized by the breakdown of the relatively closed national space economy. But, though the national scale has lost its former predominance, no single scale has replaced it as the 'primary pivot' of economic activity, regulation, or socio-political struggle (Brenner and Theodore 2002: 363). The local level has gained in prominence through an internal re-differentiation of national social space. The competitive 'place marketing' of cities is one example (Harvey 1990: 89). So also is the trend to decentralization and micro-autonomy in welfare delivery. Supra-state space has also thickened. Production and service provision are articulated across regional and global scales through outsourcing. To an extent, this is enabled and contained by emerging regulatory regimes, such as the European Union (van Apeldoorn 2003). Scalar denationalization has also been effective in representations of space. The 'global' thus underpins a rhetoric of competitiveness aimed at higher productivity and lower wage costs. This does not mean, however, that the nation has lost all salience. On the contrary, competitiveness can only be promoted through the figure of different nations contesting for investment and employment. The state is profoundly implicated in producing the phenomena of globalization (Wood 2002). Privatization and the 'opening' of national economies, along with international and regional trade law, are all unthinkable without the practical and ideological contribution of governments and official institutions.

The relativization of scales has also been evident in health care. There has been a significant withdrawal of the NHS from its former role in producing British national space. With the spread of autonomous Foundation Trusts and the Private Finance Initiative, the role of the Service in the material construction of space has dwindled.[30] Local innovation and corporate autonomy are used to justify diversity and unevenness. Critics claim that 'reforms' are interfering with the collection of population health data, as well as with mechanisms for ensuring equity of resources (Pollock 2004: 223). Capacity to represent national health space declines accordingly. At sub-national level new scales are called into being through the devolution of health-related powers to Scotland and Wales. As will be seen in the next section, the institutions of the European Union increasingly intervene to create common entitlements to provide and use health care services across the member states.[31] On the ideological plane, the 'national' form of the NHS is routinely disparaged. As will be discussed in Chapter 5, market space, locally heterogeneous, but unbounded by national frontiers, is increasingly cast as the new utopia.

Again it must be noted that national government continues to play a vital role in the production of new health spaces. As with other privatizations, it is engaged as the realtor of its own assets (Whitfield 2001: 74). Moreover some reforms seem to reassert the national scale. For example a dense system of clinical regulation and standard setting has developed since 1997 (Pridmore and Gammon 2007). In England, for example, the Care Quality Commission functions as an inspectorate evaluating and comparing clinical outcomes in NHS facilities across the country.[32] The National Institute for Heath and Care Excellence produces guidelines on the cost-effectiveness of medicines which determine prescription practice throughout the Service.[33] But, if the national has not gone away, it is also true, as I noted above, that it no longer retains the 'taken-for-grantedness' that it had in post-war health care (Jessop 2002: 180). The consequences of these developments for rhetoric and ethics have been diagnosed by Nancy Fraser. She says that:

> Although it went unnoticed at the time, [the Keynesian–national] framework lent a distinctive shape to arguments about social justice. Taking for granted the modern territorial state as the appropriate unit, and its citizens as the pertinent subjects, such arguments turned on what precisely those citizens owe one another.... Today however this framework is losing its aura of self-evidence.
>
> (2005: 76)

This loss of 'obviousness' is a vital context of the reasoning in *N*. In the next section, I explore the contested deployment of the topic of national space in that case. I compare it with a contemporaneous Court of Appeal decision which addressed patient mobility from Britain to other member states of the European Union.

The topic of space in *N*

According to their Lordships, the application in *N* was not primarily a demand to be free from deportation. It was instead an attempt to obtain medical treatment unavailable in her home country.[34] In Lord Hope's words, to allow the appeal:

> would risk drawing into the United Kingdom large numbers of people already suffering from HIV in the hope that they too could remain here indefinitely so that they could take the benefit of the medical resources available in this country. This would result in a very great

and no doubt unquantifiable commitment of resources which it is, to say the least, highly questionable the state parties to the Convention would ever have agreed to.[35]

This reasoning clearly starts from a very specific understanding of space rooted in the common sense of the national territory. Lord Brown offered a more detailed outline of the cost to the UK of *N*'s treatment:

> [a]llowing the patient to remain in the host state to enjoy decades of healthy life at the expense of that state [would constitute] an expense both in terms of the cost of continuing treatment (the medication itself being said … to cost some £7,000 per annum) and any associated welfare benefits, and also in terms of immigration control.[36]

Admittedly, as Baroness Hale noted, *N* was unaware of her HIV status on arriving in Britain. She was not, said her Ladyship:

> a would-be immigrant who came here to benefit from our superior services.[37]

However, though sympathetic, this evaluation is also anchored in a topic of national space, delimiting access to 'our' national medical resources; a territorially defined 'we' which produces and is entitled to health care. This concern with eligibility was raised in the well-known case of *Re A (Conjoined Twins: Surgical Separation).*[38] There Ward LJ felt obliged to reassure his readers and auditors that the parents were not 'Kosovan refugees unjustifiably draining our resources'.[39] It is this Keynesian common sense, rearticulated in the face of a deterritorialized attempt to access care, that defeats the analogy *N* had sought to draw between her case and that of *D v UK*. Lord Nicholls was explicit about this:

> The essential difference [between the two cases] is not to be found in humanitarian differences. Rather it lies in recognising that article 3 does not require contracting states to undertake the obligation of providing aliens indefinitely with medical treatment lacking in their home countries.[40]

Selectively deployed, the national scale remains pertinent even (perhaps especially) under pressure of increasing global mobility.

This anxiety to secure the national frontier was reproduced by the ECtHR in *N*'s case. The majority held that:

> a search for a fair balance between the demands of the general interest of the community and the requirements of the protection of

the individual's fundamental rights was inherent to the whole Convention.[41]

Advances in medical science, as well economic differences between regions of the world, meant that the level of treatment available could differ greatly depending on location. But Article 3 of the ECHR did not place an obligation on states to alleviate such disparities.[42] Interestingly, the dissenting judges in the Strasbourg court were equally concerned with the 'floodgate' argument. They sought, however, to show that it did not apply in this case. They quoted from UK asylum and immigration statistics to show that a humane decision in *N*'s favour would not lead to Europe becoming 'the sickbay of the world'.[43]

N concerns migration from the global south to the global north. Its assertion of the 'national' can be compared with the response of English courts to the movement of patients within the European Union just a few years previously. In *Secretary of State for Health v R (on the application of Watts)*[44] a patient was seeking NHS funding to travel to France for a hip-replacement operation. The European Court of Justice has long held that the freedom to provide services across borders guaranteed by the European law implies a freedom on the part of the consumer to travel to receive services in another country.[45] Mrs Watts argued that, where such services are funded by welfare agencies at home, there is a duty on governments to fund 'health tourism' in such cases. The court had already found such a duty where a patient could not be offered treatment at home 'within the time normally necessary for obtaining it'.[46] The point at issue in *Watts* was whether national NHS waiting times would exclusively determine 'the time normally necessary for obtaining' treatment. The Court of Appeal suspected that they would not. It referred the case to the European Court of Justice for a clarification of European law under Article 234 of the European treaty. In making the referral, May LJ noted the likely significance of such a finding for the NHS. Its effect would be to:

> disrupt NHS budgets and planning and undermine any system of orderly waiting lists.... [Furthermore] if the NHS were required to pay the costs of some of its patients having treatment abroad at a time earlier than they would receive it in the United Kingdom this would require additional resources.[47]

Since waiting lists were a product of scarce resources, this extra funding could only be obtained if:

> those who did not have treatment abroad received their treatment at a later time than they otherwise would or if the NHS ceased to provide some treatments that it currently does provide.[48]

May LJ's fears were confirmed when the European Court of Justice subsequently upheld Mrs Watts's claim.[49] In the language of political economy used above, we can say that the European market scale triumphed over the Keynesian national scale in Watts, as it was bound to do, given the constitutional priority of European economic law over national law.[50]

The politics of pity

Pathos plays an important role in their Lordships' speeches in *N*. However, it was not deployed directly as a means of gaining the audience's sympathy for *N* herself. To do so would have undermined the topic of national space reasserted by the House and thus, also, the decision to refuse her application to remain in the UK. Nonetheless, as discussed above, the facts of medical law cases often evoke pity or even anger, for example, at the behaviour of medical professionals or the law's failure to offer relief to the patient. Furthermore, these intense feelings are likely to be widespread, given the high profile of such cases. As a result, *pathos* figures less as a positive strategy and more as a risk to be contained in judicial rhetoric. The nature of that risk can be explored with reference to Hannah Arendt's work on the history of revolutionary politics.

Arendt based her views on certain differences between the American and French Revolutions. The aim of the former was to liberate individual men from tyranny; the aim of the latter was to free 'the life process itself from the fetters of scarcity' (1973: 64). She traced the immensely greater level of violence which followed the French Revolution to this difference. After 1789 mass poverty was no longer simply a matter of fate and an object of charity. Its elimination became the central moral purpose of political change, taken up by thinkers and revolutionaries over the following two centuries. Arendt offered a trenchant critique of this 'politics of pity'.[51] She argued that the great cruelty unleashed by the 'social' revolutions was precisely due to their instrumentalization of sentiment for political ends. Boundless misery led first to boundless sympathy and then to boundless coercion in the attempt to eliminate it. 'Pity-inspired virtue ... played havoc with justice and made light of laws' (Arendt 1973: 90). The American revolutionaries, by contrast, had ignored social issues and avoided political sentiment.[52] Consequently, 'nothing was permitted' to them 'that would have been outside the range of civil law' (Arendt 1973: 92).

The risks presented by *pathos* to the House of Lords in *N* derived from just such a combination of politics and pity. Admittedly these were not of the same magnitude as the conflagration anticipated by Arendt, writing at the height of the Cold War. Rather, they can be characterized as threats to the orderly functioning of the court and its sense of itself within the wider constitutional system. Though differing in intensity, they too can be seen to undermine legality and authority. For one thing, the strong feelings associated with *pathos* are held to be incompatible with objective deliberation. They lead to a 'disproportion' in judgment which favours prominent over more needy cases (Boltanski 1993: 27). For another, such applications offer a rallying point for social causes, whose prosecution would 'politicize' the work of the court, taking it well beyond its official task of adjudication. In the rest of this section, I seek to show how the politics of pity were an important feature of *N*.

Luc Boltanski offers an insightful application of Arendt's thought in the context of contemporary humanitarian campaigns. Drawing on this work, it is possible to elaborate three key preconditions of a politics of pity.

- 'The need for a face'. Generalized presentation of a problem such as the global AIDS pandemic is not likely to move audiences in the developed world. Statistics do not speak; they do not evoke feelings of pity (Boltanski 1993: 57). The engagement of spectators requires the visible presence of an identifiable, individual victim.
- 'Exemplarity'. There has to be a sufficient connection between the plight of the individual victim and the general problem. Though identified in her uniqueness, the victim must also be seen to be typical of the mass of sufferers (Boltanski 1993: 28). Only thus will any subsequent intervention qualify as political.
- 'Meaningful action'. The intervention of the spectator to relieve suffering requires a medium of assistance (e.g. money) and an institutional vehicle for action (e.g. the banking system). However, these are abstract and impersonal forms, tending to distance the spectator from the individual victim and 'swallow up' their beneficent intervention. Accordingly, the action taken has to be shown to be effective in specific cases, as well as responding to the broader problem (Boltanski 1993: 35).

Charities concerned with development and disaster relief attempt to meet these preconditions in their campaigning. They focus on named locations typical of a region or part of the world. For example, donors are encouraged to 'adopt' a child in an African village who subsequently corresponds with them.[53] Legal decision making cannot be straightforwardly equated with charitable campaigning. Nonetheless it is clear that each of the foregoing preconditions is met in *N* and cases like it.

- 'The need for a face'. As Tim Murphy has argued, the common law differs from other social sciences precisely through its reliance on individual disputes, rather than statistics, as a means of generating knowledge about the world (1997: 116). Thus, in *N* a detailed recitation of the painful facts of the case preceded and informed the doctrinal analysis. But more than that a particular victim was brought before the court in person. As classical writers on rhetoric noted, physical objects and the human body itself could be sources of *pathos*, as much as words (Cicero 2001: 175; Quintilian 2001: 355).

- 'Exemplarity'. For Lord Nicholls, *N*'s case as a would-be immigrant 'is far from unique.... The prevalence of AIDS worldwide, particularly in Southern Africa, is a present-day human tragedy on an immense scale'.[54]

Moreover, techniques of legal reasoning meant that *N* was reconfigured in general terms: first as an asylum seeker fleeing persecution in Uganda; and then as an applicant for relief under Article 3 of the European Convention on Human Rights. As such she stood in for a much broader class of victim.

- 'Meaningful action'. The process of abstraction just described means that decisions in such cases have (a potentially broad) precedential value. At the same time, however, a positive outcome to adjudication also confers a concrete benefit on a recognizable individual.

Thus, several important features of litigation and the legal form itself mean that a case such as *N*'s has the potential to convert the court into a 'theatre' for the politics of pity, as discussed above. 'Theatre' can be understood here in two senses:[55] first, as a stage for the display of human suffering and the evocation of sympathy in members of the audience (Marshall 1984); second, since the spectacle cannot be perceived neutrally, the court becomes a venue for global political struggles. It can be presumed that members of the House of Lords were aware of the broader ongoing politics of pity engaged in by many charities and campaigning journalists. The facts of *N*'s case formed part of this wider spectacle of suffering. As such they threatened the court's functioning as an ostensibly depoliticized zone of adjudication. In the next section I seek to show how the court addressed this risk by marginalizing the politics of pity.

Beyond pity

There are four main ways in which the House of Lords sought to pre-empt the politics of pity in *N*. First, they sought the sympathy of the audience for their own plight as decision makers. Second, they suggested that the broader issues of access to essential medicines represented by the case were better addressed by bureaucratic, than by individualized, means. Third, they emphasized the capacity of the executive to refrain from exercising its power to deport. Fourth, they substituted compassion for pity as an appropriate response to the plight of the applicant.

Ethos: sympathy for the judge

In a straightforward deployment of *ethos*, Lord Hope offered a negative oratorical definition of the tasks and competence of the court:

> The function of a judge in a case of this kind ... is not to issue decisions based on sympathy.... [T]hey must not allow their decisions to be influenced by feelings of revulsion or sympathy, judges must examine the law in a way that suppresses emotion of all kinds. The position that they must adopt is an austere one.[56]

This seeks to bolster the status of the court, by relegating argument in the pathetic mode to the margins of the decision. Similarly, Baroness Hale stated that she could not allow the appeal, 'much though [she] would like to do so'.[57] The question for the court, she said, is:

> How are we to distinguish between the sad cases where we must harden our hearts and the even sadder cases where to do so would be inhumane?[58]

As was seen in the case of Lord Bingham MR's judgment in *R v Cambridge Health Authority, ex parte B*[59] in Chapter 1, an authoritative, reasoned decision would be reached in the face of the very difficult facts of the case. To reinforce the point, Lord Hope invoked the well-worn image of judges weighing and balancing:

> [T]he fact is that there are at least two sides to any argument. The consequences if the decision goes against the appellant cannot sensibly be detached from the consequences if it is in her favour.[60]

The court in other words would not allow itself to be overwhelmed by feeling. As has been mentioned, such obvious rhetorical bids for authority are often made in novel or controversial cases. The judicial speaker is forced to address an audience that is wider than usual, including sections of the mass public as well as the legal professionals and fellow judges (Goodrich 1986: 199).

The language of feeling is not absent from *N*. On the contrary it is to be found in all of the judgments. Lord Nicholls accepted that the facts:

> encompass much human misery. No one can fail to be touched by the plight of the appellant and of others in a similar position. The prospect facing them if returned to their home country evokes a lasting sense of deep sadness.[61]

These comments seem at first glance to be aimed at evoking sympathy for the applicant. However, on closer inspection it can be observed that ethos, rather than *pathos*, is the true mode of persuasion here too. In vivid, figurative terms, Lord Nicholls recounts the facts of the case and the probable consequences of deportation:

> The cruel reality is that ... if she returns to Uganda and cannot obtain the medical assistance she needs to keep her illness under control, her position will be similar to having life support switched off.[62]

This demonstrates that the judge accepts the very difficult nature of the case, and is not reluctant to convey this difficulty to his audience ('esteem me'). Moreover a judge who is not afraid to face these facts is one who can be trusted to reach a prudent decision in the case ('follow me'). Lord Hope concluded on a similar note by avowing that he would 'resist the temptation to remit this case for further consideration of the facts'.[63] The final character-based proof is the sympathy evoked for the judge faced with a tragic choice such as this. Like the members of his audience, he is a man of feeling, appropriately troubled by the consequences of his decision ('love me'). In effect the audience's feelings for *N* are redirected towards the judges here in order to bolster its sense of the court's authority.

A bureaucratic alternative

According to Lord Hope, rather than drawing a large number of HIV sufferers into the UK in quest of treatment, the:

> better course ... would be for states to continue to concentrate their efforts on the steps which are currently being taken, with the assistance of drug companies, to make the necessary medical care universally and freely available in the countries of the third world.[64]

This presents a second alternative to an open politics of pity, one addressed briefly by Arendt. She suggests that social issues are not best dealt with by political means. Any attempt to do so will generate all the risks of lawlessness and tyranny discussed above. Rather, in so far as human need enters the public realm, this must be a matter of administration 'to be put into the hands of experts' (Arendt 1973: 91). The aggregate problem, and not the individual case, must be the focus of attention. It is in this spirit that Lord Brown prefaces his consideration of the facts of the case with a brief survey of the global scene.

> There are an estimated 25 million people living with HIV in sub-Saharan Africa (July 2004 UNAIDS report), many more million AIDS sufferers the world over. The prospects for the great many are bleak indeed.[65]

For Arendt, bureaucratic measures focused on statistics, rather than persuasion or revolutionary action, were the most appropriate means of relieving human suffering (1973: 91). The 'social question' should be depoliticized and vivid rhetoric replaced with the neutral and abstract language of science and policy.

Deus Ex Machina

Lord Brown concluded his judgment with the reflection that, although the Home Secretary could lawfully deport N, he was not obliged to do so:

> The likely impact upon immigration control (and, doubtless, National Health Service resources) of an adverse Article 3 ruling would be one thing; the favourable exercise of an administrative discretion in this individual case would be another.[66]

The possibility of clemency is raised here, though its exercise is solely a matter for government. The conflict of principle and sympathy might be resolved by a ministerial intervention in the individual case. As Raymond Williams argued, such expedient devices were a common feature of early Victorian fiction (1965: 82–84). Structurally similar conflicts between the egoistic values of a predominantly commercial society and the sufferings of individual characters were often relieved through a kind of magic, in the form of an unexpected legacy or emigration. Of course, while these interventions resolved the immediate conflict, they left the dominant social values unchallenged in substance.

Compassion beyond rhetoric

None of the judges was unmoved by N's plight. All spoke of their sympathy for her and their sadness at reaching the decision they did.[67] However, these feelings are better characterized as compassion rather than pity, to borrow another important distinction from Arendt. By contrast with pity, she argues that:

> compassion ... cannot reach out farther than what is suffered by one person and still remain what it is supposed to be, co-suffering.... [It] can comprehend only the particular, [having] no notion of the general and no capacity for generalization.

(Arendt 1973: 86)

Unlike the politicized pity of campaigners and revolutionaries and unlike the topical reasoning of the law, compassion is not aimed at achieving agreement; it is not expressed in the form of an argument. It is gestural rather than discursive, even when expressed in words. As Arendt says:

> Closely connected with this inability to generalize is the curious mute-
> ness or, at least, awkwardness with words that ... is the sign of compas-
> sion in contrast to the loquacity of pity (1973: 86).

The intimacy of compassion abolishes the 'the worldly space between men
where political matters are located' (1973: 87). Arendt draws a telling
example from Dostoyevsky's *The Brothers Karamazov* (1973: 85–86). In
response to the Grand Inquisitor's eloquent pity for suffering humanity,
Jesus remains silent. He answers the troubled monologue only with a compassionate kiss (Dostoyevsky 1958: 308).

As was seen earlier, rhetoric presumes a certain distance between
speaker and audience. The compassionate gesture abolishes this distance,
leaving no room for persuasion. We leave the realm of deliberative speech
for the purely demonstrative, the personal and idiosyncratic (Kundera
1985: 19). By contrast, as we have seen, rhetoric is inherently social. The
means of persuasion are collectively produced, so to speak. Topics embody
a social common sense, typical of a particular group in a given period. In
the present context we have seen the influence of the material and representational construction of space upon the *logos* of medical law. *Pathos*
equally depends on shared emotions, imaginations 'nourished from the
same source', including pity. The ideal character or *ethos* of the speaker is
equally social.

Conclusion

This chapter has extended our engagement with techniques of rhetorical
analysis and used them to illuminate the influence of social and economic
change on reasoning in health care law. In particular it was seen that different spaces and scales have played an important role in shaping arguments about access to medical treatment. This was true, not only as
regards the different topics of space invoked (*logos*), but also as regards
the feelings likely to be evoked among audiences (*pathos*). The element of
distance and its overcoming was a constant theme in this analysis. Obviously the physical fact of migration is likely to lead to 'access litigation', as
in *N*'s case. On the level of discourse, it is clear that the common sense of
national space has been deployed as a means of holding such migrants at
bay. However, the declining persuasiveness of that topic was noted. Scales
now multiply and compete. As the constructed nature of national space
becomes increasingly evident, distance is relativized. On the one hand
European countries with little in common are to be united in a single
community of health care users. On the other hand a firm barrier is
erected between Britain and the former colonies from which it has
historically drawn material and human resources on the most favourable
terms. These include medical knowledge and health care professionals.

Distance is also central to the deployment of *pathos* in judicial reasoning in this area. As was noted, the successful evocation of pity presumes a relationship of proximity or identification between sufferer and spectator. A number of factors serve to generate this proximity. Some are intrinsic to the operation of the common law itself. Others are a consequence of modern communications media and the educative campaigns of charities and other non-governmental organizations. With imaginations 'nourished' from a common stock of images and stories, people in the rich countries are capable of sympathizing with identifiable victims of poverty and ill health in poor countries. The overcoming of distance in this way presented risks which the House of Lords in *N* sought to avoid in different ways. On the one hand the suggested bureaucratic solution would reinstate the gap between developed and developing nations. On the other hand the demonstration of compassion for *N* made distance irrelevant by dissolving it in the immediacy of human feeling. Both moves tended to depoliticize and displace the question of access to essential medicines.

Aristotle distinguishes between 'common' and 'special' topics (1991). The former are the 'accrued wisdom' shared by all reasonable persons. 'Space' can be seen in this way as a very basic premise of understanding and argument. However, we have also seen that diverse, but quite specific spatial topics mark the common sense of the discipline of medical law in different periods (Balkin 1996: 223). The relation between them is one of competition and struggle. In the next chapter I consider the significance of 'time' in medical law reasoning. Like 'space', time is both general and specific, plural and contested. In both cases common sense is both a means of rhetorical struggle and a stake in that contest.

Notes

1 [2005] UKHL 31, [2005] 2 AC 296.
2 [1995] 1 WLR 898 (CA).
3 [2005] UKHL 31, [2005] 2 AC 296.
4 It was suggested by Baroness Hale that this matter, though not raised before the House of Lords, could have been given fuller consideration in the original decision on her refugee status: *N v Secretary of State for the Home Department* [2005] UKHL 31, [2005] 2 AC 296 [58].
5 (1997) 24 EHRR 423.
6 The fullest discussion is to be found in the judgment of Lord Hope, with which the other Law Lords concurred; see *N v Secretary of State for the Home Department* [2005] UKHL 31, [2005] 2 AC 296 [37]–[48].
7 This is acknowledged by Lord Brown: *N v Secretary of State for the Home Department* [2005] UKHL 31, [2005] 2 AC 296 [92].
8 One case, *Bensaid v UK* (2001) 33 EHRR 10, concerned a patient with long term psychotic illness. It was considered within the terms of *D v UK*. All the others involved HIV positive migrants.
9 *N v Secretary of State for the Home Department* [2003] EWCA Civ 1369, [2004] 1 WLR 1182 [37].

10 (1997) 23 EHRR 413.
11 *N v Secretary of State for the Home Department* [2005] UKHL 31, [2005] 2 AC 296 (per Lord Hope at [70]).
12 According to Laws LJ, see *N v Secretary of State for the Home Department* [2003] EWCA Civ 1369, [2004] 1 WLR 1182 [40].
13 *N v UK* (2008) 47 EHRR 39.
14 This aspect of common law reasoning and its affinities with clinical decision making are explored in Chapter 6.
15 *N v UK* App No 26565/05 (ECtHR, 27 May 2008) – Joint Dissenting Opinion of Judges Tulkens, Bonello and Spielmann at paras 12–13.
16 Ibid. at paras 18–25.
17 For an overview, see Barthes (1994: c.1).
18 [1995] 1 WLR 898 (CA).
19 By contrast it has long been common in certain forms of advocacy, such as criminal defence; see Cicero (2001).
20 *Re A (Conjoined Twins: Surgical Separation)* [2001] Fam 147 (CA per Ward LJ at 155).
21 See Goodrich (1986: 194).
22 'Space was treated as the dead, the fixed, the undialectical, the immobile. Time on the contrary was richness, life, dialectic' (Foucault 1980: 70).
23 The notion of 'lived-in' space is drawn from the work of Martin Heidegger; see further Elden (2004: 188).
24 Lefebvre calls these 'representational spaces'. I have adapted this usage for the sake of clarity.
25 For example, see Berman (1983: 173ff.).
26 General practice remained at arm's length from the new system; see Webster (2002: c.1).
27 Quoted in Newdick (2005: 52).
28 *R v Central Birmingham Health Authority, ex parte Collier* (CA, 6 January 1988) reprinted in Kennedy and Grubb (2000: 340).
29 On this process in general, see Harvey (1999).
30 For an overview of reforms, see Talbot-Smith and Pollock (2006).
31 See European Commission (2008).
32 See further Care Quality Commission (2013).
33 See further Newdick (2014).
34 See *N v Secretary of State for the Home Department* [2005] UKHL 31, [2005] 2 AC 296 (per Lord Brown at [88]).
35 *N v Secretary of State for the Home Department* [2005] UKHL 31, [2005] 2 AC 296 [53].
36 Ibid. [92].
37 Ibid. [58].
38 [2001] Fam 147 (CA).
39 Ibid. (CA at 156).
40 *N v Secretary of State for the Home Department* [2005] UKHL 31, [2005] 2 AC 296 [15].
41 *N v UK* (2008) 47 EHRR 39, para 44.
42 Ibid.
43 *N v UK* App No 26565/05 (ECtHR, 27 May 2008) – Joint Dissenting Opinion of Judges Tulkens, Bonello and Spielmann at para 8.
44 [2004] EWCA Civ 166, [2004] 2 CMLR 55.
45 Joined Cases 286/82 and 26/83 *Luisi and Carbone v Ministero del Tesoro* [1984] ECR 377.

46 Case C–56/01 *Inizan v Caisse Primaire d'Assurance Maladie des Hauts-de-Seine* [2003] ECR I–12403. See further, Hervey and McHale (2004: c.4).

47 *Secretary of State for Health v R (on the Application of Watts)* [2004] EWCA Civ 166, [2004] 2 CMLR 55 (per May LJ at [105]).

48 Ibid.

49 Case C–372/04 *R v Bedford Primary Care Trust, ex parte Watts* [2006] ECR I–4325.

50 Case C–213/89 *R v Secretary of State for Transport, ex parte Factortame (No. 2)* [1990] ECR I–2433. See further Mason and Laurie (2006: c.3).

51 This label is taken from Boltanski (1993: 15).

52 She argued that the 'primordial crime' of slavery did not invalidate this aspect of American constitutionalism (1973: 71).

53 In Britain this method was pioneered by the charity ActionAid (2008).

54 *N v Secretary of State for the Home Department* [2005] UKHL 31, [2005] 2 AC 296 [9].

55 I draw here on the reading of Adam Smith set out in Boltanski (1993: c.3). See further, Raphael (2007).

56 *N v Secretary of State for the Home Department* [2005] UKHL 31, [2005] 2 AC 296 [21].

57 Ibid. [71].

58 Ibid. [59].

59 [1995] 1 WLR 898 (CA).

60 *N v Secretary of State for the Home Department* [2005] UKHL 31, [2005] 2 AC 296 [21].

61 Ibid. [10].

62 Ibid. [4].

63 Ibid. [54].

64 Ibid. [53].

65 Ibid. [72].

66 Ibid. [99].

67 Ibid. (per Lord Nicholls at [9]; Lord Hope at [20]; Lord Walker at [55]; Baroness Hale at [71]; Lord Brown at [95]).

References

ActionAid (2008) 'Sponsor a Child' [Online]. Available at www.actionaid.org.uk/sponsor-a-child [Accessed: 6 October 2015].

Aginam, O (2000) 'Global Village: Divided World, South-North Gap and Global Health Challenges at Century's Dawn', 7 *Indiana Journal of Global Legal Studies* 603.

Arendt, H (1973) *On Revolution* (London, Penguin).

Aristotle (1991) *The Art of Rhetoric* (London, Penguin).

Arnold, PJ (2005) 'Disciplining Domestic Regulation: The World Trade Organization and the Market for Professional Services', 30 *Accounting, Organizations and Society* 299.

Balkin, JM (1996) 'A Night in the Topics: The Reason of Legal Rhetoric and the Rhetoric of Legal Reason', in P Brooks and P Gewirtz (eds), *Law's Stories* (New Haven, CT, Yale University Press) 211.

Barthes, R (1994) *The Semiotic Challenge* (Berkeley, CA, University of California Press).

Barthes, R (2000) *Mythologies* (London, Vintage).

Berman, M (1983) *All that Is Solid Melts into Air. The Experience of Modernity* (London, Verso).

Bevan, A (1978) *In Place of Fear* (London, Quartet Books).

Boltanski, L (1993) *La Souffrance à distance. Morale humanitaire, médias et politique* (Paris, Métailié).

Boseley, S (2008) 'Asylum Seekers Have Right to Full NHS Care, High Court Rules', *Guardian*, 12 April.

Bourdieu, P (1977) *Outline of a Theory of Practice* (Cambridge, Cambridge University Press).

Bourdieu, P (2000) *Pascalian Meditations* (Cambridge, Polity).

Braithwaite, J and P Drahos (2000) *Global Business Regulation* (Cambridge, Cambridge University Press).

Brenner, N and N Theodore (2002) 'Cities and the Geographies of "Actually Existing Neoliberalism"', 34 *Antipode* 349.

Burke, K (1969) *A Rhetoric of Motives* (Berkeley, CA, University of California Press).

Burris, SC, P Drahos and C Shearing (2004) 'Nodal Governance', 30 *Australian Journal of Legal Philosophy* 30.

Care Quality Commission (2013) *Annual Report and Accounts 2012/13* (London, The Stationery Office).

Chanda, R (2002) 'Trade in Health Services', 80 *Bulletin of the World Health Organization* 158.

Cicero (2001) *On the Ideal Orator (De Oratore)*, trans. JM May and J Wisse (New York, Oxford University Press).

Dodgson, R, K Lee and N Drager (2002) *Global Health Governance. A Conceptual Review. Discussion Paper No. 1* (Geneva, WHO).

Dostoyevsky, F (1958) *The Brothers Karamazov* (London, Penguin).

Doyal, L (1979) *The Political Economy of Health* (London, Pluto).

Elden, S (2004) *Understanding Henri Lefebvre. Theory and the Possible* (London, Continuum).

European Commission (2008) *Proposal for Directive of the European Parliament and Council on the Application of Patient's Rights in Cross-Border Health Care* COM 414 (Brussels, European Commission).

Foot, M (1962) *Aneurin Bevan: A Biography. Volume One: 1897–1945* (London, MacGibbon and Kee).

Foucault, M (1980) *Power/Knowledge. Selected Interviews and Other Writings 1972–77* (London, Longman).

Fraser, N (2005) 'Reframing Justice in a Globalizing World', 36 *New Left Review* 69.

Goodrich, P (1986) *Reading the Law. A Critical Introduction to Legal Method and Techniques* (Oxford, Blackwell).

Harvey, D (1990) *The Condition of Postmodernity. An Enquiry into the Origins of Social Change* (Oxford, Blackwell).

Harvey, D (1999) *The Limits to Capital* (London, Verso).

Harvey, D (2006) *Spaces of Global Capitalism* (London, Verso).

Hervey, TK and JV McHale (2004) *Health Law and the European Union* (Cambridge, Cambridge University Press).

Hollander, J (1996) 'Legal Rhetoric', in P Brooks and P Gewirtz (eds), *Law's Stories* (New Haven, CT, Yale University Press) 176.

Hutchinson, AC (2000) *It's All in the Game: A Non-Foundationalist Account of Law and Adjudication* (Durham, NC, Duke University Press).

Jessop, B (2000) 'The Crisis of the National Spatio-Temporal Fix and the Tendential Ecological Dominance of Globalizing Capitalism', 24 *International Journal of Urban and Regional Research* 323.

Jessop, B (2002) *The Future of the Capitalist State* (Cambridge, Polity).

Kennedy, I and A Grubb (2000) *Medical Law*, 3rd edition (London, Butterworths).

Kundera, M (1985) *The Unbearable Lightness of Being* (London, Faber and Faber).

Lefebvre, H (1991) *The Production of Space* (Oxford, Blackwell).

Marshall, D (1984) 'Adam Smith and the Theatricality of Moral Sentiments', 10 *Critical Inquiry* 592.

Mason, JK and GT Laurie (2006) Mason and McCall Smith's Law and Medical Ethics, 7th edition (Oxford, Oxford University Press).

Meyer, M (1999) *Histoire de la rhétorique: Des Grecs à nos jours* (Paris, Librarie Générale Française).

Murphy, WT (1997) *The Oldest Social Science? Configurations of Law and Modernity* (Oxford, Clarendon Press).

Newdick, C (2005) *Who Should We Treat? Rights, Rationing and Resources in the NHS*, 2nd edition (Oxford, Oxford University Press).

Newdick, C (2006) 'Citizenship, Free Movement and Health Care: Cementing Individual Rights by Corroding Social Solidarity', 43 *Common Market Law Review* 1645.

Newdick, C (2014) 'Health Care Rights and NHS Rationing: Turning Theory into Practice', 32 *Revista Portuguesa de Saúde Pública* 151.

Palmer, S (2005) 'AIDS, Expulsion and Article 3 of the European Convention on Human Rights', 5 *European Human Rights Law Review* 533.

Piper, AMS (1991) 'Impartiality, Compassion and Modal Imagination', 101 *Ethics* 726.

Pollock, AM (2004) *NHS plc. The Privatisation of Our Health Care* (London, Verso).

Porter, R (1997) *The Greatest Benefit to Mankind. A Medical History of Humanity from Antiquity to the Present* (London, Harper Collins).

Poulantzas, N (1978) *State, Power, Socialism* (London, Verso).

Pridmore, JA and J Gammon (2007) 'A Comparative Review of Clinical Governance Arrangements in the UK', 16 *British Journal of Nursing* 720.

Quintilian (2001) *The Orator's Education. Books 1–2* (Cambridge, MA, Harvard University Press).

Raphael, DD (2007) *The Impartial Spectator: Adam Smith's Moral Philosophy* (Oxford, Oxford University Press).

Stone, R (1965) 'Ratiocination not Rationalisation', 74 *Mind* 463.

't Hoen, E (2002) 'TRIPS, Pharmaceutical Patents and Access to Essential Medicines', 3 *Chicago Journal of International Law* 27.

Talbot-Smith, A and AM Pollock, (2006) *The New NHS. A Guide* (London, Routledge).

Timmins, N (2001) *The Five Giants: A Biography of the Welfare State*, 2nd edition (London, Harper Collins).

van Apeldoorn, B (2003) 'The Struggle over European Order: Transnational Class Agency in the Making of "Embedded Neo-Liberalism"', in N Brenner, B Jessop, M Jones and G MacLeod (eds), *State/Space. A Reader* (Oxford, Blackwell) 147.

Webster, C (2002) *The National Health Service. A Political History*, 2nd edition (Oxford, Oxford University Press).

Whitfield, D (2001) *Public Services or Corporate Welfare. Rethinking the Nation State in the Global Economy* (London, Pluto).

Williams, R (1965) *The Long Revolution* (London, Penguin).

Wood, EM (2002) *Empire of Capital* (London, Verso).

Chapter 4

Time

Introduction: taking time seriously

This chapter explores the significance of time as a dimension of argumentation in medical law. It proceeds from an understanding of time as social, plural and rhetorical. Like space, time is social in that it is not an ever-present, neutral medium within which events simply take place (Gurvitch 1964). Rather it is actively produced by various social practices, similar to the creation of space discussed in Chapter 3. Most famously perhaps, the spread of the railways in the nineteenth century led to a uniform official time in European states (Eriksen 2001: 43). Time is plural in that these practices are specific to different contexts, locations and activities (Sorokin and Merton 1937). The economy, the nation state and individual consciousness are all marked by diverse temporalities.[1] Time is rhetorical since the 'production' just mentioned is in fact a strategic process of persuasion, i.e. that a specific time frame should govern in a specific context. The success of a given temporality is substantially due to its plausible representation, whether visually (e.g. the clock) or verbally (e.g. the origin story of the nation) (Bridgeman 2007; Bell 1995). Time is, thus, both a resource and a stake in social struggles of all kinds (Baynham 2003: 351). As Ost puts it, decisive power rests with those who are in a position to impose their construction of time on other social groupings (1999: 22). For instance, the temporal nature of much industrial conflict is obvious. Disputes over the length of the working day or flexible work practices come to mind (Thompson 1967). Domains such as health care are also sites of 'intertemporal struggle' (Hope 2009: 75). The creation of the NHS, for example, can be seen as an attempt to suppress the rapid and erratic temporality of the market place in order to secure the basic health needs of the population.[2] As we saw in Chapter 1, scarcity of health care resources was to be managed instead through the waiting list, a spatio-temporal form which itself gained a certain plausibility from its association with queuing during the Second World War (Moran 2005; Syrett 2007: 47–48).

Time, medicine and law in *Mrs Dalloway*

I have introduced these aspects of time in rather abstract fashion. Before going on to outline the structure of the argument in this chapter, I turn here to Virginia Woolf's *Mrs Dalloway* to provide a vivid illustration of the interaction between time, medicine and law. In this landmark of modernist fiction, Woolf 'breaks up the narrative plane' by representing the multiple temporalities which co-exist and often conflict in different individual lives and social settings (Marder 1986: 59). Much of the novel, which unfolds over a single day in 1923, is taken up with the inner thoughts of its main characters. These partake of a subjective temporality which is qualitative (highlighting significant events, ignoring others) and non-linear (marked by flashbacks and associations) (Hasler 1982: 147). This 'time in the mind' is repeatedly counterposed to the chimes of Big Ben which punctuate the narrative, indicating a shift from scene to scene or from character to character. 'Time on the clock' is empty, uniform, and linear. It is, moreover, a means and manifestation of state power, being 'ratified by Greenwich',[3] and associated in the novel with masculinity, militarism and the law.[4] This negative association is also extended to medical power. Indeed Woolf uses the conflict between official time and other modes of temporality to produce an 'indignant' critique of psychiatric practice in that period (Showalter 1992: xli). The latter is embodied in the person of Sir William Bradshaw, a consultant whose chief strategy in treating mental illness is to stress order and regularity, or what he calls 'divine proportion' (Woolf 1992: 109). He reflects that:

> if a doctor loses his sense of proportion, as a doctor he fails; and health is proportion ... so when a man comes into your room and says he is Christ ... you invoke proportion, order rest in bed ... until a man who went in weighing seven stone six comes out weighing twelve.
>
> (Woolf 1992: 108)

Both sickness and cure are, thus, defined in the quantitative and abstract idiom of clock time (Hasler 1982: 149).

The account of Bradshaw's consultation with Septimus Smith, a veteran of the First World War apparently suffering from shell shock,[5] is dense with precise temporal references. He commences at 'precisely twelve o'clock; twelve by Big Ben'; his diagnosis is made 'in two or three minutes'; normally he gives his patients 'three-quarters of an hour'; and his earnings are imagined as a 'wall of gold, mounting minute by minute' (Woolf 1992: 103, 108, 104–105, 103). The equation of time, labour and money evident here is also a hallmark of social relations under capitalism (Castree 2009). As the close identification with official, clock time suggests, clinical practice serves a greater social purpose. 'Worshipping proportion', Sir William had 'made England prosper ... [he] secluded lunatics, forbade childbirth, penalised despair ... and made it impossible for the unfit to propagate their views' (Woolf 1992: 109). He works in the shadow of Big Ben, as it were, on legislation to deal with the 'deferred effects of shell shock' (Woolf 1992: 200–201). Not only the goals of psychiatric medicine, but also its coercive instruments are furnished by state power. Where orthodox treatment failed, Sir William was supported by 'the police and the good of society which would take care ... [that] unsocial impulses ... were held in control' (Woolf 1992: 111). For such patients there 'was no alternative ... [it] was a question of law' (Woolf 1992: 106). The damage done to individual lives by this alliance of law and medicine is forcefully expressed at the end of the consultation scene:

> Shredding and slicing, dividing and sub-dividing, the clocks of Harley Street nibbled at the June day, counselled submission, upheld authority, and pointed out in chorus the supreme advantages of proportion until the mound of time was so far diminished ...
>
> (Woolf 1992: 112)

Smith takes his own life that same day (Woolf 1992: 201). On learning of this from Bradshaw's wife, Clarissa Dalloway considers it to be 'an attempt to communicate', an act of 'defiance' (Woolf 1992: 202). Earlier, prompted by the sound of Big Ben, dissolving like 'leaden circles' in the air, she had remarked to herself on the failure of the law to represent the world around it. Those who 'love life ... can't be dealt with ... by Acts of Parliament' (Woolf 1992: 4).

Time and legal rhetoric

Virginia Woolf's challenge to the psychiatric medicine of her day suggests that struggles over time, conducted by means of competing representations, are also commonly struggles over basic ethical and political values. It will be argued in the rest of this chapter that medical law has also been marked and, in a significant way, constituted by such conflicts over time. Put differently, rival modes of temporality have been used to express and make plausible various substantive views on how the law in this area should develop. In examining time as a dimension of medical law and consistent with the approach set out in Chapter 1, we are required to take seriously its rhetorical form. In this regard it can be suggested that the persuasive tasks of lawyers and judges have both positive and negative dimensions. On the one hand, they seek to establish the plausibility of their case by invoking time frames which appear to be 'natural' and appropriate in the specific context (Hutchinson 2000: 193). For example, the imposition on doctors of extensive duties of disclosure and consultation, stretched over time, so to speak, may be justified by the need for adequate deliberation and reflection prior to treatment (Maclean 2009: 79–93; 233–259). On the other hand, they seek to show the inappropriateness and, therefore, the arbitrariness of the time frames relied on in opposing arguments. For example, a one-off approach to disclosure, mandating merely the 'imparting of information', may be discredited on the basis that, by reproducing the compressed time frame of consumer transactions, it fails adequately to respect the pre-eminent value of autonomy (Miola 2006: 113).

It can be argued that intertemporal struggle, taking the form of this rhetorical to-and-fro, is pervasive across medical law. I will focus on three broad forms of such struggle in the following discussion. In each case I offer representative samples from specific areas of medical law, rather than providing a comprehensive overview of legal doctrine. The first involves cases where the outcome proposed is congruent with a specific temporality, proper to the law itself.[6] As François Ost has argued, the doctrine of precedent, which binds the present to the past, is an important example of the law producing its own time; the law of contract, which binds the present to the future, is another (1999: 33, 37). At a more abstract level, theories in jurisprudence are commonly concerned with identifying the true temporality of the legal system as a whole (Nobles and Schiff 2006: 35). Thus, the opposition between legal positivism and common law theory can be expressed in terms of the relative importance each attributes to tradition in law. I will draw on these insights in examining the judgments in *Gillick v West Norfolk and Wisbech Area Health Authority*,[7] already mentioned in Chapter 2. I hope to show that the plausibility of both minority and majority opinions depended significantly upon their consistency with these different temporal models.

The second area of focus in this chapter is on cases in which the outcome sought is supported by reference to a temporality originating beyond the law, which is incorporated into, or 're-presented', in legal discourse. I will argue that the most significant source of such external time frames in the present context is, of course, medicine itself. Thus, through the *Bolam* test of negligence,[8] the law opens itself to change in clinical standards as the opinion of 'responsible practitioners' shifts over time, as will be discussed in Chapter 7. I pay particular attention to the temporality of the human body upon which many distinctions in medical law are also predicated. It will be seen that the idea of a natural life cycle, including a natural death, supports distinctions drawn in the case law concerning patients in PVS. A similar reliance on the developmental trajectory of the foetus has marked attempts to reform the law on abortion. As we saw in Chapter 1, the body functions to absorb and conceal the contingency of decision making in medical law.

The third focus of rhetorical struggle over temporality in medical law is the time in which legal processes themselves unfold. Thus, court procedures may be 'stretched' to allow sufficient time for wide-ranging argument and for the justification of outcomes (Scheuerman 2004: 34). Conversely, where law comes under pressure to accelerate its procedures, there is a risk that *pathos* will eclipse *logos* in legal deliberation and that emotions such as anger or pity will prevail over reasoned deliberation (Van de Kerchove 1998: 369–370). I hope to show that emergency medicine is a significant source of such pressure, considering in detail a series of cases from the 1990s which saw doctors being granted permission by the courts to carry out forced Caesarian sections upon uncooperative patients more or less at the last minute. Trenchant academic criticism sought to reparadoxify this line of cases, undermining the plausibility of their compressed temporality by pointing out its inconsistency with core legal values.

Representing law's own time: *Gillick*

The applicant in *Gillick* challenged the lawfulness of a Department of Health and Social Services Notice allowing doctors to provide contraceptive advice and treatment for patients under 16 without their parents' knowledge or approval. Though the Court of Appeal ruled in the applicant's favour, a majority of the House of Lords overruled this and held that advice and treatment would be lawful: (1) as long as it was in the child's best interests to do so; and (2) she had sufficient capacity to consent.[9] Though *Gillick* would appear to be centrally concerned with the temporality of child development, none of the nine judges who ruled in the case gave any significant consideration to relevant theories in psychology. Their reasoning was rather more informed by rival understandings of the law's own temporality. The first of these, associated with statute law, was articulated by Parker LJ in the Court of Appeal and by Lords Brandon and Templeman, who dissented in the House of Lords. (I will refer to these in the following as the 'minority'.) The second, associated with the common law, was deployed by the House of Lords majority, particularly Lord Scarman, whose judgment I focus on here. Before examining the relevant judgments, I will set out the main features of these two models of legal temporality.

Two models of legal temporality

A distinctive model of time is central to the classical liberal model of law as unified, fixed and self-sufficient. This view is most clearly articulated by positivist legal theory which views legislation as the ideal centre of the legal system (Nobles and Schiff 2006: 68). Statute law subsists in an 'eternal present': once enacted it remains in force unchanged until repealed (Fitzpatrick 2001: 88). The bounded atemporality of each individual statute means that the legal system as a whole partakes of 'alternating time' (Gurvitch 1964: 33). Things change, but only in punctual fashion: that is, by way of clearly delineated breaks, e.g. when the legislator intervenes. This allows law to be observed at any given moment as a static, synchronic system, simultaneously intelligible and applicable as a whole (Jackson 1998: 225–226). Tradition is not a significant element of this understanding of the legal system. Its past is 'no more than the continuous succession of its states of presence' (Goodrich 1992: 8). Time here is represented spatially as a series of discrete containers, helping to realize the positivist goal of sharply distinguishing law from its wider social environment (Fitzpatrick 2001: 93).

The punctual temporality associated with positivism can be contrasted with the more traditional notion that decided cases, not legislation, are the basic substance of the law (Postema 1986). The doctrine of precedent embodies what Georges Gurvitch called 'enduring time', requiring common lawyers to be ever mindful of what went before when deciding for the future (1964: 31). Here 'the past is not separated from the present by a gap, but spreads through it like an echo' (Poulantzas 1978: 109). From this perspective, the common law is seen, not as an ideally synchronous system of rules, but as the enforcement of an evolving customary order:

> [The] law develops as society develops, with new circumstances presenting new 'wrongs' which require new remedies to be developed out of existing ones.
>
> (Nobles and Schiff 2006: 65)

Indeed, according to Matthew Hale, the validity of the common law derives from its broad ongoing congruence with public life and social interaction (Postema 2004: 224). However, though change in this way is essential to the normative quality of law, the overriding value of continuity means that it has to be presented as no change at all (Nobles and Schiff 2006: 73). Hale famously illustrated this contradictory temporality with reference to the Argonauts' ship 'which returned after its long voyage the same ship as had left port years before, although every plank of it had been replaced' (Postema 2004: 224).

The minority: 'the law as it stands'

The minority in *Gillick* placed legislation at the centre of their analysis, referring repeatedly to what Parliament had done or intended, what it could have done, but had not.[10] In the Court of Appeal, Parker LJ carefully considered the Family Law Reform Act 1969, s 8 (1) of which deemed *over* 16s to have capacity to consent to medical treatment. Subsection 3 went on to state that nothing in that section should be taken to invalidate any other consent given, for example by a child *under* 16, where that had previously been lawful. Parker LJ found that such consents had not in fact been lawful prior to the 1969 Act on the basis of a number of precedents from the nineteenth century, themselves applying earlier statutes, to the effect that parents had full control over their children until the age of majority.[11] Though these rules might now be outmoded, Parker LJ affirmed that the law 'as it presently stands' must be 'observed until it is altered by the legislature'.[12] Even where the minority permitted itself to consider questions of policy, this was defined as policy which had been established by the law itself.[13] Broader considerations of public health and of ethics were excluded as 'matters for debate elsewhere'.[14] Thus, even though Lord Templeman expressed firm views on family life and sexual mores, he sought to anchor them explicitly in the existing legislative regime.[15] This was illustrated by the minority's treatment of the Sexual Offences Act 1956, s 6 of which made the consent to intercourse of girls under 16 irrelevant to a charge of rape raised against their sexual partners. That provision had been 'enacted by Parliament for the purpose of protecting the girl from herself'.[16] Absent further legislative intervention, it was not open to the courts to undermine this statutory policy in the name of widening access to contraception and reducing teenage pregnancies.[17]

By privileging the alternating temporality of statute law in this way, the minority were able to present their rulings as consistent with the over-arching values of liberal legalism. Thus, as Parker LJ noted, a fixed age for capacity promoted legal certainty, allowing all 'those dealing with children [to] know where they stand and what are their powers, rights, duties or obligations'.[18] Moreover, by refusing to establish a 'clinical' exception to the law on statutory rape, the minority saw themselves as preserving coherence across the legal system as a whole. Change should be synchronous across the law, or, in Lord Brandon's words:

> [the] criminal law and the civil law should ... march hand in hand on all issues.... [T]o allow inconsistency or contradiction between them would, in my view, serve only to discredit the rule of law.[19]

Their Lordships were, thus, concerned more with the state of the law itself than with its effects upon its social environment (Jackson 1998: 243). Para-doxically, this relative lack of concern about external consequences would have had, as its main effect, the imposition of a punctual model of change upon the realm of human development. Just as a statute is in force one day and not in force the next, so the minority judgments posited two 'eternal presents' in the life of the child, separated by a sudden rupture. In a critical essay, Ian Kennedy parodied this quantitative, segmented representation of time. The Court of Appeal, he claimed, proceeded on the basis that a girl was incapable of knowing 'her best interests until the clock strikes midnight on the eve of her sixteenth birthday' (1991: 84). Prioritizing fixity over responsiveness, the law bore 'little relation to the realities of modern life in many households' (Kennedy 1991: 80).

Lord Scarman: 'a living body of law'

By contrast with the minority, Lord Scarman placed judges, not legislators, at the ideal heart of the law. For him, statutes 'intervene' in the law, but they do not exhaust or even wholly dominate the normative field.[20] Accordingly, on his reading, the Family Law Reform Act 1969 and preceding case law provided no clear answer to the question of whether under-16s could have capacity. This left it open to the House of Lords to formulate a rule, having searched 'in the judge-made law for the true principle'.[21] Thus, where the minority were above all concerned with ascertaining how the law 'stands', for Lord Scarman, the judge's task was considerably greater, more like a voyage of discovery. The case, he asserted 'is the beginning, not the conclusion, of a legal development in a field [thus far only] glimpsed ... but not yet fully explored'.[22] He demonstrated a keen historical consciousness throughout this quest, noting that:

> features have emerged in today's society which were not known to our predecessors.... In times past contraception was rarely a matter for the doctor.... [Now] women have obtained by the availability of the pill ... a degree of independence and of opportunity undreamed of until this generation.[23]

The law ignored 'these developments at its peril'.[24] The required degree of responsiveness would be secured, not by legislation which goes rapidly out of date, but by judges willing to 'keep the law abreast of the society in which they live and work'.[25] In this regard, Lord Scarman saw himself as carrying on the traditions of 'the great masters of the judicial art'. The ability 'to look at, through, and past the decisions of earlier generations', and to discard these where necessary, was what had distinguished Coke and Mansfield, Lord Eldon and Blackstone.[26] By invoking this heroic genealogy, he confirmed that the past of the common law remained a vital and active part of its present (Goodrich 1992: 9).

In substance, Lord Scarman rejected the fixed-age test of capacity, holding instead that the parental right to determine the medical treatment of a child under 16 would terminate when she had sufficient understanding and intelligence to enable her to understand fully what was proposed by the doctor.[27] He accepted that this would introduce some uncertainty into the law. However, imposing a more precise rule in this context would:

impede the law's development, and stamp upon [it] the mark of obsolescence where what is needed is the capacity for development.[28]

The legal system is presented here as a living being, ontologically equivalent to the child whose capacity is to be determined. Each grows gradually out of its own resources and under pressure of its environment. Each changes imperceptibly, while remaining the same. This rhetorical equivalence allowed Lord Scarman to be true to the nature of the law while calling for a test of capacity which was 'sensitive to human development and social change'.[29] His rejection of 'rigid demarcations' where 'nature knows only a continuous process' applied as much to the law itself as to the growth of the child.[30]

Representing non-legal time – PVS and abortion

Legal argumentation is not exclusively concerned with its own models of time. As we saw in Chapter 2, the law develops more or less plausible representations of its non-legal environment in deparadoxifying its own operations. This process includes the incorporation of temporalities associated with other social systems or natural environment (Commaille 1998: 332). Gunther Teubner has suggested this 'porosity' is associated with the growth of subject-specific areas of law, each identifying more closely with the values and common sense of a distinct external social sphere than with that of the legal system as a whole (1990: 31, 37).[31] The twin process of fragmentation and opening up which Teubner describes is made possible through the use of open-ended standards, such as good faith and reasonableness (Teubner 1998: 135). Such tests are common in medical law, with lawfulness being commonly predicated on the exercise of professional judgment or on conformity with the practice of a responsible body of practitioners. By means of them, clinical categories, often with a significant temporal dimension, have figured prominently in medical law argumentation. I will consider the operation of these categories in this section by focusing on two areas of medical law: withdrawal of nutrition from patients in a PVS and the time limits for lawful termination of pregnancy.

PVS: 'letting nature take its course'

The jurisprudence on withdrawal of artificial nutrition and hydration (ANH) from patients in PVS provides a good example of the plausibility in law of time frames derived from clinical medicine. In such cases, the courts have effectively been required to decide the point at which a given life should come to an end. It is arguable that reasoning in the leading cases is significantly predicated upon the notion that patients subject to treatment follow one of a number of standard 'temporal trajectories'

(Reddy *et al.* 2006: 37). These 'illness trajectories' are inscribed within a broader cycle through life, from birth to death. Temporal trajectories, of both forms, are crucial to medical evaluation of the condition of patients in intensive care units. Doctors and nurses ask 'where is the patient in her recovery, where should the patient be in her recovery, what do we have to do to ensure that the patient is at the right point of her recovery' (Reddy *et al.* 2006: 38). Such reflections are not merely descriptive, they provide a normative orientation for medical decision making.

In *Airedale NHS Trust v Bland*,[32] the English courts held that ANH in PVS cases was 'futile' and could therefore be lawfully withdrawn.[33] Due to his brain injuries, Anthony Bland would never recover consciousness; yet, as long as his basic needs for food and water were met, neither would he die in the foreseeable future.[34] He was 'as good as dead', 'alive' though he had 'no life in any sense at all', subsisting in a condition of 'living death'.[35] These paradoxical formulations had two effects: they described the stalled condition of the patient; and they suggested that legal decision making was equally 'paralyzed'.[36] The extant law seemed to furnish no answer to the question posed by the applicant doctors: 'is it lawful to withdraw nutrition and hydration from a patient in PVS'. As Lord Mustill remarked, Bland had 'no best interests' such as would indicate a decision either way.[37] The idea of a path through life was central to addressing this lacuna. The paradox of being alive and dead at the same time was managed, or deparadoxified, by stretching its opposed terms over time and re-connecting them in terms of the natural trajectory of individual existence. Accordingly death is part of life, but only in its proper time at the end of a cycle. ANH was futile as it impeded progress along this trajectory. In this way, the judges in Bland were able to unblock the contradictory material situation of the patient, 'to resuscitate the living corpse' and allow him to die (Diamantides 1995: 213).

The rhetorical force of this temporal trajectory was brought out even more clearly by the Irish Supreme Court when it came to address these issues in *Re A Ward of Court (withholding medical treatment) (No. 2)*.[38] It held that withdrawal of ANH leading to the death of PVS patients was not only permissible, but positively mandated having regard to the patient's fundamental right to life, as guaranteed by the Irish constitution.[39] Hamilton CJ dealt with this apparent contradiction by arguing that:

> [as] the process of dying is part, and an ultimate, inevitable consequence, of life, the right to life necessarily implies the right to have nature take its course and to die a natural death and, unless the individual concerned so wishes, not to have life artificially maintained by the provision of nourishment by abnormal artificial means.[40]

This distinction between the artificial and the natural allowed the courts in both *Bland* and the *Ward* case to reaffirm that active killing of patients in PVS remained unlawful, notwithstanding the ruling at hand. Withdrawal of treatment, which simply allowed nature to take its course, was sharply distinguished from artificial prolongation of the patient's life through indefinite administration of ANH, on the one hand, and from the equally artificial 'acceleration' of their death by way of lethal injection, on the other.[41] The broad plausibility of natural temporalities has already been discussed in relation to the self-understanding of the common law articulated by Lord Scarman in *Gillick*. It derives, according to Gurvitch, from their association with continuity rather than contingency: all human lives follow this course; this is the rhythm that gives them meaning (1964: 32, 83).[42]

Abortion law reform: 'woven and knitted in the womb'

The idea of a natural temporal trajectory has also been central to the debate on abortion law reform in Britain. The Abortion Act 1967, as amended in 1990, s 1(1)(a) sets a 24-week limit to the lawfulness of terminations carried out on (more or less) social grounds, which I have already discussed in Chapter 2. This aspect of the Act was challenged in 2008 by MPs seeking to reduce the limit to between 14 and 20 weeks.[43] Debate focused inter alia on the time at which the foetus (or neonate) was viable and could feel pain. In 2007 the House of Commons Science and Technology Committee had found that the scientific evidence did not support the pro-life position: the threshold of viability remained close to 24 weeks (2007: 18). Moreover neurobiological studies showed that the brain of the foetus was not developed enough at that point to allow pain to be felt (House of Commons Science and Technology Committee 2007: 26). Pro-life MPs sought to outflank these arguments by describing – and, in one case, displaying[44] – ultrasound images of the foetus in three dimensions (3-D), and also moving (4-D).[45] No longer 'a medical recluse in an opaque womb', the new technology revealed the unborn to be 'one of us' at an earlier stage than previously imagined (Petchesky 1987: 276).

The rhetorical power of ultrasound images as spatialized representations of the temporality of foetal development lies in the fact that they seem to speak for themselves, 'naturally' so to speak (Palmer 2009: 173). The sonogram, like the photograph, has a simple and direct relation to reality, by contrast with the complex narratives of, say, science or bioethics (Sontag 1979: 6). Abstract medical data could, thus, be discounted in favour of what was immediately visible (Palmer 2009: 185). Contrary to what might be expected, the scan does not simply function as a momentary snapshot in this regard. Rather it also implies human growth over the time preceding.[46] This temporal trajectory is the very source of what is taken to be valuable about the foetus. As one MP put it, '[t]erminating a child that has been woven and knitted in the womb should be a choice of last resort, not the latest manifestation of Britain's throwaway society'.[47] The course of the 2008 debates, thus, exhibits the general pattern of change in medical law which I set out in Chapter 2. Pro-life campaigners effectively worked to estrange or reparadoxify the 24-week limit by showing its contingency. Like Lord Scarman in *Gillick*, as discussed above, they contrasted the artificiality of the bright-line rule with what they presented as the gradual processes of human development. In this regard, they proposed a new deparadoxification, one made plausible through being anchored in the natural temporality of the foetus.

The time of legal rhetoric – Caesarian section cases

Temporal porosity in medical law is not limited to the adoption of developmental trajectories into substantive law. In addition, clinical imperatives can set temporal horizons to the process of legal decision making itself.[48] The consequences of this openness for the law's own values are dramatically illustrated by a well-known series of cases in the 1990s permitting Caesarian sections to be imposed upon women against their wishes. In substantive terms these cases staged a conflict between medical power and patient autonomy and between the rights of the pregnant woman and the interests of the foetus.[49] These contests were resolved in principle by the Court of Appeal in favour of the autonomy of the woman, although it remains the case that a finding of incapacity or a successful application for compulsory treatment under the Mental Health Act 1983 would reinstate clinical judgment as the basis of decision making in such cases.[50] What is significant for present purposes, however, is the extreme pressure of time under which the decisions in most of these cases were reached. Given the asserted threat to the life of the woman, judges were forced to take evidence, to hear counsel's arguments regarding the law and to reach a decision in periods from 15 to 30 minutes.[51] Not merely a background datum, this urgency was established rhetorically in the terms of the judgments themselves. Judges were careful to produce a precise timeline of events; the facts were presented in a heightened and vivid idiom to emphasize that the decision was a 'matter of life and death'.[52]

Medical evidence as to the necessity of intervention played a central role in these cases. Given the short period available for decision, this evidence was usually uncontested and often delivered in summary form, over the telephone, for example.[53] Moreover, in several instances independent psychiatric evidence was unavailable and the obstetricians involved were also called on to testify as to the competence of the patient.[54] All told, these cases demonstrate an extreme degree of openness on the part of the law as regards the temporality of clinical urgency. This porosity led to a significant loss of the law's own substantive and procedural values. For example, critics pointed out that the ruling in *Re S (Adult: Refusal of*

Treatment)[55] was 'fatally flawed' in relying on an American decision which had in fact been overruled, while overlooking essential principles of English law regarding the status of the foetus (De Gama 1993: 122; Thomson 1994: 128). In *St George's Healthcare NHS Trust v S, R v Collins, ex parte S*[56] not only did the patient go unrepresented at the original hearing, but she and her solicitors were unaware that the application had been made in the first place. Moreover, 'nothing was done subsequent to the hearing to make sure that the proper formalities were complied with ... no affidavit evidence from the hospital confirming what [counsel] had said to the judge was filed'.[57] In the view of the Court of Appeal, 'technically no proceedings ever existed' in this case.[58]

These developments can be illuminated with reference to the notion of a 'state of exception', familiar to constitutional lawyers and political theorists. This arises when:

> a sudden, urgent, usually unforeseen event or situation ... requires immediate action, often without time for prior reflection and consideration.
>
> (Gross 1999–2000: 1833)

Given that substantive legal principle and procedural constraints are suspended, executive action in the state of exception can only be judged with reference to the 'public good' (Gross 1999–2000: 1843). All that law and the constitution can do is to indicate who is to act, not when or what action shall be taken (Gross 1999–2000: 1845). Logic suggests, furthermore, that the person or body with the power of decision in the state of exception also decides on when circumstances triggering it have arisen (Gross 1999–2000: 1845). Indeed this capacity was seen by Carl Schmitt as the very definition of sovereign power (1985). Though traditionally limited to military threats to the life of the nation, the state of exception is now a widespread feature of law and governance. In particular, as William Scheuerman has suggested, the increased speed of financial movements associated with globalization has led to an entrenched 'economic state of exception'; e.g. 'the executive must act quickly, drawing up austerity measures to calm the markets' (2004: 144ff.). This tends to undermine the operation of the slower, more deliberative branches of government – the legislature and the judiciary: e.g. 'parliamentary consideration of this austerity package must be cut short in order to calm the markets' (Scheuerman 2004: 44–60).

The Caesarian section cases illustrate the potential for an analogous 'medical state of exception' whereby pressure of speed leads the law to accelerate or abandon its own processes of deliberation. Sovereign power in these cases was exercised not by king or cabinet, but by medical professionals. Not only did they define what needed to be done in the state of exception, but their evidence as to the urgency of the situation and the patient's lack of competence determined whether the exception arose in the first place. Moreover, the normal self-referential standard of legal adjudication (i.e. decision in accordance with the law) appeared to be subordinated to a clinical understanding of the public good. Thus, a number of reserved judgments concluded by noting, as a favourable outcome of the case, that the mother was well and that the child had been safely delivered.[59] The triumph of medicine in the intertemporal struggle at the heart of these cases had a number of negative consequences remarked on by academic commentators and by the Court of Appeal. The compressed and *ex parte* nature of the proceedings meant that judicial decision making was marked more by emotion (*pathos*) than by reason (*logos*). Speaking extrajudicially about these cases, Lord Justice Thorpe noted that it had been difficult for trial courts to discern and apply legal principle 'in the face of judicial instinct, training and emotion' (1997: 663). If speedy criminal trials are likely to be dominated by anger, then these hearings were marked by fear. A loss of reason was also central to the legal and medical construction of the emergency. Thus, Johnson J indicated that 'acute emotional stress and physical pain in the ordinary course of labour' led in and of itself to a loss of competence.[60] As Hilary Lim noted, the pregnant woman was wholly identified with her physical body, thus falling outwith the realm of liberal rights (1999: 168). This is consistent with Giorgio Agamben's argument that in the state of exception the 'nexus between human being and citizen' is broken (2000: x). Persons subject to the emergency regime are treated as 'bare lives', subject in these cases to the direct power of an obstetric medicine freed from the normal constraints of the law.[61] In the course of a critical review, Anne Morris wondered at 'what point did the wish to do good become an act of coercion of such magnitude?' (1999: 76). The foregoing discussion suggests that an answer to that question may be found in the specific temporality of the medical state of exception, a temporality encapsulated in Paul Virilio's aphorism that 'speed is violence' (Virilio and Lotringer 1983: 20).

Conclusion: the chronopolitics of medical law

Intertemporal struggles in medical law are political struggles. As I argued in Chapter 2, this does not mean that they simply reflect or reproduce conflicts originating elsewhere, say in the parliamentary system or in the economy. Rather, they are authentic struggles, conducted through legal rhetoric over the diverse terms of social life. As anticipated in our reading of *Mrs Dalloway*, the stakes in this 'chronopolitics' of medical law are high.[62] Rival representations of time were seen to be at the heart of profound legal controversies over the provision of contraceptive treatment to minors, access to abortion, the removal of life-sustaining treatment from patients in PVS and the medical control of pregnancy. The variety of temporalities at play in these debates indicates that this is politics in the plural. It cannot be neatly reduced to a single basic opposition between time frames. Rather than attempting that, and by way of conclusion, two generic features of time as a dimension of medical law may be picked out in very broad terms. These are: on the one hand, the tendency for natural temporalities relied on in medical law to lose their plausibility as a result of technological development; and, on the other, the enduring role of law as a forum for intertemporal contest in the face of significant 'de-temporalizing' tendencies within and beyond the legal system.

As I noted earlier, the positive plausibility of a specific temporality depends on how appropriate it is made to appear in a given context. In *Bland* and in the abortion law reform debate, it was seen that this involved drawing direct normative consequences from natural trajectories, in particular the life cycle of the human being. Somewhat less directly, Lord Scarman in *Gillick* portrayed the growing child and the common law as participating in the same natural process of development. As feminist writers have argued, 'man-made' social arrangements have long been justified with reference to notions of what is natural (Butler 1990). Such notions, with their strong temporal dimensions, function in this context to conceal the contingency of the categories and distinctions which structure important areas of medical law. We noted, however, that the legal rhetorician also has a negative task: showing the implausibility of the common sense assumptions relied on by the other side. This critical task becomes easier, the more the naturalness of the human life cycle is undermined, or reparadoxified, by scientific developments, for example, as we saw in Chapter 2. Ironically, increasing medical capabilities at both ends of life, showcased in the debates on abortion and PVS, have hollowed out the notion of a natural path from conception to death.[63] Purposeful intervention is both possible and demanded at every stage. The problem is that relevant, new regulatory measures can no longer be grounded in the natural processes which these interventions have already replaced. The mode of temporality here has changed from a flow to a series of points at which decisions can and have to be made about how to proceed. It is unsurprising then that legislation, with its own punctual temporality, has grown in importance in medical law. It may be wondered, however, whether deferring to the bare will of the sovereign, in the form of statute law, will contribute to the stability or, in the terms used here, the plausibility of the new regime of categories and distinctions.[64]

The chronopolitics of medical law is also a struggle between what Ost has termed 'de-temporalization' and 're-temporalization' (1999: 14, 29). De-temporalization involves the loss of a sense of time appropriate to the issues at hand. The compression of legal procedures identified in the case law on Caesarian sections is one example. Not only was there a quantitative scarcity of the (clock) time needed for argument and deliberation, but this lead to a qualitative loss of the law's sense of its own past. While legal adjudication demands engagement with the historical materials of the law, judges in these cases appeared to function more like 'test pilots', reacting only to the pressures of the moment (Virilio 2006: 159). The threat of compression is also evident in the area of informed consent, mentioned briefly above. As Alasdair Maclean argues, to the extent that current rules privilege the moment of choice over any more extended model of reflection and dialogue, the temporal effect is to strand the patient in the present, cutting them off from both previous commitments and future interests (2006). We can observe here what Virilio has called a liquidation of 'the reflective capacity of the citizen', including the citizen judge, in favour of merely 'reflex responses' (quoted in James 2007: 101). Ost sees a vital role for law in responding to this tendency, as an agent of re-temporalization. Through its diverse substantive doctrines, as well as its temporally stretched procedures, law can reinstate the lost connections to past and future (Ost 1999: 29, 33). It does this, not necessarily by imposing a single time in place of others, but by providing space (and time) for rhetorical contest between multiple temporalities.

Finally it should be noted that the phenomena considered here can be related to the changing form in which the capitalist economy exercises ecological dominance over the rest of society, as discussed in Chapter 1. I noted there that the rise of neo-liberalism has been marked by a disembedding of the economy: a decline in the limits to markets and an increase in their influence over other social systems. I argued further in Chapter 3 that this change had an important spatial dimension: the national territory losing its status as the 'natural' frame for regulation. But it has also been matched by a temporal shift from the long horizon of government planning to the rapid turnover of global commercial transactions. Indeed this acceleration in the operations of financial markets has been central to the loss of states' capacity to control the economy and the imperative on them to compete for mobile capital (Jessop 2000). Put very briefly, the drive to competitiveness has included the privatization of public services and the mimicking of markets in welfare provision. The radical 'short-termism' in informed consent law, feared by commentators such as Maclean, is increasingly plausible in the context of an ascendant patient consumerism associated with these developments. In the next chapter, I will focus more directly on the commodification of medicine and its significance for the development of medical law in Britain. That discussion will follow the rise and fall of the utopian conception of the National Health Service as an exemplary space, set apart from the market, in which a new society could be pioneered in advance of its time.

Notes

1 See, respectively, Armitage and Graham (2001); Edensor (2006); Toombs (1990).
2 See more generally Poulantzas (1978: 112).
3 See Woolf (1992: 112).
4 For examples, see Woolf (1992: 52, 55, 4).
5 Showalter has argued that the symptoms described in the novel suggest a condition rather more severe than shell shock, possibly schizophrenia (1992: xl).
6 See further, Melissaris (2005).
7 [1986] 1 AC 112 (CA & HL).
8 See *Bolam v Friern Hospital Management Committee* [1957] 1 WLR 582 (McNair J at 592).
9 See *Gillick v West Norfolk and Wisbech Area Health Authority* [1986] 1 AC 112 (CA & HL per Lord Fraser at 174).
10 Ibid. (CA & HL per Parker LJ at 136; Lord Brandon at 196, 198; Lord Templeman at 199, 201, 203).
11 Ibid. (CA & HL per Parker LJ at 127–129). The relevant precedents were *R v Howes* (1860) 3 El & El 332, 121 ER 467 and *In Re Agar Ellis (No. 2)* (1883) 24 ChD 317 (CA). Most notable among the statutes was the Tenures Abolition Act 1660.
12 Ibid. (CA & HL per Parker LJ at 133).
13 Ibid. (CA & HL per Parker LJ at 121; Lord Brandon at 195).
14 Ibid. (CA & HL per Parker LJ at 133).
15 Ibid. (CA & HL per Lord Templeman at 203, 207).
16 Ibid. (CA & HL per Lord Brandon at 196).
17 Ibid. (CA & HL per Parker LJ at 137; Lord Templeman at 203).
18 Ibid. (CA & HL per Parker LJ at 132).
19 Ibid. (CA & HL at 198–199).
20 Ibid. (CA & HL per Lord Scarman at 185–186).
21 Ibid. (CA & HL per Lord Scarman at 185, 182).
22 Ibid. (CA & HL per Lord Scarman at 176).
23 Ibid. (CA & HL per Lord Scarman at 182–183).
24 Ibid. (CA & HL per Lord Scarman at 183).
25 Ibid.
26 Ibid. (CA & HL per Lord Scarman at 183, 186).
27 Ibid. (CA & HL per Lord Scarman at 188–189).
28 Ibid. (CA & HL per Lord Scarman at 186).
29 Ibid.
30 Ibid.
31 I discuss this point further in Chapter 8.
32 [1993] AC 789 (FamD, CA & HL).
33 *Airedale NHS Trust v Bland* [1993] AC 789 (FamD, CA & HL per Butler Sloss LJ at 818; Lord Goff at 869).
34 Ibid. (FamD, CA & HL per Lord Keith at 856; Lord Goff at 867; Lord Browne Wilkinson 884).
35 Ibid. (FamD, CA & HL per Sir Stephen Brown P at 804; Hoffmann LJ at 828; Lord Goff at 863).
36 As discussed in Chapter 2, paradoxes have the effect of paralyzing observation and judgment; see Teubner (1997: 765).
37 *Airedale NHS Trust v Bland* [1993] AC 789 (FamD, CA & HL at 897).
38 [1995] IESC 1, [1995] 2 IR 73.
39 Article 30.3.2 *Bunreacht na hÉireann* (Constitution of Ireland).

40 *Re A Ward of Court (withholding medical treatment) (No. 2)* [1995] IESC 1, [1996] 2
    IR 73 [139]. For a trenchant criticism of this aspect of the Supreme Court's
    reasoning, see Keown (1996).
41 *Airedale NHS Trust v Bland* [1993] AC 789 (FamD, CA & HL per Hoffman LJ at
    831; Lord Keith at 859; Lord Goff at 865); *Re A Ward of Court (withholding
    medical treatment) (No. 2)* [1995] IESC 1, [1996] 2 IR 73 (per Hamilton CJ at
    [140]; Flaherty J at [198]).
42 This distinction is further developed in the work of Henri Lefebvre; see Elden
    (2004: 192–198).
43 These amendments were presented in the course of a more wide-ranging and
    arguably quite distinct Bill to reform the Human Fertilisation and Embryology
    Act 1990; see further, Fox (2009).
44 Mark Pritchard MP HC Deb Vol 476 Col 235 (20 May 2008).
45 Edward Leigh MP Vol 476 Col 227 (20 May 2008); Claire Curtis-Thomas MP
    Vol 476 Col 232 (20 May 2008); Nadine Dorries MP Vol 476 Col 263 (20 May
    2008); Anne Widdecombe MP Vol 476 Col 271 (20 May 2008).
46 See further, Franklin (1991).
47 Mark Pritchard MP Vol 476 Col 235 (20 May 2008).
48 On temporal horizons, see Reddy *et al.* (2006: 42–46).
49 See Stern (1993); Morris (1999); and Scott (2000).
50 See *Re MB (An Adult: Medical Treatment)* [1997] 2 FCR 541 (CA per Butler Sloss
    LJ at 549, 554) and *St George's Healthcare NHS Trust v S, R v Collins, ex parte S*
    [1999] Fam 26 (CA per Judge LJ at 45, 46–47).
51 See, respectively, *Rochdale Healthcare NHS Trust v C* [1997] 1 FCR 274 (per
    Johnson J at 275); and *Re MB (An Adult: Medical Treatment)* [1997] 2 FCR 541
    (CA per Butler Sloss LJ at 546 referring to decision of Hollis J at first instance).
52 For example, see, respectively, *Re L (Patient: Non-Consensual Treatment)* (1996) 35
    BMLR 44 (per Kirkwood J at 45); and *Re S (Adult: Refusal of Treatment)* [1993]
    Fam 123 (per Stephen Brown P at 124).
53 For example, see, respectively, *Re L (Patient: Non-Consensual Treatment)* (1996)
    35 BMLR 44 (Kirkwood J at 47); and *Norfolk and Norwich Healthcare NHS Trust v
    W* [1997] 1 FCR 269 (Johnson J at 270).
54 See *Re L (Patient: Non-Consensual Treatment)* (1996) 35 BMLR 44 (Kirkwood J at
    47); *Rochdale Healthcare NHS Trust v C* [1997] 1 FCR 274 (per Johnson J at 275).
55 [1993] Fam 123 (Stephen Brown P).
56 [1999] Fam 26 (CA).
57 *St George's Healthcare NHS Trust v S, R v Collins, ex parte S* [1999] Fam 26 (CA per
    Judge LJ at 41).
58 Ibid.
59 See *Re L (Patient: Non-Consensual Treatment)* (1996) 35 BMLR 44 (per Kirkwood
    J at 47); *Rochdale Healthcare NHS Trust v C* [1997] 1 FCR 274 (per Johnson J at
    276); *Norfolk and Norwich Healthcare NHS Trust v W* [1997] 1 FCR 269 (per
    Johnson J at 273).
60 *Norfolk and Norwich Healthcare NHS Trust v W* [1997] 1 FCR 269 (per Johnson J
    at 272). He applied the same reasoning in *Rochdale Healthcare NHS Trust v C*
    [1997] 1 FCR 274 (per Johnson J at 275).
61 See Agamben (1998: 5).
62 The term 'chronopolitics' is borrowed from James (2007: 104).
63 As Lord Browne Wilkinson put it in *Bland,* whereas 'death in the traditional
    sense was beyond human control' it is now increasingly 'determined by human
    decision': *Airedale NHS Trust v Bland* [1993] AC 789 (FamD, CA & HL at 878).
64 On the theme of instability in medical law, see Montgomery (2006).

References

Agamben, G (1998) *Homo Sacer. Sovereign Power and Bare Life* (Palo Alto, CA, Stanford University Press).

Agamben, G (2000) *Means Without End. Notes on Politics* (Minneapolis, MN, University of Minnesota Press).

Armitage, J and P Graham (2001) 'Dromoeconomics: Towards a Political Economy of Speed', 7 *Parallax* 111.

Baynham, M (2003) 'Narratives in Space and Time: Beyond "Backdrop" Accounts of Narrative Orientation', 13 *Narrative Inquiry* 347.

Bell, A (1995) 'News Time', 4 *Time and Society* 305.

Bridgeman, T (2007) 'Time and Space' in D Herman (ed.), *The Cambridge Companion to Narrative* (Cambridge, Cambridge University Press) 52.

Butler, J (1990) *Gender Trouble. Feminism and the Subversion of Identity* (New York, Routledge).

Castree, N (2009) 'The Spatio-Temporality of Capitalism', 18 *Time and Society* 26.

Commaille, J (1998) 'La regulation des temporalités juridiques par le social et le politique', in F Ost and M van Hoecke (eds), *Temps et droit. Le droit a-t-il pour vocation de durer?* (Brussels, Bruylant) 317.

De Gama, K (1993) 'A Brave New World? Rights Discourse and the Politics of Reproductive Autonomy', 20 *Journal of Law and Society* 114.

Diamantides, M (1995) 'Ethics in Law: Death Marks on a "Still Life". A Vision of Judgment as Vegetation', 6 *Law and Critique* 209.

Edensor, T (2006) 'Reconsidering National Temporalities, Institutional Times, Everyday Routines, Serial Spaces and Synchronicities', 9 *European Journal of Social Theory* 525.

Elden, S (2004) *Understanding Henri Lefebvre. Theory and the Possible* (London, Continuum).

Eriksen, TH (2001) *Tyranny of the Moment. Fast and Slow Time in the Information Age* (London, Pluto).

Fitzpatrick, P (2001) *Modernism and the Grounds of Law* (Cambridge, Cambridge University Press).

Fox, M (2009) 'The Human Fertilisation and Embryology Act 2008: Tinkering at the Margins', 17 *Feminist Legal Studies* 333.

Franklin, S (1991) 'Fetal Fascinations: New Dimensions to the Medical-Scientific Construction of Fetal Personhood', in S Franklin, C Lury and J Stacey (eds) *Off-Centre. Feminism and Cultural Studies* (London, Harper Collins) 190.

Goodrich, P (1992) 'Poor Illiterate Reason: History, Nationalism and the Common Law', 1 *Social and Legal Studies* 7.

Gross, O (1999–2000) 'The Normless and Exceptionless Exception: Carl Schmitt's Theory of Emergency Powers and the "Norm-Exception" Dichotomy', 21 *Cardozo Law Review* 1825.

Gurvitch, G (1964) *The Spectrum of Social Time* (Dordrecht, Nijhoff).

Hasler, J (1982) 'Virginia Woolf and the Chimes of Big Ben', 63 *English Studies* 145.

Hope, W (2009) 'Conflicting Temporalities: State, Nation, Economy and Democracy under Global Capitalism', 18 *Time and Society* 62.

House of Commons Science and Technology Committee (2007) *Scientific and*

Technology Committee, *Scientific Developments Relating to the Abortion Act 1967*, Twelfth Report of Session 2006–7, vol 1, HC 1045–1 (Norwich, The Stationery Office).

Hutchinson, AC (2000) *It's All in the Game. A Non-Foundationalist Account of Law and Adjudication* (Durham, NC, Duke University Press).

Jackson, B (1998) 'On the Atemporality of Legal Time', in F Ost and M van Hoecke (eds), *Temps et droit. Le droit a-t-il pour vocation de durer?* (Brussels, Bruylant) 225.

James, I (2007) *Paul Virilio* (London, Routledge).

Jessop, B (2000) 'The Crisis of the National Spatio-Temporal Fix and the Tendential Ecological Dominance of Globalizing Capitalism', 24 *International Journal of Urban and Regional Research* 323.

Kennedy, I (1991) *Treat Me Right. Essays in Medical Law and Ethics* (Oxford, Clarendon).

Keown, J (1996) 'Life and Death in Dublin', 55 *Cambridge Law Journal* 6.

Lim, H (1999) 'Caesareans and Cyborgs', 7 *Feminist Legal Studies* 133.

Lord Justice Thorpe (1997) 'The Caesarean Section Debate', 27 *Family Law* 663.

Maclean, AR (2006) 'Autonomy, Consent and Persuasion', 13 *European Journal of Health Law* 321.

Maclean, AR (2009) *Autonomy, Informed Consent and the Law* (Cambridge, Cambridge University Press).

Marder, H (1986) 'Split Perspective: Types of Incongruity in *Mrs Dalloway*', 22 *Papers in Language and Literature* 51.

Melissaris, E (2005) 'The Chronology of the Legal', 50 *McGill Law Journal* 839.

Miola, J (2006) 'Autonomy Rued OK?', 14 *Medical Law Review* 108.

Montgomery, J (2006) 'Law and the Demoralisation of Medicine', 26 *Legal Studies* 185.

Moran, J (2005) 'Queueing Up in Postwar Britain', 16 *Twentieth Century British History* 283.

Morris, A (1999) 'Once Upon a Time in a Hospital: The Cautionary Tale of *St George's Health Care NHS Trust v S, R v Collins and others, ex parte S* [1998] 3 All ER 673', 7 *Feminist Legal Studies* 75.

Nobles, R and D Schiff (2006) *A Sociology of Jurisprudence* (Oxford, Hart Publishing).

Ost, F (1999) *Le Temps du droit* (Paris, Odile Jacob).

Palmer, J (2009) 'Seeing and Knowing: Ultrasound Images in the Contemporary Abortion Debate', 10 *Feminist Theory* 173.

Petchesky, RP (1987) 'Fetal Images: The Power of Visual Culture in the Politics of Reproduction', 13 *Feminist Studies* 263.

Postema, GJ (1986) *Bentham and the Common Law Tradition* (Oxford, Clarendon Press).

Postema, GJ (2004) 'Melody and Law's Mindfulness of Time', 17 *Ratio Iuris* 203.

Poulantzas, N (1978) *State, Power, Socialism* (London, Verso).

Reddy, WC, P Dourish and W Pratt (2006) 'Temporality in Medical Work: Time Also Matters', 15 *Computer Supported Cooperative Work* 29.

Scheuerman, WE (2004) *Liberal Democracy and the Social Acceleration of Time* (Baltimore, MD, Johns Hopkins University Press).

Schmitt, C (1985) *Political Theology. Four Chapters on the Concept of Sovereignty* (Cambridge, MA, MIT Press).

Scott, R (2000) 'The Pregnant Woman and the Good Samaritan: Can a Pregnant Woman Have a Duty to Undergo a Caesarean Section', 20 *Oxford Journal of Legal Studies* 407.

Showalter, E (1992) 'Introduction', in V Woolf, *Mrs Dalloway* (London, Penguin) i.

Sontag, S (1979) *On Photography* (London, Penguin).

Sorokin, PA and RK Merton (1937) 'Social Time: A Methodological and Functional Analysis', 42 *American Journal of Sociology* 615.

Stern, K (1993) 'Court-Ordered Caesarean Sections: In Whose Interests?', 56 *Modern Law Review* 238.

Syrett, K (2007) *Law, Legitimacy and the Rationing of Health Care. A Contextual and Comparative Perspective* (Cambridge, Cambridge University Press).

Teubner, G (1990) ' "And God Laughed": Indeterminacy, Self-Reference and Paradox in Law', 7 *Stanford Literature Review* 15.

Teubner, G (1997) 'The King's Many Bodies: The Self-Deconstruction of Law's Hierarchy', 31 *Law and Society Review* 763.

Teubner, G (1998) 'The Two Faces of Janus: Rethinking Legal Pluralism', in K Uusitalo, Z Bankowski and H Thor (eds), *Law and Power. Critical and Socio-Legal Essays* (Liverpool, Deborah Charles) 119.

Thompson, EP (1967) 'Time, Work Discipline and Industrial Capitalism', 38 *Past and Present* 56.

Thomson, M (1994) 'After Re S', 2 *Medical Law Review* 127.

Toombs, SK (1990) 'The Temporality of Illness: Four Levels of Experience', 11 *Theoretical Medicine* 227.

Van de Kerchove, M (1998) 'Accéleration de la justice pénale et traitement en "temps réel" ' in F Ost and M van Hoecke (eds) *Temps et droit. Le droit a-t-il pour vocation de durer?* (Brussels, Bruylant) 367.

Virilio, P (2006) *Speed and Politics. An Essay on Dromology* (Los Angeles, Semiotext(e)).

Virilio, P and S Lotringer (1983) *Pure War* (New York, Semiotext(e)).

Woolf, V (1992) *Mrs Dalloway* (London, Penguin).

Chapter 5

Utopia

Introduction

Medical law in Britain is characterized by a series of anti-market prohibitions. The sale of organs, gametes and surrogacy services is either banned or subject to severe restrictions.[1] Brokering and advertising are outlawed. These restrictions have been subject to harsh criticism, particularly from ethicists. Ethicists argue that such paternalistic restrictions cannot be justified in terms of coherent rational argument (Wilkinson 2003). They reflect instead a set of ill-defined taboos and prejudices. But this approach abandons rather too soon the analysis of statutory limitations on markets in medicine. In particular it fails to take seriously the historical and cultural context of anti-market arguments.

In this chapter, I attempt to remedy that defect, drawing on rhetorical analysis and literary criticism to trace the political background to legislative prohibitions on trade in the human body and some of its functions. In short I propose that anti-market arguments instantiate and extend certain utopian aspirations shared by the founders of the National Health Service. Their rhetorical plausibility depended significantly on their resonance with this general vision of the health service as an enclave, an exemplary zone of non-commodified human relations. It is equally true that the declining plausibility of anti-market arguments is linked with the perceived failure of this broader vision of the NHS. In the last two decades the commodity form has been gradually reasserted across the range of medical practice. Patient autonomy, which is used to justify commerce in human tissue or surrogacy services, resonates with market-based reforms to the structure of the NHS.

The chapter is organized as follows. The next section takes as its particular focus the ethical and legal debate regarding commercial surrogacy. The utopian backdrop to this debate is then elaborated using contemporary literary and social theory. I pay particular attention to the formal aspects of fictional and political utopias. The notion of the utopian enclave can be discerned in the speeches and writings of Aneurin Bevan, founder of the NHS, and in the work of Richard Titmuss, its most important academic proponent. Decommodification of clinical work is framed in utopian terms with reference to the writings of the nineteenth-century visionary William Morris. The following section reads Professor Ian Kennedy's germinal Reith Lectures of 1980 as an anti-utopian attack on the enclave status of health care under the NHS. This stance has also been shared by Health Secretaries over the last two decades seeking to reform the Service in the name of choice and accountability. In the penultimate section I seek to reveal the hidden utopian dimensions of this new dispensation. Drawing on the work of David Harvey and Zygmunt Bauman, I argue that the enclave form has been replaced by a utopian idealization of processes, such as market exchange, rational ethical debate and the law itself. In conclusion I suggest a number of anti-utopian critiques of this new common sense.

Surrogacy and the gift in medical law

This section explores debates regarding the commercialization of surrogacy in the United Kingdom. These debates illustrate the conflict between pro- and anti-market perspectives on medicine in general and on the National Health Service as an institution. It will be seen that an inherited set of common-sense assumptions supporting the limitation of commerce in health care has recently been challenged by ethical reasoning which emphasizes autonomy and choice. This debate is inherently political: it cannot be resolved in the abstract. As our discussion in Chapter 1 showed, relevant arguments gain in force from the plausibility of the visions of society by which they are underpinned. These visions are moreover closely connected to broader material and institutional contexts, which are themselves subject to challenge and change.

Surrogacy – the Brazier report

In 1998, a team chaired by Professor Margaret Brazier was established by the Health Ministers of the United Kingdom to review the regulation of surrogacy (Brazier et al. 1998). Prior to this, attempts had already been made to forestall the marketization of surrogacy by legislative prohibition. Commercial brokering and advertising in this area were banned by the Surrogacy Arrangements Act 1985.[2] Contracts between surrogate mothers and commissioning couples were deemed to be unenforceable.[3] Moreover, under the Human Fertilisation and Embryology Act 1990, a court could deny a parental order in favour of the commissioning couple where money had been paid in consideration of the surrogate mother handing over the child.[4] However, increased use of non-profit agencies in the 1990s, as well as rumours of a thriving unofficial market in surrogacy, led the UK Health Ministers to instigate a fresh review and to seek proposals for law reform.

In its report the review team recommended a more detailed system of regulation, based on a code of practice for non-profit surrogacy agencies who would be licensed and monitored by the respective health ministries of the different nations of the UK.[5] Existing restrictions on commercialization would be maintained and strengthened by an explicit limit on payments to surrogate mothers. These would be restricted to genuine expenses, as laid down in a detailed catalogue, with a ban on additional remuneration. Violation of the new restrictions would constitute additional grounds for denying a parental order to commissioning parents.

Brazier's justification

The Brazier report offered several justifications for these proposals. It sought to protect the welfare of children born as a result of surrogacy. Admittedly there was no direct evidence of psychological harm to such children, but the potential for this demanded a precautionary approach from the state (Brazier *et al.* 1998: 32–33). The Report was also concerned with possible exploitation of the surrogate mother, who usually came from a lower socio-economic background than the commissioning parents (Brazier *et al.* 1998: 35). On this point, the report was criticized for exhibiting an unjustifiably paternalistic attitude to surrogates (Freeman 1999: 5). The effectiveness of the proposed regulatory regime was also challenged (Freeman 1999: 10). For whatever reason, the Health Ministers opted not to change the law and the regulation of surrogacy in the United Kingdom went unchanged.

Of greatest importance in the present context was the final justification given by the review team for its restrictive stance. This arose from a concern with the 'commodification of childbearing' (Brazier *et al.* 1998: 38). Whether the payment to the surrogate was classified as a fee for services or the price of a product, the resulting child would be viewed, and would view itself, in terms of a monetary equivalent. Consequently the law should ensure that bearing a child for others was only ever 'a fully informed and free act of giving' (Brazier *et al.* 1998: 39). The review team drew support for its position from the fact that:

> as a society, we believe that the use of our procreative capacities to assist others should … be a gift, not a commercial transaction.
>
> (Brazier *et al.* 1998: 39)

This was the 'core value' on which many social arrangements in the United Kingdom were based, including legislative prohibitions on markets in organs and gametes. Consistency demanded that surrogacy be regulated in the same manner.

The reality and acceptability of commodification in surrogacy has been widely debated before and since the Brazier report (van Niekerk and van Zyl 1995; Wilkinson 2003: c.8). I will not engage directly with this ethical dispute here. Rather I focus on the style of argument adopted in the Report itself and by some of its critics in order to reveal the rhetorical strategies and political stakes in the controversy over surrogacy. These are made clear in the response of McLachlan and Swales to Brazier. They raise a familiar set of anti-paternalist arguments in support of a freer market in surrogacy (McLachlan and Swales 2000). On commodification, they charge the report with failing to give adequate reasons for its position. The 'core values' of British society invoked by the review team are merely:

> assertions of their own views rather than arguments for them, far less arguments against opposing ones.
>
> (McLachlan and Swales 2000: 10)

For McLachlan and Swales it cannot be a matter of what 'we as a society' believe, but rather what can be argued for in reasoned discussion. In essence this criticism prescribes a certain type of speech in relation to controversial issues of health policy, namely that which adopts the abstract and detached style of liberal bioethics. Speech which fails to meet the formal qualities of ethics discourse is stigmatized as redundant or 'rhetorical' (McLachlan and Swales 2000: 10).

Brazier's rhetoric

McLachlan and Swales's argument exhibits the 'scientistism' characteristic of orthodox legal scholarship and of much work in economics and bioethics. For them, 'rhetoric' functions as a term of abuse, a negative pole by which to define their own more scientific enterprise. As we discussed in Chapter 1, that aspiration neglects the indeterminate nature of reasoning and the inherently political nature of speech in all disciplines, apart perhaps from mathematics and formal logic. Consistent with the approach taken in this book, the form and purpose of Brazier's affirmations can be better grasped if their nature as rhetoric is taken seriously and analysed as such. In short, we should read this crucial part of the report, not as a failed ethical argument, but as an exercise in political persuasion, oriented to the needs and values of a concrete, historical community. The 'gift relationship' invoked by Brazier as a 'core value' amounts to a further topic of medical law: a piece of common sense shared between the review team and its wider audience (Perelman 1982: 21). They sought to extend to the conclusion (i.e. a prohibition on commercial surrogacy) the allegiance of the audience to the original common place (i.e. the 'gift') (Perelman 1982: 21). Put in classical terms, we can say that in this respect the Brazier report was a form of 'deliberative speech', aimed at moving the audience to action (or more accurately inaction) (Robrieux 2000: 36). But the report was also 'epideictic' in form: confirming the values and identity of its readers in the manner of an oration. As James Boyd White has argued, rhetoric does not just find its audience, it also actively creates it as a moral community (White 1985: 695). These were also the political stakes for Brazier's critics: the creation of a new mentality, a new community of values to replace that formed around the gift in medicine.

A utopian vision?

The persuasive force of Brazier's ideal of non-commodification can be understood by attending to its specific historical resonances. I will argue that the topic of the 'gift' crystallizes a utopian vision of a better society, one from which money has typically been banished. This goal gained force in the post-war years with the creation of the National Health Service and through the ideological labours of its founders and promoters. More broadly it needs to be understood within the context of the Keynesian settlement, which set considerable limits to the scope of the market. Brazier's championing of the 'gift' partakes of this utopian vision, however implicitly. It gains in resonance from a particular institutional setting. It appeals to and constitutes an ideal audience of fellow citizens committed to non-market relations in this sector. This is the performative effect of eliding 'we as a society' with 'we' meaning the review team (Brazier et al. 1998: 39).

The widespread criticism of Brazier's reasoning would indicate that, by 1998 at least, the topic of the 'gift' had declined greatly in plausibility. Indeed not long afterwards Professor Brazier herself remarked on this shift and its connection to institutional and economic change. She noted that regulation was based:

> on the supposition that fertility services would be integrated into the NHS.... The enormous commercial potential of developments in reproductive medicine was hardly foreseen, and opposition to commodification of reproduction was almost a given. Yet debate on commodification and commercialization is at the forefront of debate today.

> (1999: 191)

Returning briefly to McLachlan and Swales, we can observe the active contribution made by critics to creating a new common sense regarding human reproduction and health care. At a formal level, their proscription of non-ethical language has already been noted. Ironically, they themselves no less than Brazier, make a number of rhetorical moves to bolster their case. In a typically rhetorical appeal to the obvious they state that 'Britain, like any society is a "multi-values" one' (McLachlan and Swales 2000: 10). The 'we' in their argument is now constituted by the 'rest of us' who may not agree with the review team. A new mode of address is required for this new audience. Social disaggregation, they imply, calls for neutral technocratic expertise, rather than value-laden political rhetoric. Significantly they query the failure to include an economist in the review team (McLachlan and Swales 2000: 14). In conclusion, they assert that the perceived weaknesses of the Brazier report demonstrate a broader:

> need for ... radical re-assessment of the nature and proper scope of pecuniary transactions in connection with the provision of health care and related services.
>
> (2000: 17)

Legislative bans on organ and gamete sales can be challenged, even the core NHS settlement itself.

Dimensions of utopia

I have argued in earlier chapters that the NHS made an important contribution to the post-war settlement. It helped to achieve social peace between capital and labour and to discharge the responsibility of the state to maintain a suitably fit workforce. It also served as source of demand for the growing pharmaceutical and medical equipment industries (Jessop 2002). But this fairly functional perspective is not the only possible view of the NHS. The attachment of many intellectuals and much of the general public to the Service cannot simply be accounted for in instrumental terms. Political economy alone cannot explain the purchase of the 'core values' adumbrated in the Brazier report for example. As I have suggested above, these values are supported by a broader, utopian vision of the NHS as an idealized zone exempted from the morals of the marketplace.

Like 'rhetoric', 'utopia' now largely functions as a term of abuse in political speech. It is synonymous with fanciful and impractical schemes on the one hand and coercion on the other.[6] As we have seen, the NHS is sometimes condemned in this vein as a doomed attempt to make everyone healthy or to provide limitless care to everyone regardless of the cost. However, there is a great deal more to 'utopia' than the simple dream of abundance. Historically utopians have often laid more emphasis on the moral renewal that would follow upon institutional change (Levitas 2007: 300–301). The study of utopias is wide ranging and draws on literary criticism, political philosophy and the history of ideas. I cannot do justice to this varied body of insights here. Instead I will pick out a number of themes which help to illuminate the key utopian features of the NHS as represented in political, legal and academic rhetoric. These themes are intelligible across two interrelated dimensions: the form taken by real and imaginary utopias; and the functions which such utopias are intended to perform (Levitas 1990: 178).

Utopias have traditionally been conceived as enclaves, separated from the wider world. Practical utopias such as garden cities and rural communes are physically carved out of the rest of society. Literary utopias are often set in another time or place. But they are not implemented or imagined in a vacuum. They always maintain a significant relationship with the actual social and political situation within which they were conceived. Indeed it is this combination of separation and connection that gives utopias their critical power. As the American critic Fredric Jameson notes, they:

> are something like a foreign body in the social ... they remain as it were momentarily beyond the reach of the social and testify to its political powerlessness, at the same time they offer a space in which new wish images of the social can be elaborated and experimented on.
>
> (2005: 16)

This 'pre-figurative' trait has been a key temporal feature of concrete utopian communities. Thus the mediaeval monastery was an island of rationality and discipline, later to be generalized across all of Western society with the Reformation (Kumar 1991: 65). Robert Owen's settlement at New Lanark was intended to anticipate a just society in contradistinction to the harsh world of early British industrialism (Polanyi 2001: 174–182). But concrete utopias do not simply constitute a message to the outside world. Their inhabitants gain a moral education through following a distinctive regime of rules and routines. Practical utopias are schools for the future.

In the terms used by Harvey, the enclave is a 'utopia of spatial form' (2000: 160). It presumes a sequestered space within which the messy process of historical change and social conflict has been repressed. To achieve this, it is often necessary to banish certain key features of the world outside. Thus Thomas More constituted his original *Utopia* as 'a closed space economy' by excluding the disruptive forces of money, private property and wage labour (Harvey 2000: 160). As Harvey puts it, 'the happy perfection of the social and moral order depends upon these exclusions' (2000: 160). Human relations are no longer mediated by money and property. Altruism and solidarity replace alienation and competition (Levitas 1990: 6–7). Life within such an enclave utopia is, therefore, an education in non-commercial morality.

The final generic theme in utopianism to be considered here is the 'blueprint'. In utopia, the 'messy play of social processes' is often replaced by a precisely specified machine (Jameson 2000: 385). According to Jameson, this 'apparatus' gathers up necessity, absorbing unfreedom, and allowing freedom to flourish all around itself' (2000: 385). In the context of medicine, necessity connotes the bodily constraints imposed by pain and sickness. The associated machine might then be a diagnostic device or a new drug. But the apparatus need not take the concrete form of a machine or a therapy. It can also be understood more broadly to include the administrative system within the utopian enclave. This is especially true when it is recognized that bodily necessity is often matched by economic necessity. In a market system, lack of resources may block access to the apparatuses of clinical medicine, reinforcing the unfreedom caused by ill health. From this perspective, the organizational blueprint for free health care can itself be viewed as a utopian machine. At one and the same time it serves to gather up the chaos of the market and to conquer the necessity of poverty and ill health. Its implementation allows the enclave to function as a zone of moral exemplarity.

In the next section, I trace the utopian aspects of the NHS with reference to the characteristics discussed above. It is, of course, true that the NHS was not programmatically designed as an ideal community in the manner of the fictional or practical utopias just considered. But, as the philosopher Ernst Bloch argued, the 'anticipatory consciousness' typical of utopia is 'embedded in a vast range of human practice and culture' going well beyond traditional schemes (Levitas 2007: 291). This broader category includes 'piecemeal social democratic and "liberal" reforms allegorical of a wholesale transformation of the social totality' (Jameson 2005: 4). The most prominent and enduring social reform in post-war Britain, the NHS was invested with just such an allegorical meaning by many of its early proponents.

The NHS as utopian enclave

The Beveridge report of 1941, on which the NHS and other welfare state initiatives were based, can be read as a utopian blueprint (Beveridge 1942). In prose evoking the redemptive travelogue of John Bunyan's Pilgrim, the report enumerated the five giant evils which its programme would challenge: Want, Ignorance, Idleness, Squalor, and Disease.[7] Beveridge aimed to liberate the people from the brute embodied necessity of sickness and ill health. The basic mechanism for achieving this was clear: a system of health care available to all and free at the point of use.[8] However, Beveridge's blueprint was no more than a framework. In particular there was little detail on provision for health care (Timmins 2001: 24). The task of creating a national system fell to Aneurin Bevan, Minister of Health in the Labour government of 1945.

Building socialism: Aneurin Bevan

The essence of Bevan's scheme was to remove health care from the market in two significant respects.[9] On the one hand, patients' access to care would no longer depend on their income. Clinical relations would not be mediated by money. On the other hand, professional autonomy was guaranteed within a wholly state-funded service. Doctors were exempted from many of the disciplines imposed on wage labourers in the rest of the economy. As will be seen, this 'double decommodification' was not simply a matter of strategy, i.e. to induce co-operation among doctors or to gain favour with the public. In his speeches and writings, Bevan cast these features of the NHS in distinctively moral terms.

At bottom Bevan shared the traditional utopian view that the human character will be improved by the abolition of money and private property (Carey 1999). In this respect the NHS prefigured a broader transformation in British life:

> A free health service is pure Socialism and as such it is opposed to the hedonism of capitalist society.... It takes away a whole segment of private enterprise and transfers it to the field of public administration ... by means of which the new society is gradually being articulated.
>
> (Bevan 1990: 106)

The pre-war patchwork of insurance, charity and commercial provision was to be replaced by an orderly system. Collective planning would eliminate the insecurity produced by sickness and economic necessity. Beyond this, a moral bonus would accrue to the wider population, as the general inclination to solidarity and altruism was satisfied. Society, said Bevan:

> becomes more wholesome, more serene and spiritually healthier, if ... its citizens have at the back of their consciousness the knowledge that not only themselves, but all their fellows have access when ill to the best that medical skill can provide.
>
> (Quoted in Foot 1962: 105)

'Serenity' was one of Bevan's favourite words. According to his biographer, it expressed the widespread desire for a settled 'sense of order, not imposed, but cooperatively established' (Foot 1962: 105).

The capacity of the NHS to achieve moral renewal was not simply a matter of free access. It also derived from the nature of medical work. For Bevan, doctors were exemplars of a non-capitalist way of life. Scientific pioneers such as Pasteur, Jenner and Lister were, he said:

dedicated men and women whose work was inspired by values that have nothing to do with the rapacious bustle of the stock exchange.... Few would have described themselves as Socialists, but they can hardly be considered representative types of the competitive society.

(Bevan 1990: 99)

In practice, however, commercial imperatives limited the profession's autonomy and stifled its impulse to serve the public without discrimination. Bevan reserved special disapprobation for the buying and selling of doctors' practices, which was banned under the National Health Service Act 1946 (Rintala 2003: 51). Bevan argued that a doctor's work should be determined, not by external criteria or the requirement to turn a profit, but by 'the standards of his profession and the requirements of his oath' (1990: 112). By underwriting clinical practice without specifying its content, the NHS would restore the moral integrity of medicine. By constituting itself as an enclave of non-commodified labour, it anticipated a general refashioning of the world of work.

I explore in greater detail the utopian aspects of this double decommodification in the rest of this section. The influential commentator Richard Titmuss portrayed the NHS as a practical utopian community, participation in which would educate patients in the values of solidarity and altruism. The nineteenth-century fiction of William Morris articulated a vision of labour beyond the market, common to socialists and elite professionals alike.

Altruism and solidarity: Richard Titmuss

Titmuss is best known to contemporary medical lawyers for his work on commercial markets in human blood (1997). His book *The Gift Relationship* has been so influential that its title is often taken as shorthand for a range of anti-market positions in health care, such as that adopted in the Brazier report discussed above. The book's argument is woven from material in anthropology, economics and ethics, and has been subject to extensive critique.[10] However, I will only focus here on its nature as political rhetoric. Titmuss was clear that there was more at stake in the 'commodification' debate than the sale of human tissue. He predicted that:

> if human blood be legitimated as a consumption good ... [a]ll policy would become in the end economic policy, and the only values that would count are those that can be measured in terms of money and pursued in the dialectic of hedonism.
>
> (1987: 191)

Keeping blood out of the market was an expression of his broader utopian ambitions for the NHS and the welfare state. Titmuss challenged the idea that people were essentially incapable of altruism. Human motives were not fixed in this way. Rather they could be encouraged or discouraged by specific practices and social arrangements (Titmuss 1997: 306). Accordingly the NHS, as an institution, was capable of transforming the quality of human relationships through fostering 'a sense of mutual responsibility' (Kynaston: 2007: 543).

Titmuss vividly set forth this vision in one of his last essays: a description of his experiences as a cancer patient at the Westminster Hospital in 1972. Originally delivered in lecture form to an academic audience, this is framed as a travel narrative in the manner of much utopian fiction (Jameson 2005: 18). Sitting on a bench in the waiting room of a radiotherapy department, Titmuss evokes the democratic and egalitarian nature of the NHS from the outset (Abel-Smith and Titmuss 1987: 269). He introduces a series of representative fellow patients, all from modest or disadvantaged backgrounds, but each benefiting equally from NHS treatment. Next to him on the bench, for example, is a 'harassed middle-aged woman, married to a postman, who had two children' (Abel-Smith and Titmuss 1987: 269). Who went first depended 'quite simply on the vagaries of London traffic – not race, religion, colour or class' (Abel-Smith and Titmuss 1987: 275). There follows an evocative description of his time as an inpatient. He is helped by a 53-year-old man named Bill, who is receiving treatment for spinal injuries sustained in North Africa during the Second World War:

> Since the National Health Service came into operation in 1948 Bill has spent varying periods from two to four or five weeks every year at the Westminster Hospital receiving the latest micro-developments [in] care and rehabilitation.
>
> (Abel-Smith and Titmuss 1987: 270)

With help from Titmuss, Bill worked out that he has 'cost the National Health Service' roughly half a million pounds over the previous 24 years (Abel-Smith and Titmuss 1987: 270).

Titmuss conveys an atmosphere of friendly co-operation on the ward, notwithstanding technical shortcomings. Patients assist each other to use the sole portable telephone, though the lines keep getting crossed. Titmuss himself helped:

> with the tea trolley at 6 o'clock in the morning when all the mobile patients served the immobile patients, and one shuffled around not caring what one looked like and learning a great deal about other human beings and their predicaments.
>
> (Abel-Smith and Titmuss 1987: 275)

Interestingly the medical and nursing staff are not brought to life in any rounded way, Titmuss being concerned to detail the 'fellowship' between patient-citizens above all else.[11] Clinical practice is evoked instead through a depersonalized description of the expensive 'theratron' used for radiotherapy. The control panel of this 'apparatus':

> looked like what I imagine might resemble the control panel of the Concorde cockpit.... [Y]ou lie naked on a machine and you are raised and lowered and this machine beams at you from various angles radium at a cost, so I am told, of £10 per minute.
>
> (Abel-Smith and Titmuss 1987: 273)

Titmuss's enumeration of costs here and throughout the essay highlights the role of the NHS itself as a utopian machine absorbing economic necessity and freeing up space for what he called 'social growth': a process which 'cannot be quantified' (1997: 274). However, it also suggests a constant awareness that this non-market enclave is subject to pressure from wider economic and political forces. In this respect, Titmuss's NHS shares certain features with the pastoral ideal of England, which, as I noted in Chapter 1, was depicted in many of Lord Denning's judgments. Admittedly Denning looked back regretfully, whereas Titmuss looked forward in hope. Nonetheless each conjured up a precarious zone of unmediated and fraternal relations between people (Klinck 1994: 45). The atmosphere of fellowship and harmony within is contrasted with the complexity and alienation threatening from outside (Tonsor 1973).

Labour as art: William Morris

The creation of the NHS was made possible by a remarkable convergence of opinion between the socialist minister Bevan and the ennobled leaders of the medical profession in the 1940s.[12] Both sides agreed that medical work was a matter of 'privacy, sacredness and inviolable clinical judgment' exempt from 'overtly political or economic considerations' (Lawrence 1994: 76–77). Though unexpected, this convergence was not unprecedented when viewed in the context of English cultural history. As Raymond Williams pointed out, many conservatives and socialists had been united in denouncing industrial society from the late eighteenth century on (1962: 23–24). Critics focused in particular on the growing use of machinery in production, the routinization and specialization of work and the mass manufacture of goods. This critique was expressed in the aesthetic theories of the English Romantics who denounced mere 'imitation' as an inauthentic mode of artistic production involving only the following of rules. They contrasted it with the unique emanations of artistic genius (Williams 1962: 61). For Karl Marx, industrial capitalism entailed the alienation of workers from the process of production, from each other and from themselves as human beings (1970: 106–119). All condemned what Shelley called the 'unmitigated exercise of the calculating faculty' (quoted in Williams 1962: 59).

The different elements of this tradition come together in the writings of Morris, nineteenth-century artist, craftsman and utopian socialist. For him, the arts defined a quality of living and working 'which it was the whole purpose of political change to make possible' (Williams 1962: 23–24). His views on labour developed in opposition to those of the novelist Edward Bellamy and other 'state socialists' who expected technical progress and bureaucratic administration to abolish poverty and eventually eliminate the need for work (2007).[13] For Morris, this goal of maximum leisure denied the nature of man to 'take pleasure in his work under certain conditions' (Morris 1973b: 87). What was needed was not the abolition of labour, but its transformation into 'honourable and fitting work' (Morris 1973a: 129).

Set in the twenty-first century, *News from Nowhere* is Morris's fictional response to Bellamy's position. In it, 'commercial morality' is extinct, money abolished, and factories replaced by 'banded-workshops' (Morris 2003: 39–40). The decommodification of work is central to the new order. The narrator is told that:

> men make for their neighbours' use as if they were making for themselves, not for a vague market of which they know nothing and over which they have no control.
>
> (Morris 2003: 83)

Producers are instinctively self-governing. The external discipline of the factory owner is not required:

> It is each man's business to make his own work pleasanter and pleasanter, which of course tends to raising the standard of excellence, as no man enjoys turning out work which is not a credit to him.
>
> (Morris 2003: 79)

The new society does not repudiate scientific progress. But machines serve the worker rather than dominating him (Leopold 2003: xvii).[14] Here, as elsewhere in Morris's writings, labour freed from 'the brutalities of competitive commerce' is equated with art (Morris 1973a: 118). Although sectoral and defensive, the medical profession's view of itself partook of this wider ideal of free labour. As such it chimed with Bevan's aspirations for workers more generally.

From utopia to anti-utopia

At its inception then, the institutional form of the NHS promised to over-come the alienation inherent in much pre-war medical practice.[15] Doctors would no longer have to compete with each other for patients. Medical work would be fulfilling as an end in itself, not simply a means of making a living. Individual clinical judgement would prevail over economic and technical concerns. Patients would be set free from the brute necessity of ill health: citizens bound together in a community of altruism and solid-arity. This vision was utopian, not only in the sense that it offered a better life for all, but also because it held out the prospect of transformed human relations in health care and in the wider society. The banning of trade in surrogacy, organs, blood and gametes, discussed earlier, was plausible against the backdrop of this broader vision. But plausibility is always contingent on the specific circumstances within which an argument is made. The declining persuasiveness of anti-market prohibitions was noted in the discussion of the Brazier report on surrogacy arrangements. The next section examines the important contribution of anti-utopian critique to this decline in plausibility.

Anti-utopian critique

Context and themes

Anti-utopia has 'stalked' utopia since its beginnings in literature and polit-ical theory (Kumar 1987: 99). But, as Krishan Kumar points out:

> the relationship is not symmetrical or equal. The anti-utopia is formed by utopia, and feeds parasitically on it…. [It] draws its material from utopia and reassembles it in a manner that denies the affirmation of utopia.
>
> (1987: 100)

Anti-utopian critique is often closely related to a specific utopian vision, picking out those negative aspects and unforeseen consequences which tend to thwart its practical realization. It will be seen that the NHS ideal, elaborated by Bevan and Titmuss, has been critiqued in just this way. Thus, the enclave is equated, not with shelter, but with closure and authoritari-anism (Harvey 2000: 182). By suppressing social processes, it promotes stagnation rather than moral growth. The blueprinted apparatus expands uncontrollably, absorbing freedom rather than releasing it. Ideals of peace and harmony are realized as repression and conformity. If anything is pre-figured, it is 'the horror of a society in which utopian aspirations' have actually been fulfilled (Kumar 1987: 100). Fear, not hope, is the keynote.

This anti-utopian challenge to the 'NHS settlement' was vividly formulated in Ian Kennedy's Reith Lectures of 1980.

Published as *The Unmasking of Medicine*, Kennedy's intervention came at the end of a decade of intense conflict within the NHS which formed part of the broader crisis besetting the Keynesian order in Britain (Timmins 2001). Doctors and other health staff had taken unprecedented industrial action in pursuit of pay claims. Government and consultants clashed over the acceptability of private practice within NHS hospitals. The unravelling of the 1948 compromise between doctors and the state was matched by a growing challenge to orthodox medicine from activist patient groups, focused on mental health and maternity care, for example. As I suggested in Chapter 2, these initiatives took the rhetorical form of challenges to the common sense of medicine and welfare at the time. In its hostility to medical privilege, Kennedy's argument is unmistakably influenced by these radical trends. Charting what he saw as the errors of modern medicine, he proposed ethics, law and patient consumerism as correctives. It is true that Kennedy was not the only or the first scholar to investigate and conceptualize medical law or medical ethics in Britain (Wilson 2014).[16] Nonetheless these lectures are worthy of particular attention owing to their wide dissemination and their keen reception by the medical profession (Miola 2007: 40–46). Beyond this, it is clear that more was at stake than the demarcation of academic disciplines. Indeed Kennedy's later work as a regulator allowed him to realize many of the ambitions for medical reform articulated in the Reith Lectures.

'Unmasking medicine'

The anti-utopian target of *The Unmasking of Medicine* is not the NHS as such. Though he condemns its neglect of prevention and primary care, Kennedy declares himself a 'committed supporter' of the Service (1983: 48). Rather, his main focus is on the model of clinical medicine that Bevan and the medical leaders had installed at the heart of the health care system (Kennedy 1983: 48). Doctors are represented in *The Unmasking of Medicine* as benevolent guardians, paternalistically securing the population against the negative consequences of industrial society. Medicine in this mode aims at defusing political tensions through social control.[17] Kennedy illustrates the point with a series of fictional vignettes. For example, the 35-year-old housewife Mrs Jones 'has grown to dread and despise the tedium of her life' (Kennedy 1983: 12). The doctor who diagnoses her as ill and who prescribes tranquilizers:

> endows himself with power over her.... [He] cannot change the economic and social order, but, with drugs he can stop her worrying

about it. So that is what he does. He returns her to the ranks of unhappy women who no longer feel the pain.

(Kennedy 1983: 12)

Mr Smith, exhausted from his 'dull and tedious' job on an assembly line, seeks a sick note. His doctor's decision is again more an exercise of power than of skill (Kennedy 1983: 8). These atomized and unhappy figures are sharply distinguished from the community of patients and staff conjured up by Titmuss. Far from overcoming alienation, NHS medicine seems to reinforce it in Kennedy's account.

The 'apparatus of medicine', so esteemed by Bevan, is thus seen to colonize broad areas of life. While liberating the citizen from the bodily necessity of illness, it also subjects her to an insidious kind of social coercion. It is supported in this effort by the 'vested interest' of the pharmaceutical industry and the 'connivance' of the general public (Kennedy 1983: 13, 22). Such exchanges of 'freedom for bread' have been thematized in anti-utopian literature since Dostoyevsky's Grand Inquisitor.[18] For Kennedy, clinical power in this mode is underwritten by a vision of the doctor as 'engineer/mechanic applying the techniques of medical science to cure a sick engine' (1983: 28). As Boltanski and Chiapello have pointed out, the engineer was emblematic of mid-twentieth century society, embodying a general:

> belief in progress, hope invested in science and technology, productivity and efficiency ... but also [a civic ideal of] institutional solidarity, the socialization of production, distribution and consumption ... in pursuit of social justice.

(2007: 18)

But this image is wholly inverted in Kennedy's account. Rationalized medicine has lead ironically to 'the appearance of new magicians and priests wrapped in the cloak of science and reason' (Kennedy 1983: 25). Medical technology and clinical autonomy are united in spectacularly futile and costly interventions at the end of life. Echoing Mary Shelley's *Frankenstein*, Kennedy describes this as a:

> pursuit of immortality with the respirator symbolizing some kind of Promethean eternity.

(1983: 28)

The respirator here can be taken to stand for the medical system as a whole, conceived in anti-utopian terms as a machine out of control. It contrasts clearly with the cool benevolence and efficiency of the 'theratron', itself a microcosm of the utopian NHS, in Titmuss's account.

Dissolving the enclave

For Kennedy, the dystopian features of contemporary medicine flow from its enclave status. Doctors, he says, 'have a highly developed sense of territoriality' which had been ratified by government and the courts (1983: 28). In his academic writing, Kennedy trenchantly criticized the tendency of English courts to defer to medical opinion.[19] He argued that this had the twin defects of producing 'idiosyncratic' decision making and sheltering the doctor from 'social responsibility' to the rest of society (1983: 119–120). Thus, in discussing uncontrolled medical research, he notes that:

> we, the consumers are rarely heard. But it is we who are affected by these developments, whether as patients or as members of the community.... And if any of us should be bold, or naïve, enough to raise his voice [in protest] ... the scientific establishment reacts with wounded indignation.
>
> (1983: 154)

Kennedy here calls forth an ideal audience of sovereign patient-consumers. His actual audience may not have conceived of themselves in this way. Indeed, he argues elsewhere that they have 'chosen to surrender' their power to medicine (1983: 152). Consequently, he implies, it is not just liberty, but the authentic appetite for liberty which needs to be restored. The medical profession is not directly addressed here. Kennedy merely intends doctors to overhear his condemnation of their high-handedness. This demotion contrasts with the status of medical leaders as Bevan's privileged and sole interlocutors during the creation of the NHS. Taken together these rhetorical moves aim to fracture the harmonious community of staff, patients and the general public on which Titmuss rested his hopes for the NHS. In its place, *The Unmasking of Medicine* unites idealized health care consumers with their idealized tribunes: ethicists and lawyers such as Kennedy himself.

Kennedy's reform proposals proceed from this basic alliance. Sensitive clinical decisions could not be left to the 'unarticulated judgment of individual medical practitioners' or the 'undefined collectivity of the medical profession' (Kennedy 1983: 102). The enclave would have to be dissolved into the general normative order. We are entitled, he says:

> to expect not only some regularity ... in the decisions doctors arrive at, but also some conformity between these decisions and those which the rest of us might make.
>
> (1983: 124)

Law and ethics are central to this levelling out. Indeed they are deeply interconnected in discharging this function. On the one hand, 'good law' reflects and promotes 'good medical ethics' (Kennedy 1983: 125). On the other hand, ethics takes the distinctively legalistic form of rules, principles and standards. These norms are clear, explicit and of general application. I explore in detail those formal properties of ethics which made it a plausible vehicle for reforming medical law in Chapter 8. For now it is sufficient to note that both allow medical practice to be understood and evaluated by lay people, as well as professionals, in the same terms as any other form of work (Montgomery 2006: 206). In Kennedy's words, this model holds out the promise of democratic control: 'standards set by all of us' (1983: 85). In practice, he envisages that clinical and ethical norms will be generated by an extensive system of standing committees.[20] The consumerist challenge is energized by the first of Kennedy's four basic moral principles: 'individual autonomy' (1983: 121). Along with a supply of reliable comparative information on care, effective choice requires the ethical and legal elevation of the self-determining patient.

Return of the commodity form

The effect of Kennedy's legalistic proposals for dissolving the NHS enclave is to re-impose the commodity form on medical practice where Bevan and Titmuss had hoped to exclude it. This consequence can be explained with reference to the work of Evgeny Pashukanis (1978). He argued that the forms of modern law are intimately connected with the dominant model of economic relations in capitalist society (Arthur 1978: 13). In previous eras, production was largely aimed at satisfying the immediate needs of producers themselves. Markets were not widespread and money played a marginal role in the economy. The legal subject was defined by status: for example, guilds and other groups enjoyed exclusive privileges at law based on their distinct identity. Under capitalism, by contrast, production is carried on for sale in the market.[21] In the process of market exchange, or contracting, quite heterogeneous things are brought into a relationship of equivalence with each other or with a 'third entity', i.e. money. Abstracted from their material substance and from the circumstances of their production, these things are treated as commodities. Moreover the contracting parties who exchange them are treated in similarly abstract fashion by the law. They encounter each other as formally equal (Marx 1976: 178).

The Unmasking of Medicine proposes just such a system of equivalences in health care.[22] Professional privileges are to be abolished and the clinical relationship modelled, instead, as a process of contractual bargaining: consent being exchanged in return for information and treatment. The general, abstract capacity to own and exchange also offers a basis for markets in formerly inalienable material such as blood and gametes, as well as surrogacy services. Furthermore, contract-style accountability characterizes the envisaged relationship between practitioners and health care funders. Different medical interventions are to be compared and evaluated in terms of general standards, not subsumed to the clinical judgment of the individual practitioner or his peers. In the next section, I consider briefly the extent to which these proposals have been implemented in practice and seek to elaborate the distinctive vision underpinning them.

A new utopia?

Remaking the NHS

The Unmasking of Medicine anticipated subsequent NHS reforms to a remarkable degree. Recent decades have seen the development of an extensive regulatory apparatus around the practice of clinical medicine in Britain. The legitimacy of professional self-regulation was in part undermined by a series of scandals involving criminal behaviour and extreme malpractice.[23] As a consequence, ultimate responsibility for clinical standards has been taken away from consultants, and now rests with the (non-medical) chief executives of hospitals. NHS management is now equipped with (and to an extent bound by) explicit standards of care under the guidance of the National Institute for Health and Care Excellence on the effectiveness of drugs and other interventions. Since 2001, the Service has collected data on medical accidents to enable it to learn from its mistakes.[24] Beyond the NHS, initiatives such as the Cochrane Collaboration have entrenched 'evidence-based medicine' at the heart of clinical practice (Iliffe 2008). Whereas a 1970 review of medical regulation could assert that 'the most effective safeguard of the public is the self-respect of the profession itself', in 2004 the President of the General Medical Council was moved to say that 'medicine is far too important a subject simply to be left to doctors' (quoted in Davies 2007: 305). The shift to external regulation was also marked by the creation of the Healthcare Commission in 2004 to assess the quality of management and care in NHS and private facilities (Davies 2007: 320). Significantly, until its merger with other inspectorates in 2009, it was chaired by Ian Kennedy.

The effect of these reforms has been reinforced by significant changes in the financial and operational structure of the NHS. Historically, resources were distributed as block grants to NHS facilities on the basis of established health needs and accounted for as expenditure *ex post* at the end of the financial year (Pollock 2004: 73–75). By contrast, since 1988 the Service has operated a 'fixed-tariff' system, whereby specific clinical interventions are priced in advance allowing them to be transacted over *ex ante* by different providers and funders. Furthermore, there has been growing commercial involvement in the provision of care following a 'concordat' between the Department of Health and the private sector in 2000, as well as extensive use of public–private partnerships to fund and build new facilities (Pollock 2004: 66). The public face of this reform programme has been the so-called 'choice agenda', which sees the NHS as being 'in the business of customer service' (Department of Health 2003: 63).

It is true that most NHS care remains free at the point of use. However, taken cumulatively, these reforms have meant the end of the Service as a distinctive enclave of non-market production and consumption. It is increasingly defined, not by its concrete activities and institutional form, but by its more intangible 'ethos' and 'values base' (Timmins 2002: 130). As with other franchise operations, the 'NHS' brand will float free, a quality mark attached to diverse sources of health information and service providers (Department of Health 2003: 48). Indeed the 'NHS' logo has become more prominent at eye level in Britain (e.g. on buildings, signs and vehicles) just as the institution itself is being hollowed out.

Utopia without a topos

Anti-utopian rhetoric has been prominent in explaining and justifying these reform initiatives. Thus, it is common to describe the inherited Service as a 'monolithic centrally run monopoly provider' or the 'second largest employer in Europe after the Red Army' (Milburn 2002; Blunkett 2008). It was in this vein that Alan Milburn, Health Secretary at the time of many of these crucial changes, often returned in speeches to:

> his childhood on a County Durham council estate – where the council not the tenants chose what colour the front door was painted.
>
> (Walker 2005: 9)

In the 1940s, the population were said to be deferential and grateful for benefits doled out by paternalistic professionals working for the state (Timmins 2002: 133). However, the more recent emphasis is on 'liberating the potential of each individual as an individual' (Milburn 2005). The NHS simply has to adapt to a 'more avidly consumerist world' (Timmins 2002: 133).

The Keynesian settlement had given real force to the prefigurative vision of the NHS shared by Bevan and Titmuss. But, as Jameson notes, any given utopia is vulnerable to the 'all-encompassing forward momentum' of political and economic change (2005: 16). The crisis of the 1970s, articulated and realized in rhetorical form by commentators such as Kennedy, undermined the plausibility of the NHS as an exemplary zone beyond the market. Bauman attributes the force of this challenge to a general decline in the role of territory as a frame for political aspiration and social reform. He argues that through most of the twentieth century the exercise of power and sovereignty were 'blatantly and self-consciously territorial', with the nation-state as their pre-eminent form (Bauman 2003: 14). As we have seen in this chapter, utopian thought partook of this spatial imaginary. The good life was held to proceed from a certain order and that order would be achieved through organization and planning within a given space. However, this pre-eminence has been lost over the last three decades of neo-liberal restructuring. The commodity form has penetrated deeply into social life, including, as we have seen, health care and the human body itself. Moreover, the phenomena of globalization mean that capitalist market relations have also spread over the whole globe. Withdrawal into a social enclave defined in national terms, such as the NHS, is no longer possible (Jameson 2005: 20). As Bauman puts it, there are 'no more plots left to which one could escape and in which one could hide' (2003: 16).

Process-utopia

Structural change and anti-utopian critique mean that aspirations for the future are no longer framed in terms of collective planning and territorial engagement. Pro-market reformers emphasize their own pragmatism, stigmatizing opponents as ideological, utopian, rhetorical. However, this does not mean that all notion of the good life has been abandoned. On the contrary, happiness is to be pursued, but only through individual choices. In this new dispensation, weightlessness and mobility are prized over the solidity and predictability associated with enclave utopias. As Bauman puts it:

> 'place' (whether physical or social) has been replaced by the unending sequence of new beginnings, inconsequentiality of deeds has been substituted for fixity of order, and the desire for a different today has elbowed out concern with a better tomorrow.
>
> (2003: 24)

According to Ruth Levitas, this vision is nonetheless utopian, albeit of a 'self-denying' and 'self-hating' kind (2007: 298). Its novelty lies in its idealization, not of a perfect end-state, but of social processes themselves. The most important of these is, of course, the free market. As Harvey has argued, neo-liberal reformers propose:

> a utopianism of process in which individual desires, avarice, greed, drives, creativity, and the like [can] be mobilized through the hidden hand of the perfected market to the social benefit of all.
>
> (2000: 175)

Utopian aspirations in this mode are directed to an unfettered, unencumbered and unending process of free bargaining and choosing. This is the positive desire accompanying the anti-utopian rhetoric of Health Ministers and sympathetic academic commentators. Not only individual choice, but the marketization of public services is characterized as open-ended in this way. Thus, for Alan Milburn:

> Yesterday's solution may not be the answer to tomorrow's challenge. Reform is not a process that starts one day and ends the next: it must go on and on.
>
> (2005)

The task of the state then is not simply, or primarily, to secure the material well-being of all its citizens. Rather, it must ensure an ever more equitable 'distribution of aspiration' and choice (Reid 2005: 68). The new utopian common sense was embraced as such in a report of the King's Fund which asserted that, since 'choice defines the democratic capitalist state', the case for its extension 'scarcely needs to be argued' (Appleby *et al.* 2003, 14).

Conclusion

This chapter has charted the rise and fall of a utopian vision of health care in the United Kingdom. The substance of this vision related to the nature of medical work and the use of health care services by patients. The utopian form was given equal stress in this discussion. Non-commodified medicine was realized within the enclave of the NHS. Legislative bans on commercial surrogacy and the sale of human tissue were plausible within the context of these wider arrangements. They were sustained, in other words, as much by political common sense as by more abstract ethical reasoning. However, the utopian vision of 1948 has been challenged in principle and undermined in practice. A new anti-utopian common sense repudiates the enclave and supports the generalization of the commodity form in medicine as elsewhere. It was argued that the current marketization of health care rests, in its turn, on a distinctive utopian vision; but one which emphasizes the process of individualized bargaining and exchange over the solid spatial form of collective provision of health care. This new conjuncture of practical reforms and political common sense tends to support the removal of the legislative restrictions considered above.

It has been seen that critique played an important role in reshaping the understanding and organization of post-war health care. But, given the entrenched nature of the ongoing reform process, it may be asked whether any significant critique of current arrangements is possible. A starting point for such a critique is suggested by the work of Boltanski and Chiapello, mentioned above, which focuses on changes in the capitalist organization of work over the last five decades (2007). In their account, the late 1960s were characterized by a widespread rejection of the bureaucratic and hierarchical structures then prevalent in industry and in other sectors. An important strand of this critique, which they term 'artistic', was directed at the lack of control and authentic choice available to workers under these arrangements (Boltanski and Chiapello 2007: 36–40). They show how capitalism survived this period of crisis, in part through absorbing the critique and restructuring work arrangements to meet some of the demands raised. This process, which they label 'recuperation', is evident in health care too (Boltanski and Chiapello 2007: 424).

As has been seen, a similar and related demand for control and authentic choice, raised by Kennedy and others, has informed the restructuring of health care in the UK. Any renewed critique must focus on the manner in which this original critique was recuperated and, to an extent, distorted. Boltanski and Chiapello argue that the main mechanism by which capitalism can respond to the desire for authenticity is through expressing it as a demand for products or services (2007: 443). Individual autonomy, the desire for authentic choice, can only be extended through an expansion of markets. The crux is, of course, that the commodity form presumes a system of equivalences which is the very antithesis of authenticity.

The crowding out of non-market values is examined in Allyson Pollock's influential book *NHS plc: The Privatisation of Our Health Care* (2004). This offers a persuasive evaluation of NHS reforms in terms of value for money and the evidence basis for change. However, it also includes an 'artistic critique' of the emerging market system of health care. This focuses on the material spaces of the NHS: hospitals and general practitioners' surgeries, which are now commonly subject to the control of private ventures. In the quest to maximize shareholder returns, spare land is sold off for 'golf courses, luxury homes and supermarkets' (Pollock 2004: 29). NHS premises themselves now host fast-food outlets and chain stores, where once voluntary organizations served the public (Pollock 2004: 112). To draw a parallel from recent cultural theory, a modernist faith in progress, under the direction of charismatic artist–doctors, has been forsaken for a kind of market populism that celebrates the 'decorated sheds' of the retail park (Jameson 1991: 2).

Pollock depicts the new NHS in 'anti-pastoral' terms quite at odds with the original vision of Bevan and Titmuss. Patients pay to watch TV on their own, rather than free in a common room. The rationalization of care systems means that doctors now frequently treat unknown patients, breaking the continuity of care. The 'camaraderie of the doctors' mess is lost – in fact it is now usually deserted' (Pollock 2004: 113). The genuineness of patient emancipation has also been challenged. As Rachel Aldred showed, in practice the public have little control over the direction of NHS reform (2008: 40–42). Privatization brings with it stricter rules of commercial secrecy. Commercially produced health data is subject to monopoly control under intellectual property law. Long-term public–private contracts preclude democratic control.

Notwithstanding the publicity about choice and responsiveness, no local challenge to the policy of marketization will be entertained. As Kenneth Veitch has noted, although patients may choose between doctors, hospitals and other services in the NHS, they may not reject choice itself (2007: 42). The demand for autonomy is conceded, then recuperated. New forms of domination channel and confine patient choice.

Notes

1 See, respectively, Human Tissue Act 2004, as amended 2014, s 32; Human Fertilisation and Embryology Authority Code of Practice 8th edition as revised 2012, para 13A; Surrogacy Arrangements Act 1985, as amended 2008, s 2.

2 Respectively, Surrogacy Arrangements Act 1985, ss 2 and 3. Note that following the amendment of the Act by the Human Fertilisation and Embryology Act 2008, s 59(4) non-profit-making bodies are permitted to charge a reasonable fee in order to recoup their costs.

3 Surrogacy Arrangements Act 1985, s 1A. Adoption arrangements were subject to similar control under Adoption Act 1976, s 57, a provision now substantially carried over in the Adoption and Children Act 2002, s 95.

4 Human Fertilisation and Embryology Act 1990, s 30(7). This provision has been carried over by Human Fertilisation and Embryology Act 2008, s 54(8).

5 See the 'Summary of Recommendations' in Brazier *et al.* (1998: 71–72).

6 For example, see Gray (2008).

7 This insight on style is drawn from Timmins (2001: 23). Bunyan's millennial vision was a staple of radical political culture in England up until the early twentieth century. See Thompson (1980: 34).

8 Beveridge has been accurately described as a 'non-socialist collectivist', indicating the broad faith in planning at the time. See Rintala (2003: 16).

9 For an overview, see Webster (2002: 12–30).

10 For example, see Rapport and Maggs (2002); Arrow (1972); Stewart (1984).

11 For further discussion, see Titmuss (1997: 311).

12 For a philosophical perspective on this 'alliance', see Jacob (1988: 181–184).

13 See Morris (1889).

14 This reference to male workers is deliberate. Morris envisaged a continuing, if much more highly valued, role for women as homemakers (2003: 51–53).

15 For an overview, see Timmins (2001: 102–109).

16 For an evaluation of Kennedy's role in creating British medical law, see Veitch (2007: 8–25).

17 This part of the lectures relies heavily on the 'medicalization of life' thesis developed by commentators such as Ivan Illich and Thomas Szasz. See Kennedy (1983: 132).

18 'Man has no more agonizing anxiety than to find someone to whom he can hand over with all speed the gift of freedom with which he was born' (Dostoyevsky 1958: 298).

19 For example, see Kennedy (1988).

20 For details, see Kennedy (1983: 179–180).

21 On the transition between these modes of production, see Marx (1981: 440–455).

22 For an insightful critique in this regard, see Jacob (1988, 165–172).

23 See Davies (2007: 123ff.).

24 For an introductory discussion, see Davies (2000).

References

Abel-Smith, B and K Titmuss (1987) *The Philosophy of Welfare. Selected Writings of Richard M Titmuss* (London, Allen and Unwin).

Aldred, R (2008) 'NHS Lift and the New Shape of Neo-Liberal Welfare', 95 *Capital and Class* 31.

Appleby, J, A Harrison and N Devlin (2003) *What Is the Real Cost of More Patient Choice?* (London, King's Fund).

Arrow, KJ (1972) 'Gifts and Exchanges', 1 *Philosophy and Public Affairs* 343.

Arthur, CJ (1978) 'Editor's Introduction' in EB Pashukanis, *Law and Marxism: A General Theory* (London, Pluto).

Bauman, Z (2003) 'Utopia with No Topos', 16 *History of the Human Sciences* 11.

Bellamy, E (2007) *Looking Backward 2000–1887* (Oxford, Oxford University Press).

Bevan, A (1990) *In Place of Fear* (London, Quartet Books).

Beveridge, W (1942) *Social Insurance and Allied Services*, Cmnd. 6404 (London, HMSO).

Blunkett, D (2008) 'Time to Slash NHS Red Tape', *Sun*, 8 July.

Boltanski, L and E Chiapello (2007) *The New Spirit of Capitalism* (London, Verso).

Brazier, M (1999) 'Regulating the Reproduction Business?', 7 *Medical Law Review* 166.

Brazier, M, A Campbell and S Golombok (1998) *Surrogacy: Review for Health Ministers of Current Arrangements for Payments and Regulation*, Cmnd. 4068 (London, Department of Health).

Carey, J (1999) 'Introduction', in J Carey (ed.), *The Faber Book of Utopias* (London, Faber) xi.

Davies, A (2000) 'Don't Trust Me I'm a Doctor: Medical Regulation and the 1999 NHS Reforms', 20 *Oxford Journal of Legal Studies* 437.

Davies, M (2007) *Medical Self-Regulation: Crisis and Change* (Aldershot, Hampshire, Ashgate).

Department of Health (2003) *Building on the Best: Choice, Responsiveness and Equity in the NHS*, Cmnd. 6079 (London, The Stationery Office).

Dostoyevsky, F (1958) *The Brothers Karamazov* (London, Penguin).

Foot, M (1962) *Aneurin Bevan: A Biography. Volume One: 1897–1945* (London, MacGibbon and Kee).

Freeman, M (1999) 'Does Surrogacy Have a Future after Brazier?', 7 *Medical Law Review* 1.

Gray, J (2008) *Black Mass. Apocalyptic Religion and the Death of Utopia* (London, Penguin).

Harvey, D (2000) *Spaces of Hope* (Edinburgh, Edinburgh University Press).

Iliffe, S (2008) *From General Practice to Primary Care. The Industrialization of Family Medicine* (Oxford, Oxford University Press).

Jacob, JM (1988) *Doctors and Rules. A Sociology of Professional Values* (London, Routledge).

Jameson, F (1991) *Postmodernism: or, the Cultural Logic of Late Capitalism* (London, Verso).

Jameson, F (2000) 'Utopianism and Anti-Utopianism', in M Hardt and K Weeks (eds), *The Jameson Reader* (Oxford, Blackwell) 382.

Jameson, F (2005) *Archaeologies of the Future. The Desire Called Utopia and Other Science Fictions* (London, Verso).

Jessop, B (2002) *The Future of the Capitalist State* (Cambridge, Polity).

Kennedy, I (1983) *The Unmasking of Medicine* (London, Granada).

Kennedy, I (1988) *Treat me Right. Essays in Medical Law and Ethics* (Oxford, Clarendon).

Klinck, D (1994) ' "This Other Eden": Lord Denning's Pastoral Vision', 14 *Oxford Journal of Legal Studies* 25.

Kumar, K (1987) *Utopia and Anti-Utopia in Modern Times* (Oxford, Basil Blackwell).

Kumar, K (1991) *Utopianism* (Open University Press, Buckingham).

Kynaston, D (2007) *Austerity Britain 1945–51* (London, Bloomsbury).

Lawrence, C (1994) *Medicine in the Making of Modern Britain 1700–1920* (London, Routledge).

Leopold, D (2003) 'Introduction', in W Morris (ed.), *News from Nowhere* (Oxford, Oxford University Press).

Levitas, R (1990) *The Concept of Utopia* (Cambridge, Polity).

Levitas, R (2007) 'Looking for the Blue: The Necessity of Utopia', 12 *Journal of Political Ideologies* 289.

Marx, K (1970) *Economic and Philosophic Manuscripts of 1844* (London, Lawrence and Wishart).

Marx, K (1976) *Capital. A Critique of Political Economy* vol 1 (London, Penguin).

Marx, K (1981) *Capital: A Critique of Political Economy* vol 3 (London, Penguin).

McLachlan, HV and JK Swales (2000) 'Babies, Child Bearers and Commodification: Anderson, Brazier et al., and the Political Economy of Commercial Surrogate Motherhood', 8 *Health Care Analysis* 1.

Milburn, A (2002) 'Diversity and Choice within the NHS', Speech to the NHS Confederation, 24 May. Available at http://webarchive.nationalarchives.gov.uk/20050208211442/www.dh.gov.uk/NewsHome/Speeches/SpeechesList/SpeechesArticle/fs/en?CONTENT_ID=4000764&chk=m2BA0o.

Milburn, A (2005) 'Speech to the Fabian Society New Year Conference' 17 January. Available at www.theguardian.com/politics/2005/jan/17/thinktanks.uk.

Miola, J (2007) *Medical Ethics and Medical Law. A Symbiotic Relationship* (Oxford, Hart Publications).

Montgomery, J (2006) 'Law and the Demoralisation of Medicine', 26 *Legal Studies* 185.

Morris, W (1889) 'Bellamy's "Looking Backward" ', *Commonwealth*, 21 June. Available at www.marxists.org/archive/morris/works/1889/backward.htm.

Morris, W (1973a) 'Art and Socialism', in AL Morton (ed.), *Political Writings of William Morris* (London, Lawrence and Wishart) 109.

Morris, W (1973b) 'Useful Work versus Useless Toil', in AL Morton (ed.), *Political Writings of William Morris* (London, Lawrence and Wishart) 87.

Morris, W (2003) *News from Nowhere* (Oxford, Oxford University Press).

Pashukanis, EB (1978) *Law and Marxism. A General Theory* (London, Pluto).

Perelman, C (1982) *The Realm of Rhetoric* (Notre Dame, IN, University of Notre Dame Press).

Polanyi, K (2001) *The Great Transformation. The Political and Economic Origins of Our Time* (Boston, MA, Beacon Press).

Pollock, AM (2004) *NHS plc. The Privatisation of Our Health Care* (London, Verso).

Rapport, FL and CJ Maggs (2002) 'Titmuss and the Gift Relationship: Altruism Revisited', 40 *Journal of Advanced Nursing* 495.

Reid, J (2005) 'Aspiration Moves the World', in Fabian Commission on Life Chances and Child Poverty, *Why Life Chances Matter* (London, Fabian Society) 66.

Rintala, M (2003) *Creating the National Health Service. Aneurin Bevan and the Medical Lords* (London, Frank Cass).

Robrieux, JJ (2000) *Rhétorique et argumentation*, 2nd edition (Paris, Nathan Université).

Stewart, RM (1984) 'Morality and the Market in Blood', 1 *Journal of Applied Philosophy* 227.

Thompson, EP (1980) *The Making of the English Working Class* (London, Penguin).

Timmins, N (2001) *The Five Giants. A Biography of the Welfare State*, 2nd edition (London, Harper Collins).

Timmins, N (2002) 'A Time for Change in the British NHS: An Interview with Alan Milburn', 21 *Health Affairs* 129.

Titmuss, RM (1997) *The Gift Relationship. From Human Blood to Social Policy* (New York, New Books).

Tonsor, SJ (1973) 'The Conservative Element in American Liberalism', 35 *Review of Politics* 489.

van Niekerk A and L van Zyl (1995) 'Commercial Surrogacy and the Commodification of Children: An Ethical Perspective', 14 *Medicine and Law* 163.

Veitch, K (2007) *The Jurisdiction of Medical Law* (Aldershot, Hampshire, Ashgate).

Walker, D (2005) 'Vision of the Future', 51 *Public Eye* 8.

Webster, C (2002) *The National Health Service. A Political History* (Oxford, Oxford University Press).

White, JB (1985) 'Law as Rhetoric, Rhetoric as Law. The Arts of Cultural and Communal Life', 52 *University of Chicago Law Review* 684.

Wilkinson, S (2003) *Bodies for Sale: Ethics and Exploitation in the Human Body Trade* (Routledge, London).

Williams, R (1962) *Culture and Society 1780–1950* (London, Pelican).

Wilson, D (2014) *The Making of British Bioethics* (Manchester, Manchester University Press).

Chapter 6

Progress

Introduction

Professional judgement has been central to the determination of rights and obligations in many areas of medical law, such as access to abortion and contraceptive treatment, the level of disclosure prior to treatment and the standard of care in negligence.[1] It has functioned as a place or 'black box' to which the indeterminacy of legal decision making can be displaced. The effectiveness of this deparadoxification strategy depends on its persuasiveness within wider legal and political contexts. Given the ecological dominance of the economy in a capitalist society, as discussed in Chapter 1, a rhetorical analysis needs to take account of the influence of concrete institutional and economic arrangements upon the substance of medical law argumentation. In previous chapters, I pursued this broadly materialist approach, examining the key role played by the national and utopian dimensions of the NHS in the development of legal doctrine.

A materialist perspective also needs to take medical practice seriously as a form of labour. This is not to claim that professional work is the 'real' base which determines the cultural superstructure of medical law. What I am concerned with here, rather, are the terms in which medicine has been *represented* as a form of work and the manner in which they have helped to sustain the plausibility of law's deference to clinical judgment. Indeed, as we saw in Chapter 5, the utopian vision underpinning the NHS involved sheltering medical practice from market forces and other external direction. This vision was framed negatively, however, in terms of what medicine is not. In this chapter and the next I want to extend that analysis by considering the positive framing of clinical work as both 'science' and 'art'. These involved respectively the understanding that medicine as a whole exhibits the features of a progressive science and that clinical work involves the exercise of fine judgement. Of course these key topics of medical law are not wholly consistent. They have supported judicial deference like the 'legs of a table' or the strands of a rope rather than as part of any coherent ideological system. I hope to show each gained rhetorical force from its affinities with traditional conceptions of the common law and its resonance with enduring national stories and self-images.

The present chapter investigates the dimensions and plausibility of the topic of medicine as a science. It will first provide some evidence of the importance of the idea of scientific progress to doctors' collective self-perceptions since the early nineteenth century. Thereafter an attempt will be made to reconstruct this idea in terms of Karl Popper's work on epistemology. The ideal-typical attributes of the scientific method thus elaborated provide an interpretative framework for understanding the English case law on medical malpractice. It will then be shown that the notion of scientific medicine evolving through a competitive pluralism of ideas resonates with the historical idea of the common law progressing through dissent and conflict. This overlapping self-understanding can also be linked with broader ideologies of progress current in Western society since the Enlightenment. These ideologies valorize liberal political ideals and the institutional arrangements through which they are realized. Both doctors and lawyers have found it useful to draw upon these discursive resources in order to achieve and legitimate their professional status. I conclude by examining a counter-theory of scientific development. The work of Thomas Kuhn disputes the notion of orderly progress and identifies instead a secretive and non-cumulative sequence of scientific revolutions: an opaque world which neither reflects nor validates liberal ideals. This darker vision is reflected in critiques of medical work by both radical sociologists and consumer-oriented legal scholars.

Medicine as a progressive science

According to sociologists, the development of a unified and autonomous scientific knowledge base has been essential to the professional status of medicine (Larson 1977: 23–51). The association of medicine with science has never been complete or uniform, however. Rival conceptions of medicine have been advanced to further the strategic ambitions of the profession as a whole, or of specific groups within it. In the early decades of the nineteenth century, English general practitioners and provincial doctors sought to overcome the social and occupational barriers to their advancement erected by the metropolitan, consultant elite. They did so by promoting a scientific idea of medicine in imitation of that which had emerged in post-revolutionary France. In the eyes of marginalized English medics, 200 of whom were found to be studying pathological anatomy in Paris in 1828 (Warner 1991: 144), French success was based upon a rigorously empiricist approach to medical knowledge and a legislatively supported 'medical polity' which linked medical work with the interests of the state. If established in England, a scientific basis to practice would allow the cleverest, rather than the most refined or best connected, to advance furthest. Equally, a system of medical legislation would proscribe and de-legitimate the work of competitors from below, so to speak, such as herbal-ists and midwives. As well as having a keen admiration for France, it is significant that members of the scientific faction in English medicine at the time were frequently associated with political radicalism and religious dissent.[2] More likely to have been educated at Edinburgh or Glasgow, than Oxford or Cambridge, they viewed the ideal doctor not as a gentleman ministering to the needs of the upper classes, but as an agent of physical and moral improvement in society as a whole (Lawrence 1994: 42).

In *Middlemarch*, George Eliot provides us with a convincing portrait of one such reforming provincial doctor in the character of Tertius Lydgate. For him:

> there was fascination in the hope that the two purposes [i.e. of healing and research] would illuminate each other: the careful observation and inference which was his daily work, the use of the lens to further his judgment in special cases, would further his thought as an instru-ment of larger inquiry. Was this not the special pre-eminence of his profession?
>
> (Eliot 1994: 142)

Lydgate's commitment to science is contrasted with the practice of his traditionalist rival Wrench (1994: 250–251). When called to attend the young Fred Vincy, Wrench hastily concludes that the stricken man is suf-fering from 'a slight derangement' which he treats with 'the usual white parcels' with their 'black and drastic contents'. When these prove useless Lydgate is called. He observes the patient closely, taking a detailed history. He diagnoses Vincy precisely as suffering from 'the pink-skinned stage of typhoid fever' and successfully treats him. Lydgate stands here for the new scientific medicine identified with careful observation and reasoning, and aiming for public well-being rather than the financial exploitation of patients.[3]

A unified profession was achieved in Britain with the passing of the Medical Act 1858, which created a single register of practitioners and bestowed a legal monopoly of medical work on doctors. Fundamental con-flict over the form and content of medical knowledge ceased and medi-cine attained a position of unprecedented prestige and influence. First physiology, then microbiology emerged as the 'lead' disciplines in medical practice during the latter half of the nineteenth century. Science-driven progress in these areas was personified in a new elite of physician and surgeon scientists, of whom the most famous was perhaps Joseph Lister. Self-styled leader of the 'antiseptic revolution', Lister was regarded by late Victorians and Edwardians as a hero in the manner of engineers and colonial explorers, and was made a baron in 1900 (Porter 1997: 428–461).

Bacteriology, on which antiseptic techniques were based, also provided the platform for some of the most famous medical advances in the late nineteenth and early twentieth centuries: the identification of the micro-organisms which caused cholera, tuberculosis, diphtheria and rabies, and the subsequent development of cures and vaccines (Maulitz 1979). These breakthroughs established the laboratory as the hub of medical progress and a 'fresh source of power for modifying society' (Latour 1983: 158; see also Worboys 1992: 85). Indeed:

> far from just turning to science as an established source of authority, nineteenth-century medical practitioners were themselves among the most influential proponents of a new culture in which science was so regarded.
>
> (Sturdy 1992: 127)

Consequently, during this period the once marginal view of medical advance as essential to the well-being of the general population and to the prosperity of the nation became professional and political orthodoxy (Canguilhem 1994: 280). Medical categories of thought began to replace those of religion as the dominant frame of reference for understanding the world; inequalities of class, gender and race coming to be invested with naturalistic, medically sanctioned meanings (Lawrence 1994: 70).

In the twentieth century, the profession adapted to democratic and welfarist politics by successfully translating the problems of established and emerging interest groups into health care issues (see Latour 1983: 144). Medicine spoke to the concerns of the military that troops be fighting fit, and to the need of industrialists for a healthy workforce. These tendencies culminated in an extension of state sponsorship beyond the statutory monopoly of practice to the point where, as we have seen, the government took over the funding of almost all medical work in Britain with the establishment of the NHS in 1948 (Berridge 1999: 15).

The notion of scientific progress remained crucial to the effective translation of others' interests in the decades after the Second World War (Cantor 1992). Indeed we shall see that most of the case law on medical negligence, the substance of which is premised upon a public interest in such progress, dates from this period. The 'lead' discipline in medicine at the time was indisputably pharmacology, which gained massively in prestige from the introduction into practice of penicillin, cortisone, sulphonamides and a sequence of other 'wonder drugs'. Drug development itself represented a fusion of the interests of medical scientists and capital: systematic synthesis of possible drug compounds was only possible with massive financial support and this depended on the likelihood of a substantial return on investment (Le Fanu 2000: 206). In addition, as will be discussed in Chapter 7, clinical practice itself became the site of a new experimental science which sought to rationalize diagnosis and treatment. Each case came to have a significance beyond the interests of the individual patient. Each presented the scientifically minded practitioner (usually male) with an opportunity to gather 'clinical material' which he could analyse and publish, thereby improving his colleagues' practice and advancing his own career. This flourishing scientific culture was promoted by governments, aware of the importance of the pharmaceutical industry to the British economy; indeed state support for medical research increased fivefold from the 1950s to the mid-1970s (Strong 1984: 341). As will be seen later, significant critique has been directed at the notion of scientific progress, with the effect of weakening its plausibility as a support for judicial deference to medical professional opinion. Before considering those trends, however, I will itemize key elements of the notion of progress as discussed in theories of scientific development and as articulated in the English case law on medical negligence.

The dynamic of scientific progress

We have seen the importance of the idea of scientific progress to medical professionalism in the nineteenth and twentieth centuries. In this section, I draw on the work of Karl Popper in elaborating a number of ideal-typical components of this idea. These will help to structure the following analysis of the law on medical malpractice. For Popper 'the history of science [was], by and large, a history of progress' (Popper 1981: 94). Many activities are taken as exhibiting change and improvement over time: crafts and technologies, for example. But progress is only 'scientific' if it is understood by practitioners and observers to happen in an orderly, open and intelligible manner. Popper's work on this is a particularly useful source since he promoted a model of rational progress accepted by many scientists and by the wider lay public (Magee 1985: 10; Lakatos 1981: 113). The model was also anticipated by the pioneering French physiologist Claude Bernard in his *Introduction à l'étude de la médecine expérimentale* (1865).[4] Bernard repudiated the scholastic method which had proceeded dogmatically on the basis of fixed theological and philosophical texts and personal authority. In science and medicine there could be no immutable truths. Authority was independent and impersonal, derived from the methods of experience and observation.[5] In line with the trajectory of contemporary European political history, Bernard argued that an initial rupture establishing the experimental method would be followed by the evolutionary development of science and latterly medicine.[6]

Change in science, Popper argued, can be modelled upon Darwinian evolutionary biology (1979a). Like plant and animal life, scientific knowledge develops through repeated stages of variation and selection. At the first stage, just as the gene structure of an organism responds to environmental pressures by internal mutation and recombination, so science responds to theoretical problems by developing tentative new theories. At the second stage, just as there is selection between available genetic mutations and variations, so scientific theories are tested experimentally and the erroneous eliminated. The process of testing (or falsification) generates further problems which scientists respond to with further theories and so on. For Popper as for Bernard, 'there are no more scientific revolutions ... [rather] science grows gradually and steadily' (quoted in Canguilhem 1994: 139).

The evolutionary model and the method of falsification allow us, with Popper, to elaborate certain characteristics of scientific activity and, thus, to distinguish it from non-science. These are:

1   Statements which are not capable of being falsified by observation and experiment are by definition not scientific.
2   Scientists take (or should take) a thoroughly critical attitude both to their own theories and to those which are already well established. It is not permitted systematically to reject experimental results which confound theoretical explanations. The latter is generally characteristic of dogma or ideology and is a hindrance to progress (Popper 1981: 96).
3   Scientific truth is emergent rather than transcendental; its rationality is procedural. Thus, the content of scientific knowledge is contingent and revisable.
4   The evolutionary model is based on a process of rational learning by feedback (Popper 1979b: 117). This is aided by the availability of scientific knowledge for study and criticism in the form of written sources. Although contingent, scientific knowledge is thus objective (Popper 1979b: 106).
5   Science is most likely to evolve under conditions of free and open competition. In other words, theoretical pluralism drives progress.[7] As another philosopher of science has written, '[d]ialectical confrontations are essential to the growth and improvement of scientific knowledge; like nature science is red in tooth and claw' (Laudan 1981: 153). Centralization and uniformity in the production of scientific ideas lead inevitably to a failure of adaptation and, thus, to stagnation and backwardness.
6   Finally, the existing state of scientific knowledge sets limits to the extent of theoretical pluralism at any given time. New theories can only be generated recursively; they must draw upon, modify and explain previous theories. In Popper's words scientific discovery depends 'on a conservative or traditional or historical element, and on a revolutionary use of trial and the elimination of error by criticism' (1981: 87).

From this discussion we can extract a number of ideal-typical attributes of science which will be found in judicial representations of medical activity.

These are: change as progress; progress through pluralism; ordered or bounded pluralism; objective knowledge; and rational learning.

Representing medicine as a progressive science in the common law

Judges seized of malpractice cases have frequently emphasized both the progressive nature of medicine and the benefits which this has conferred upon society as a whole. In furtherance of this public interest, doctors have generally been allowed to define the standard of care in negligence by which their peers are held to account (Jackson and Powell 1997: 639). To recall our discussion in Chapter 2, the test of negligence in *Bolam v Friern Hospital Management Committee*[8] lays down that a doctor will not be held responsible if her practice conformed to that of a responsible body of medical practitioners. Consistent with the ideal of science as plural and competitive, a practice may be acceptable even where it is only followed by a minority of doctors or specialists. Until the House of Lords; decision in *Bolitho v City and Hackney Health Authority*,[9] expert witnesses had a more or less sovereign role in deciding on fault in cases of malpractice (Dugdale and Stanton 1998: 319). This liability regime was exceptional: in cases involving all other occupational groups, the courts had reserved the power to set the standard of care in negligence themselves.[10] We shall see that even after *Bolitho* the scope for judicial reconsideration of medical evidence has in practice been rather slim. In addition, as will be shown, the ideal-typical elements of scientific activity outlined above continue to structure English case law to the benefit of the medical profession.

Change as progress

Recitations of great medical breakthroughs appear consistently in the case law on malpractice; for example, in *Bolam*[11] which concerned a psychiatric patient who suffered fractures because he had not been restrained during the administration of electro-convulsive therapy (ECT). In his direction to the jury on the question of negligence, McNair J traced the development of ECT. He noted 'the enormous benefits which are conferred upon unfortunate men and women by this form of treatment'.[12] In order to facilitate such advances in clinical science, therapeutic and diagnostic negligence must be judged according to a standard set by the profession itself. A similar homage to progress preceded the House of Lords' decision in *Sidaway v Board of Governors of the Bethlem Royal Hospital*[13] to extend the *Bolam* test to cover a doctor's duty to make disclosure of the risks accompanying treatment. For Lord Diplock:

> [P]ractices are likely to alter with advances in medical knowledge. Experience shows that, to the great benefit of humankind, they have

done so, particularly in the recent past. That is why fatal diseases such as smallpox and tuberculosis have within living memory become virtually extinct in countries where modern medical care is generally available.[14]

English law seems accordingly to have adopted the notion of medicine as dynamic and experimental. As such it is necessarily accompanied by the possibility of mishaps. In *Roe v Ministry of Health*[15] Lord Denning stated that:

> Medical science has conferred great benefits on mankind, but these benefits are attended by considerable risks.... We cannot take the benefits without taking the risks. Every advance in technique is also attended by risks.[16]

This tragic dimension to progress corresponds, in Popper's terms, to the error-elimination stage of the falsification procedure. It is at this point that the public interest in medical science begins to bite. To quote again Lord Diplock in *Sidaway*:

> Those members of the public who seek medical or surgical aid would be badly served by the adoption of any principle that would confine the doctor to some long-established, well-tried method of treatment only, although its past record of success might be small, if he wanted to be confident that he would not run the risk of being held liable in negligence simply because he tried some more modern treatment, and by some unavoidable mischance it failed to heal but did some harm to the patient.[17]

The law has thus constructed an image of the doctor as an intrepid researcher and of the patient as a bundle of 'clinical material' whose greatest significance lies, not necessarily in his or her immediate physical needs, but in being one moment in a sequence of scientific experiments.

Progress through pluralism

Cognitive pluralism is normally suppressed by the law as a threat to effective decision making. Carol Jones has shown, for example, how expert witnesses are effectively forced by legal procedures to conceal dissent within their ranks (1994: 9). A flight into monism shores up the credibility and legitimacy of both medicine and law in the context of fact finding. The law on medical malpractice is different, however, in that it is based on an acceptance of diversity. As has been stated, a practitioner may follow a minority practice and still not be held liable for any damage resulting from his or her work. In *Maynard v West Midlands Regional Health Authority*[18] the plaintiff suffered damage to her vocal cords as a result of the conduct of invasive tests for Hodgkin's disease; less risky, non-invasive tests for tuberculosis had been equally indicated but were not carried out until later. At first instance the trial judge found for the plaintiff on the basis of his substantive preference for the testimony of her expert witnesses. Unusually, this finding of fact was overturned by the House of Lords. The trial judge was severely criticized by Lord Scarman who held that:

> Differences of opinion and practice exist, and will always exist, in the medical as in other professions. There is seldom any one answer exclusive of all others to problems of professional judgment. A court may prefer one body of opinion to the other, but that is no basis for a conclusion of negligence.[19]

In *Bolam* it was held to be permissible for a psychiatrist not to restrain a patient undergoing ECT, where professional opinion was divided as to whether this was necessary. The practitioner had applied his 'inquiring mind'[20] to the possible alternatives and that was sufficient. This option, which indeed is also an obligation, to exercise individual judgement in the specific case, will not be removed by the existence of a treatment guideline covering the procedure (Hurwitz 1999).

At bottom, courts have valorized intra-medical conflict in this way because they have assumed it to be the engine of scientific progress. As Lord Clyde put it in the Scottish case of *Hunter v Hanley*;

> [A] deviation from ordinary professional practice is not necessarily evidence of negligence. Indeed it would be disastrous if this were so, for all inducement to progress in medical science would be destroyed.[21]

This reasoning 'could not be bettered' according to McNair J who adopted it as the basis of the relevant English law in *Bolam*. It is set in the context of medical history (or mythology) by Kenneth Norrie's comment that:

> Every medical advancement since Hippocrates has at some stage been a departure from the normal and accepted practice, and to castigate such departure as per se negligence is a nonsense.
>
> (1985: 158)

Like Popper's ideal science, medical practice is thus necessarily and productively plural: only where there is variation, in the form of a range of recommended practices, can the system select and thus progress. The Canadian scholar and judge Allen Linden recast the importance of tolerating this diversity in quasi-religious language:

The courts recognizing that the heresy of today may become the orthodoxy of tomorrow have wisely refused to halt all experimentation.

(1968: 165)

In other words, monism is equivalent to dogmatism and therefore against
the public interest.

Bounded pluralism

Dissent is, however, confined by canons of rationality, particularly as to the
methods of discovering new truths. In medical negligence law, we find
recognition of this procedural rationality in the requirement that the
defendant's practices have been in conformity with those of a *responsible*
body of practitioners. This qualification was widely seen as redundant until
the decision of the House of Lords in *Bolitho*.[22]

The facts of that case were that the plaintiff's child, who suffered from
croup, developed breathing difficulties while in hospital. He was not
attended to in time and died from respiratory failure. As well as issues of
causation, their Lordships addressed the matter of fault. It appeared that
there was division in the profession as to whether a child in that position
should have been intubated or not. Lord Browne-Wilkinson held that this
plurality of views did not automatically decide the issue in favour of the
defendants. To be held to be 'responsible', a body of opinion must also be
shown to have a logical basis.[23] This clarification of the *Bolam* test was
greeted by commentators as a first move towards substantial judicial
control over medical decision making (Brazier and Miola 2000); and
indeed, the Lord Chief Justice Lord Woolf drew on *Bolitho* as a warrant of
greater judicial intrusiveness into the domain of professional judgement.[24]
The decision in *Bolitho* itself did not give grounds to anticipate a truly
radical change in the liability regime, however. Lord Browne-Wilkinson
stated there that medical opinion is likely to be upheld as rational and
responsible in the vast majority of cases.[25] What *Bolitho* mandates is a form
of procedural, as opposed to substantive, control over the exercise of clinical judgment. As long as a process of risk assessment has been gone
through by the proponents of a course of action, that is sufficient to excul-
pate the practitioner who follows it. This is indeed a weak standard of
review. It simply seeks to promote among doctors the critical attitude
which Popper holds to be definitive of good faith among researchers and
essential to the progress of science.

In the eyes of the law, plural medical opinion is generally constituted as
'schools of thought'.[26] A defendant who deviates from orthodoxy, without
being able to show that she was following any such school, will be required
to justify this departure.[27] The progressive nature of medicine does not, in
other words, provide a licence for random or unsupported experimentation

by the individual practitioner. Like Popper's scientists, doctors are forced in the first instance to refer to the accrued knowledge of the discipline. A 'conservative or traditional or historical element' to medical practice is thus preserved (Popper 1981: 87). The limits of tolerated plurality are also reached in cases where the defendant is charged with having made basic errors such as failing to count swabs after an operation or amputating the wrong limb.[28] Mistakes of this sort are effectively treated as being beneath medical science, allowing the court to set the standard of care itself. By contrast with doctors, moreover, nurses, radiographers and so on are treated by the law as performing more or less routine functions. Their work does not in itself obey the experimental dynamic of science. As members of 'lesser professions', they do not benefit from the *Bolam* regime (Dugdale and Stanton 1998: 318), testimony surely to the triumph of medical ideology.

Objective knowledge and rational learning

The progressive nature of medicine, as ratified by the courts, means that a doctor may also be held liable if she falls behind universally implemented improvements in practice. In *Bolam* itself it was stated that the doctor-centred test of professional negligence:

> does not mean that a medical man can obstinately and pig-headedly carry on with some old technique if it has been proved to be contrary to what is substantially the whole of informed medical opinion. Otherwise you might get men today saying: "I don't believe in anaesthetics. I don't believe in antiseptics. I am going to continue to do my surgery in the way it was done in the eighteenth century". That would clearly be wrong.[29]

This passage evokes a heroic history according to which medicine moves continually from a state of (relative) unknowing to one of (relative) enlightenment. Its discoveries have become part of general common sense knowledge; those who resist its dynamic are condemned as dangerous dogmatists.

Medical practitioners participate in the scientific enterprise by adapting to change produced by trial and the elimination of error. They also contribute to it by recording their own experiences and feeding them back into the scientific system through medical records and publications. The status of this corpus as objective scientific knowledge is reinforced by the legal obligations on doctors to maintain comprehensive and detailed files and to keep abreast of recent developments in their fields (Jackson and Powell 1997: 614; Giesen 1988: 114). Furthermore, law cases themselves may be a means by which the risks of a given procedure are discovered and publicized, as for example in *Roe v Ministry of Health*.[30] There the anaesthetic used on the plaintiff had been contaminated by near-colourless disinfectant liquid, which had seeped through invisible cracks in the phial in which it was stored. As a result, the plaintiff was left permanently paralysed after the operation. The Court of Appeal, however, refused to hold the defendants liable in negligence since the possibility of contamination was wholly unforeseeable at the time. As Lord Denning put it, '[w]e must not look at the 1947 accident with 1954 spectacles'.[31] Nonetheless, the medical profession would be on notice, partly as a result of the case, of the perils presented by the old method of storing anaesthetic substances.[32] In future the disinfectant liquid would have to contain dye to facilitate recognition of leakages.

Progress in the common law

In the present section, I seek to show how the scientific understanding of medicine resonates with the self-perceptions of common law judges and theorists. It is, of course, impossible to demonstrate an exact correspondence between these ideological formations. Historically the natural sciences have been much more deeply implicated in medical practice and talk about it, than in law. Furthermore, although I treat both as social systems reproducing themselves through recursively linked communications (as demonstrated in Chapter 2) the social roles and functions of each discipline are significantly different. Medicine operates primarily on the phenomenal level, aiming to produce tangible effects on or in the bodies of its subjects; law operates primarily on the noumenal level, defining values and stabilizing normative expectations (Luhmann 1999: 73–91). The 'logic of scientific discovery' is, thus, more prominently displayed in medicine than in law. Nonetheless strong mutual affinities can be found which reflect the central elements of Popper's thesis: the notion of cumulative progress; and the proposition that this is achieved through competitive pluralism of ideas. The first can be found in pervasive and influential theories of legal history, which portray law as evolving over centuries from primitive origins to modern complexity. The second is evident in the quotidian phenomenon of the dissenting judgement.

Evolutionary progress in Western law: the influence of Maine

The most important formulation of the evolutionary understanding of the common law is contained in Henry Maine's *Ancient Law* (1861/1870). Maine sketched a history of law, from pre-customary decrees, through the law of the Roman republic and empire, and on to the legal systems of Western Europe in the nineteenth century. Law had developed, he argued, from custom to rule-based systems, from disparate to centralized power structures, and from dominating its subjects to guaranteeing individual self-determination. He encapsulated this dynamic in the famous maxim that 'the movement of the progressive societies has hitherto been a movement *from Status to Contract*' (1861/70: 170). Two features of Maine's work are significant for this discussion. First, he distinguished evolving from stationary societies. This was necessary to explain the divergence between contemporary European law and that of colonized regions such as India. The colonies were Europe's past made present to itself, affirming both its origins and the immense progress which it had achieved (Fitzpatrick 1992: 100). Second, Maine's work was influenced by the uniformitarian doctrine of Charles Lyell, a contemporary geologist. According to this, changes in the Earth's surface were constant, gradual and imperceptible, the result of regular physical forces. As Peter Stein has noted, 'this provided an attractive analogy with the traditional view of the common law' (1980: 88).

Maine's grand generalizations rapidly became 'the common currency of legal thought', notwithstanding his lack of detailed research (Stein 1980: 98). Their popularity was due to both a formal and a substantive association with contemporary science. As regards form, Maine's work was born of a concern to provide an empirico-historical account of law's growth after the fashion of Savigny. To distinguish himself from his rivals, he invoked the positivist, experimental methodology typical of the leading natural and medical sciences, claiming that:

> The inquiries of [other jurists] are in truth prosecuted much as inquiry in physics and physiology was prosecuted before observation had taken the place of assumption. Theories, plausible and comprehensive, but absolutely unverified ... enjoy a universal preference over sober research into the primitive history of society and law.
>
> (1861/1870: 3)

As regards substance, contemporary law gained depth and order through being shown to contain its past within itself, rather like plant and animal life in Darwin's evolutionary schema (Fitzpatrick 1992: 93). This perspective was keenly taken up by Maine's contemporaries, susceptible as they were to theories ascribing the immense changes through which they were living to ineluctable and irresistible forces. To lawyers in particular, the evolutionary perspective revealed that the law was able to adapt itself gradually, that is without convulsion or revolution, to new social and economic circumstances. The good was thus equated with the existent (Stein 1980: 99; Sugarman 1986: 43). As we have seen, this pattern was also taken to be characteristic of medicine in the later 1800s, whereby the sectarianism and epistemic disjunctures of the early century were replaced by a unified knowledge base and a dispensation of orderly progress (Lawrence 1994: 55).

Progress through pluralism: the dissenting judgment

The common law, it can be argued, progresses, not just over the *longue durée* from time immemorial to the present, but also from case to case. The engine of this progress is, in the higher courts at least, the production of plural opinions and dissenting judgments. Both phenomena can be seen, in Darwinian terms, as instances of variation produced by the legal system in response to changes in its environment: for example, social and economic developments (Luhmann 1994: 241). The system selects from the variety of judgments in future cases where a similar point arises. Any selection can be revised or overturned subsequently with the result that the content of legal knowledge, like that of science, is inherently contingent. The necessary variation (and selection) is possible because of the tolerance, indeed the valorization, of a vigorous contest of judicial opinions in the common law tradition. It is not surprising that English judges, embedded as they are in that tradition, have taken pluralism to be emblematic of progressive and beneficent medical science as well.

Majority, as opposed to consensus, decision making has been practised in the English courts since at least the fifteenth century. John Alder has illuminated some of the practical justifications for, and political resonances of the dissenting judgment (2000). He surmises, for instance, that the possibility of open contradiction serves to sharpen majority judgements. Like science and nature, the common law too would appear to be 'red in tooth and claw'. In addition, whatever the outcome of the case, minority opinions endure in the law reports and constitute a resource for future correction and reform of the law. To paraphrase EH Carr they are the '[p]regnant failures ... of today [which] may turn out to have made a vital contribution to the achievement of tomorrow' (1987: 128–129). Benjamin Cardozo went even further, inserting the minority judge into a (lightly) secularized version of Judæo-Christian tradition:

> The dissenter speaks to the future and his voice is fixed to a key that will carry through the years.... The prophet and the martyr do not see the hooting throng. Their eyes are fixed on eternities.
>
> (Quoted in Alder 2000: 241)

On Alder's account, however, the ultimate justification for plurality and dissent in the common law is moral rather than practical. From a moral perspective, judgments in the higher courts have a double nature: expressive on the one hand, representative on the other (Alder 2000: 223). As regards the first, judges must be taken to have their own profoundly held views on matters of ethical and political importance. Their rights as ordinary citizens demand that these views should not be suppressed. As regards the second, judges can be said to give utterance in their reasoning to the range of moral positions held in society. Thus, a move to single-judgment decisions would effectively stigmatize unorthodox beliefs and disenfranchise their adherents. Furthermore, with increasing disputes over human rights, bioethics and governance, dissent has become more likely and the need for toleration more pressing. The foregoing, essentially liberal and democratic reasons only run so far, however: plurality must be managed, as well as tolerated (Luhmann 1994: 325). As we will see in Chapter 7, it is successfully managed by the shared professional culture of judges and also by the need to incorporate previous authorities in any valid decision, even if only to distinguish them. As in science, operations of the legal system are necessarily recursive. These ideological and operational constraints on dissent correspond to the 'conservative or traditional or historical element' in Popper's model of scientific advance (1981: 87).

The idea of progress

In the foregoing sections, it has been shown that judicial evaluation of doctors' work is structured by an understanding of medicine as a progressive, conflict-driven science, and that this resonates with lawyers' understanding of their own discipline. The idea of progress that informs these insights is best apprehended from three overlapping perspectives (philosophical, religious and political), which are the focus of this section of the chapter. By attending to the 'background metaphorics'[33] of the idea, it should be possible for us to specify its enduring significance in elite, professional discourses.

Some idea of progress has provided an orientation for philosophical and practical endeavour in Europe since Pascal proposed that the course of all humanity was as 'one man always subsisting and incessantly learning' (Bury 1955: 68). There has been no agreement on the content of the idea. Scholars note, however, that it occupies the position formerly held by providence in the worldview of Europeans (Nisbet 1980: 124; Blumenberg 1999: 39). The latter set the horizon of Christian faith and expectation in the future, all earthly history tending towards the Second Coming of Christ.[34] As much is captured in the extended title of John Bunyan's *The Pilgrim's Progress* (1678): 'from this world to that which is to come'.[35] With the fragmentation of religious belief in the late seventeenth century, this eschatology was secularized (Löwith 1949: 83). For moderns, the fulfilment of time will no longer take the form of a transcendental intervention. Rather the new providence is immanent to the world, its duration infinite, its *telos* unspecified. The attitudes of faith and expectation remain, but they are now imbued with confidence in steady human self-improvement (Löwith 1949: 202). 'Progress' thus functions as an integrating ideal, providing security and stability to the individual and the collective in the face of a hostile environment and the indifference of God. It has been felicitously described as 'the continuous self-justification of the present by means of the future that it gives itself, before the past with which it compares itself' (Blumenberg 1999: 32).

Thus the profound importance of the idea of progress derives, at least indirectly, from its theological antecedents. Beyond this we can suggest that the precise mode of progress, valorized in judicial discourse, is informed by distinct confessional forms which are themselves deeply implicated in ideas of Britishness. As Linda Colley has well demonstrated, the creation of a common British political identity in the eighteenth and nineteenth centuries was crucially dependent on the shared Protestant-ism of its otherwise diverse peoples (1992: 232). This identity was achieved by contra-distinction with the 'other' of Catholicism, which menaced it from across the Channel. Britain's economic and scientific advances, as well as its parliamentary practices, were consequently taken to be part of the nation's 'Protestant inheritance' (Colley 1992: 52). Con-tinental equivalents had developed slowly, or not all, wherever the dead hand of church authority and the threat of persecution stifled enterprise and inquiry.[36] It is certainly true that, from the mid-nineteenth century onwards, the specifically religious influence of Protestantism on the British began to wane; indeed, as we have noted, the rise of modern medical science contributed significantly to this. Nonetheless, the now latent national self-understanding continued to facilitate an association of pluralism and dissent with the achievement of progress.[37] As much is evident in the terminology ('dogma', 'heresy', 'martyr', 'visionary', 'prophet') which we have seen used to describe the nature and function of minority opinions in medicine and law. Clearly the rhetoric of dissent still has purchase in an otherwise secular context.

Liberal political theory, itself built upon the same 'Protestant inherit-ance', also contributes to the background metaphorics of the idea of progress in medicine and law. Most important in this regard is JS Mill's defence of free speech on the ground that truth is most likely to emerge from unregulated competition in ideas (1989: 23).[38] Mill condemned censorship as a restraint upon 'the invisible hand' of the intellectual marketplace, which risked privileging the false and suppressing the true (Schauer 1982: 15). A robust competition of ideas was responsible for the progressive dynamic of European nations, which, like Maine, he dis-tinguished from the stationary societies of the Orient (Mill 1989: 72). Accordingly freedom of expression deserved protection on instrumental grounds first and foremost. As we have seen, a survivalist theory of truth also underpins Popper's philosophy of science, a philosophy which he extended to the political sphere in *The Open Society and its Enemies* (1966). There, Popper recommended an incremental, problem-solving approach to social questions rooted in the method of trial and elimination of error which characterized good science. A Darwinian concern with adaptation and evolution, as well as a fallibilist scepticism concerning established truths, led him to see progress as infinite, but unpredictable. Both Mill and Popper thus appear to locate the origins of liberal political arrangements and progressive science in the struggles of nature and in the naturalized realm of the marketplace. Change is accordingly absorbed into mythic processes; 'the new appears as predetermined' and the present is justified endlessly (Adorno and Horkheimer 1997: 27). Furthermore, each area of social activity is constructed and legitimated as a sphere of free and beneficent competition pursued by formally equal actors, in which scientific theories and political opinions gain acceptance solely by reason of their plausibility.[39] Considered as an ideal, this model of scientific and social development is an obvious example of 'process-Utopia' as considered in Chapter 5.

The radical critique

The complex interlacing of critical–rational science, medical advance and weak legal regulation, discussed in this chapter, has been fundamentally challenged in recent decades. At each point, a radical critique has disputed the transparency, order and beneficence of progress. The English common law has been indicted as an accomplice in the exploitation of patients by a rapacious medical science. Cumulatively this critique confirms our inductive conclusion as to the ideological and, therefore, contestable nature of the idea of progress in science, medicine and the law. In the following discussion we examine its three main moments.

The work of Thomas Kuhn throws into question the Popperian ideal of scientific activity which underpinned the legal representation of medicine. According to Kuhn, scientific work is only possible within 'paradigms' which mark out the phenomena to be investigated and indicate appropriate research questions. Research in this mode is in the nature of puzzle solving; that is, continually refining the paradigm without ever transcending it (Kuhn 1996: 35). Normal science is, therefore, characterized not by a vigorous competition of ideas, but by a high degree of consensus and closure. Kuhn also rejects the notion of an orderly, cumulative increase in knowledge which underlies Popper's notion of rational learning by feedback in science. Change only occurs when a given paradigm is beset by a multiplicity of experimental anomalies and is ultimately abandoned in favour of a new paradigm. The latter is often wholly incommensurable with its predecessors, and its adoption by individual scientists is more a matter of conversion than of rational persuasion (Kuhn 1996: 151). Scientific progress thus manifests itself in the form of a series of ruptures or revolutions. These are like their political equivalents in seeking to change institutions in a manner prohibited by the institutions themselves (Kuhn

1996: 93). The connotations of violence and subversion are clearly negative.[40] Kuhn's theories break the closed circle of legitimation which Popper
establishes between the liberal polity and the 'republic of science'. According to Steve Fuller, while Popper's science can be understood as part of
the Enlightenment tradition, Kuhn's is arcane and closed, its practitioners
maintain their autonomy through uniform displays of their authority
(1997: 5, 26). The latter clearly suggests an enduring dogmatism of the
sort condemned by Popper's precursor Claude Bernard.

Ivan Illich's similarly influential critique of modern medicine is structured around the classical idea of nemesis. In Greek mythology, this divine
revenge was called down by human impudence, or hubris. Prometheus
stole fire from Mount Olympus and was cruelly punished over centuries by
Zeus; Narcissus was bound to suffer for spurning Echo's affections.
Nemesis also structured the Greek view of profane history as cyclical. The
passage to each new stage was marked by the downfall of the precedent
order as a result of hubris (Löwith 1949: 7). This worldview is sharply distinct from that of the secular, post-Christian era. As we have seen, the
latter is oriented towards the open horizon of the future and supports an
idea of cumulative, linear progress in science and in human affairs. Illich
reverts to the classical model precisely in order to place himself beyond
the consensus in favour of therapeutic advance (1976: 43). Medical
nemesis, he contends, is a specific form of cosmic retribution for industrial hubris; that is, the pursuit of material progress without regard to the
limits of taboo or myth.[41] Consequent human suffering takes three forms
(Illich 1976: 41–43): first, clinical iatrogenesis: the fact that patients are
increasingly sickened not so much by external agents, as by the medical
system itself; second, social iatrogenesis: the growing power of the profession and the economic costs of its untramelled monopoly;[42] third, cultural
iatrogenesis: the commodification of health which degrades the capacity
of the laity to respond to illness and mortality.[43] Nemesis is structural and
endemic, a product of the ambitions of the medical profession, the passive
greed of the general public, and the penetration of capital into all corners
of social life. Things get worse, not better. For Illich, medical solutions to
the crisis, drawing as they do on the bankrupt logic of scientific progress,
are doomed simply to reinforce the iatrogenic loop. Escape from medical
nemesis is only possible through political action aimed at a recovery of
authentic, pre-scientific meanings of illness and mortality, and at the restoration of autonomous capacities for curing and healing (1976: 233, 239).

Conclusion: reparadoxifying scientific progress

These radical critiques of science and medicine provided crucial rhetorical
resources to medical law scholars seeking, as Kenneth Veitch has argued,
to assert jurisdiction over clinical practice (2007: 21–25). Most prominent

among these scholars was Ian Kennedy, whose anti-utopian critique of the NHS was discussed in Chapter 5. Kennedy applied Illich's theses to the British context. The force of this critique was augmented with reference to revisionist medical histories of the 1970s. These sought to demonstrate that the great progress in health since the Victorian era had been largely due, not to scientific progress, but to improvements in the diet and environment of the population (Kennedy 1980: 53, citing McKeown 1979). According to Kennedy this undermined, or in our terms 'repara-doxified' the common-sense link between clinical medicine and general welfare used by judges to justify the relatively weak regime of liability for medical malpractice in English law.

Kennedy's empirical challenge is complemented in Sheila McLean's *Old Law, New Medicine. Medical Ethics and Human Rights* (1999) by the claim that the more medicine becomes 'scientific', the more doctors are trans-formed into elite custodians of an arcane knowledge. Law's deference to scientific medicine is seen to rest on a paradox and is thereby rendered implausible. McLean gives form to this critique by repeatedly drawing on the type of religious language used by judges to describe themselves and their medical peers. This terminology is deployed here to opposite effect however. Thus she notes a widespread understanding that:

> all ills, social, personal, societal and global, can somehow be refash-ioned, neutralised and even eradicated, by the miracles generated by the modern religion that is medical science. The power to dispense its goods is vested in its priests – namely physicians.... [Our] culture turns to the doctor as a latter day Messiah.
>
> (1999: 8)

This rhetorical effect is sustained throughout: doctors' views are 'revered'; they possess 'awe-inspiring power'; medical diagnosis is 'a bandage for the spiritually wounded'; scientists are 'deified' and so on (McLean 1999: 9, 10, 11, 19). The irony and hyperbole evident here work on the basis of an implicit contrast between the established association of scientific progress with secu-larization and debate, on the one hand, and the superstition and deference to authority which surround modern medicine, on the other.[44] This self-presentation of the academic commentator in defiance of the medical papacy is also suggested by the very title of Kennedy's published Reith Lectures. *The Unmasking of Medicine* combines a pun based on the surgeon's mask, with a religious idea of desacralization and the basic physical experience of not seeing and then seeing. For both McLean and Kennedy, the ideal role of law and ethics lies in restoring transparency, opening up the conclave of profes-sional opinion. That ambition will be considered more fully in the final chapter of this book. Before that, however, I will examine the topic of medi-cine as an art and its specific purchase in the rhetoric of medical law.

Notes

1 See above, Chapter 2.
2 For a compelling introduction to this milieu, see Paulin (1998).
3 For a fuller discussion, see Furst (1993).
4 See Bernard (1927); this debt is acknowledged in Popper (1979a: 258).
5 See Cohen (1985: 541–544) and Porter (1997: 337).
6 Bernard admitted that medicine was slower to develop since its practice was more shaped by the personality of the doctor than, say, physics or chemistry, see Cohen (1985: 542).
7 This corresponds to 'organized scepticism', one of the four organizational norms of science according to Merton (1973).
8 [1957] 1 WLR 582 (McNair J at 592).
9 [1998] AC 232 (HL).
10 *Edward Wong Finance Co Ltd v Johnson Stokes & Master* [1984] AC 296 (PC); *Cavanagh v Ulster Weaving Co Ltd* [1960] AC 145 (HL).
11 [1957] 1 WLR 582 (McNair J).
12 [1957] 1 WLR 582 (at 586).
13 [1985] AC 871 (HL).
14 [1985] AC 871 (HL at 893). Support for such an approach is spelled out in Linden (1968: 154).
15 [1954] 2 QB 66 (CA).
16 Ibid. (CA at 83).
17 [1985] AC 871 (HL at 893).
18 [1984] 1 WLR 634 (HL).
19 Ibid. (HL at 638).
20 [1957] 1 WLR 582 (per McNair J at 592).
21 1955 SLT 213 (SC at 217).
22 [1998] AC 232 (HL)
23 Ibid. (HL per Lord Browne Wilkinson at 241–242); cf. also, *Joyce v Merton, Sutton and Wandsworth Health Authority* [1996] 7 Med LR 1 (CA).
24 In the inaugural Provost's Lecture at University College London, 16 January 2001. See Dyer (2001).
25 [1998] AC 232 (HL at 243); for patterns in the case law after *Bolitho* see Mulheron (2010).
26 *De Freitas v O'Brien* [1995] 6 Med LR 108 (CA). For further discussion, see Khan and Robson (1995).
27 *Hucks v Cole* [1993] 4 Med LR 393 (CA) (1968); *Clark v MacLennan* [1983] 1 All ER 416 (Peter Pain J).
28 *Mahon v Osborne* [1939] 2 KB 14 (CA); *Anderson v Chasney* [1949] 4 DLR 71 (Manitoba CA).
29 *Bolam v Friern Hospital Management Committee* [1957] 1 WLR 582 (per McNair J at 587).
30 [1954] 2 QB 66 (CA).
31 [1954] 2 QB 66 (CA per Denning LJ at 84).
32 Denning LJ noted that the lesson of the case had already been publicized in a relevant medical textbook: [1954] 2 QB 66 (CA at 86).
33 This has been defined as 'a process of reference to a model that is operative in the genesis of a concept but is no longer present in the concept itself' (Blumenberg 1960: 73).
34 'So Christ was once offered to bear the sins of many: and unto them that look for him shall he appear the second time without sin unto salvation' (Hebrews 9:28).

35 See further, Williams (1983: 244).

36 For a historical and comparative review, see Troeltsch (1986).

37 See Jardine (1999).

38 This view of the uses of free speech was also adopted into the First Amendment jurisprudence of the US Supreme Court under the influence of Oliver Wendell Holmes. See Cohen (1989).

39 See further, Eagleton (1984: 26).

40 See Williams (1983: 273–274).

41 For a philosophical consideration of the 'limits to medicine', see Jonas (2003).

42 The 'medicalization of life' thesis was first developed by Zola (1972).

43 Illich borrows the legal term 'dissezin' to describe this 'wrongful putting out' of people from their capacity to cope and care for each other (1976: 70).

44 This contrast and the paradox of rationality which it sets up is famously articulated in Weber (1919).

References

Adorno, T and M Horkheimer (1944/1997) *Dialectic of Enlightenment* (London, Verso).

Alder, J (2000) 'Dissents in Courts of Last Resort: Tragic Choices?', 20 *Oxford Journal of Legal Studies* 221.

Bernard, C (1865/1927) *An Introduction to the Study of Experimental Medicine* (New York, Macmillan).

Berridge, V (1999) *Health and Society in Britain since 1939* (Cambridge, Cambridge University Press).

Blumenberg, H (1960) 'Paradigmen zu einer Metaphorologie', 6 *Archiv für Begriffsgeschichte* 69.

Blumenberg, H (1999) *The Legitimacy of the Modern Age* (Cambridge, MA, MIT Press).

Brazier, M and J Miola (2000) 'Bye-Bye Bolam: A Medical Litigation Revolution?', 8 *Medical Law Review* 85.

Bury, JB (1955) *The Idea of Progress. An Inquiry into its Origin and Growth* (New York, Dover).

Canguilhem, G (1994) *A Vital Rationalist. Selected Writings* (New York, Zone Books).

Cantor, D (1992) 'Cortisone and the Politics of Drama, 1949–55', in JV Pickstone (ed.), *Medical Innovations in Historical Perspective* (London, Macmillan) 165.

Carr, EH (1987) *What Is History?* 2nd edition (London, Penguin).

Cohen, IB (1985) *Revolution in Science* (Cambridge, MA, Harvard University Press).

Cohen, J (1989) *Congress Shall Make No Law: Oliver Wendell Holmes, the First Amendment, and Judicial Decision Making* (Ames, IA, Iowa State University Press).

Colley, L (1992) *Britons. Forging the Nation 1707–1837* (New Haven, CT, Yale University Press).

Dugdale, AM and KM Stanton (1998) *Professional Negligence*, 3rd edition (London, Butterworths).

Dyer, C (2001) 'Courts Too Deferential to Doctors, says Judge', 322 *British Medical Journal* 129.

Eagleton, T (1984) *The Function of Criticism. From 'The Spectator' to Post-Structuralism* (London, Verso).

Eliot, G (1872/1994) *Middlemarch* (London, Penguin).

Fitzpatrick, P (1992) *The Mythology of Modern Law* (London, Routledge).

Fuller, S (1997) *Science* (Buckingham, Open University Press).

Furst, LR (1993) 'Struggling for Medical Reform in Middlemarch', 48 *Nineteenth Century Literature* 341.

Giesen, D (1988) *International Medical Malpractice Law* (Tübingen, JCB Mohr).

Hurwitz, B (1999) 'Legal and Political Considerations of Clinical Practice Guidelines', 318 *British Medical Journal* 661.

Illich, I (1976) *Limits to Medicine. Medical Nemesis: The Expropriation of Health* (London, Penguin).

Jackson, RM and JL Powell (1997) *Professional Negligence*, 4th edition (London, Sweet and Maxwell).

Jardine, L (1999) *Ingenious Pursuits. Building the Scientific Revolution* (London, Little, Brown & Co).

Jonas, H (2003) *Das Prinzip Verantwortung. Versuch einer Ethik für die technologische Zivilisation* (Frankfurt-am-Main, Suhrkamp).

Jones, CAG (1994) *Expert Witnesses. Science, Medicine and the Practice of Law* (Oxford, Clarendon).

Kennedy, I (1980) *The Unmasking of Medicine* (London, Allen and Unwin).

Khan, M and M Robson (1995) 'What Is a Responsible Body of Medical Opinion?', 11 *Professional Negligence* 121.

Kuhn, TS (1996) *The Structure of Scientific Revolutions*, 3rd edition (Chicago, University of Chicago Press).

Lakatos, I (1981) 'History of Science and its Rational Reconstructions', in I Hacking (ed.), *Scientific Revolutions* (Oxford, Oxford University Press) 107.

Larson, MS (1977) *The Rise of Professionalism. A Sociological Analysis* (Berkeley, CA, University of California Press).

Latour, B (1983) 'Give Me a Laboratory and I Will Raise the World', in KD Knorr-Cetina and M Mulkay (eds), *Science Observed. Perspectives on the Social Study of Science* (London, Sage) 141.

Laudan, L (1981) 'A Problem Solving Approach to Scientific Progress' in I Hacking, *Scientific Revolutions* (Oxford, Oxford University Press) 144.

Lawrence, C (1994) *Medicine in the Making of Modern Britain 1700–1920* (London, Routledge).

Le Fanu, J (2000) *The Rise and Fall of Modern Medicine* (London, Abacus).

Linden, AM (1968) 'Custom in Negligence Law', 11 *Canadian Bar Journal* 151.

Löwith, K (1949) *Meaning in History* (Chicago, University of Chicago Press).

Luhmann, N (1994) *Das Recht der Gesellschaft* (Frankfurt-am-Main, Suhrkamp).

Luhmann, N (1999) *Ausdifferenzierung des Rechts. Beiträge zur Rechtssoziologie und Rechtstheorie* (Frankfurt-am-Main, Suhrkamp).

McKeown, T (1979) *The Role of Medicine. Dream, Mirage or Nemesis?* (Oxford, Blackwell).

McLean, S (1999) *Old Law, New Medicine. Medical Ethics and Human Rights* (London, Pandora).

Magee, B (1985) *Popper*, 3rd edition (London, Fontana).

Maine, HS (1861/1870) *Ancient Law. Its Connection with the Early History of Society and its Relation to Modern Ideas* (London, John Murray).

Maulitz, R (1979) '"Physician versus Bacteriologist": The Ideology of Science in Clinical Medicine', in MJ Vogel and CE Rosenberg (eds), *The Therapeutic Revolution. Essays in the Social History of American Medicine* (Philadelphia, PA, University of Pennsylvania) 91.

Merton, RK (1973) *The Sociology of Science* (Chicago, University of Chicago Press).

Mill, JS (1859/1989) *On Liberty and Other Writings* (Cambridge, Cambridge University Press).

Mulheron, R (2010) 'Trumping Bolam: A Critical Legal Analysis of Bolitho's "Gloss"', 69 *Cambridge Law Journal* 609.

Nisbet, R (1980) *History of the Idea of Progress* (London, Heinemann).

Norrie, K (1985) 'Common Practice and the Standard of Care in Medical Negligence', *Juridical Review* 145.

Paulin, T (1998) *The Day-Star of Liberty. William Hazlitt's Radical Style* (London, Faber).

Popper, K (1966) *The Open Society and its Enemies* (London, Routledge and Kegan Paul).

Popper, K (1979a) 'Evolution and the Tree of Knowledge', in K Popper, *Objective Knowledge. An Evolutionary Approach* (Oxford, Clarendon) 256.

Popper, K (1979b) 'Epistemology without a Knowing Subject', in K Popper, *Objective Knowledge. An Evolutionary Approach* (Oxford, Clarendon) 106.

Popper, K (1981) 'The Rationality of Scientific Revolutions', in I Hacking (ed.), *Scientific Revolutions* (Oxford, Oxford University Press) 80.

Porter, R (1997) *The Greatest Benefit to Mankind. A Medical History of Humanity from Antiquity to the Present* (London, Harper Collins).

Schauer, F (1982) *Free Speech. A Philosophical Inquiry* (Cambridge, Cambridge University Press).

Stein, P (1980) *Legal Evolution. The Story of an Idea* (Cambridge: Cambridge University Press).

Strong, PM (1984) 'The Academic Encirclement of Medicine', 6 *Sociology of Health and Illness* 339.

Sturdy, S (1992) 'The Political Economy of Scientific Medicine: Science, Education and the Transformation of Medical Practice in Sheffield, 1890–1922', 36 *Medical History* 125.

Sugarman, D (1986) 'Legal Theory, the Common Law Mind and the Making of Tradition', in W Twining (ed.), *Legal Theory and the Common Law* (Oxford: Basil Blackwell) 26.

Troeltsch, E (1912/1986) *Protestantism and Progress. The Significance of Protestantism for the Rise of the Modern World* (Philadelphia, PA, Fortress Press).

Veitch, K (2007) *The Jurisdiction of Medical Law* (Aldershot, Hampshire, Ashgate).

Warner, JH (1991) 'The Idea of Science in English Medicine: The "Decline of Science" and the Rhetoric of Reform, 1815–1845' in R French and A Wear (eds), *British Medicine in an Age of Reform* (London, Routledge) 136.

Weber, M (1919) 'Wissenschaft als Beruf', in M Weber, *Geistige Arbeit als Beruf* (München, Duncker & Humblot).

Williams, R (1983) *Keywords. A Vocabulary of Culture and Society* (London, Fontana).

Worboys, M (1992) 'Vaccine Therapy and Laboratory Medicine in Edwardian Britain', in JV Pickstone (ed.), *Medical Innovations in Historical Perspective* (London, Macmillan) 84.

Zola, IK (1972) 'Medicine as an Institution of Social Control', 20 *Sociological Review* 487.

Chapter 7

Art

Introduction

At the outset of the last chapter, I proposed that judicial and legislative deference to professional opinion was supported rhetorically by images of clinical practice as a distinctive form of work which resonated with the self-perceptions of lawyers. I noted that there were two significant such images and went on to explore in some detail the first of these, the idea of medicine as a scientific practice, driven by an ongoing contest of opinions. In this chapter I will investigate the second, the art model of medicine, investigating its plausibility, again with reference to influential understandings of the nature of the common law. I consider first the prominence of 'judgement' and the 'individual case' in the language of medical leaders from the late nineteenth century and note its continuing salience in polemics regarding the nature and purpose of medical work. I then examine briefly the manner in which this model was reproduced in leading medical law decisions from the period around the foundation of the NHS onwards. In the following two sections, I draw on work in the philosophy of medicine and in legal theory to clarify the elements of this model and to show how they are shared by both disciplines. These elements include the idea that the true nature of practitioner knowledge cannot be captured in explicit rules and prescriptions; that clinical and legal reasoning are primarily analogical in form; and that, as a result, skills are best transmitted subliminally through a period of apprenticeship. In conclusion, I locate these common representations with reference to broader conservative political theories. I note the irony that a hierarchical model of professional authority, ratified and depended on by the law, contributed to the functioning of the egalitarian welfare state.

Professional ideology: 'the art of medicine'

The elevation of professional judgment in medical law and in the operation of the NHS reflected a long held self-perception or 'ideology' of the profession (Osborne 1998: 260). In resisting external political and commercial control, late Victorian and Edwardian commentators had deployed the language of 'privacy, sacredness and the inviolability of clinical judgement.... [This] made medical work accountable only to other doctors – only to those with experience of the clinical situation' (Lawrence 1994: 77).

Correspondingly many leading doctors denied that explicit scientific principles could have any direct role in clinical practice. As a contributor to *The Lancet* put it in 1900:

> [w]e must never allow theories or even what appear to be logical deductions or explanations, however ingenious, or statistics, however apparently conclusive, or authority, however venerable, to take the place of the one touchstone of practical medicine, experience.
>
> (Pye-Smith quoted in Lawrence 1985: 511)

Indeed new instruments such as the stethoscope were condemned for threatening to 'pauperize the senses and weaken clinical acuity' (Lawrence 1985: 513). Professional experience was matched in this model by an emphasis on the uniqueness of each patient. Thus, the introduction of randomized controlled trials of new drugs in the 1940s was resisted on the basis that 'medicine never will be an exact science because the normal variations in individuals have such a wide range' (Armstrong 1977: 600).

The emphasis on 'producer virtualities'[1] which characterized the profession in the first half of the twentieth century was strategically aligned with a view of medicine as 'a powerful instrument for effecting ... social progress and national prosperity' (Lawrence 1994: 76). The labour movement claimed clinically focused health care as a right, a claim made good with the creation of the NHS in 1948. As we saw in Chapter 5, there was no conflict on the question of medical autonomy between Aneurin Bevan, the founder of the Service, and the elite medical leaders with whom he negotiated.[2] In a speech to the Royal Medico-Psychological Association in 1945, he asserted that just as 'the individual citizen must be free to choose his doctor' so 'the doctor must be able to treat his patient in conditions of inviolable privacy' (quoted in Foot 1962: 119).

This opposition between pristine, individually focused professional judgement and the scientistic conception of clinical work as mere rule following also informs more recent critiques of the organization and goals of medicine. In *The Rise and Fall of Modern Medicine* (1999) James Le Fanu identifies two emblematic personalities in this regard. The first, Lord 'Tommy' Horder (1871–1955), was the most celebrated physician of his day, enjoying the patronage of leading politicians, cultural figures and royalty. Drawing on 'vast experience and shrewd judgement' in history taking and observation, he was able to infer what was amiss with the patient without recourse to the technology which became popular in later decades (Le Fanu 1999: 199). The essential objective of any doctor was, he held, to act in the best interests of the particular patient. Le Fanu's brief account of Horder's career is enhanced by the reproduction of a photograph of him in the garden of his home in Kent. Secateurs in hand, Horder looks not into the camera, but at the tangle of a rambling rose which has grown around an arched gap in the garden wall. The composition, surely allegorical and set moreover in the 'garden of England', speaks of patience, watchfulness and restrained intervention.

The career of Sir Thomas Lewis (1881–1945) is offered by Le Fanu as a counterpoint to that of Lord Horder. The son of a Welsh mining engineer, Lewis's reputation was founded on his pioneering study *The Mechanisms and Graphic Registration of the Heartbeat.* Work on this tome involved thousands of precise recordings of human hearts and continuous experimentation on animals. Lewis's application of science to human physiology embodied what he saw as 'the university spirit in medicine' (Le Fanu 1999: 200). For him the individual patient was significant not only, or even primarily, in and of herself. Rather doctors should look for what they could 'get out of [each] case in order to do better the next time' (Le Fanu 1999: 200). Lewis sought in other words to raise clinical practice to the level of a science which advances through an inductive accumulation of knowledge. As before, Le Fanu supports his analysis with a photographic representation: of Lewis standing between a dark cabinet and a bench on which is placed a cluster of mechanical devices, all dials and wires. The caption informs us that this is an electrocardiogram, the chief instrument of his research. Apart from Lewis himself, no living thing can be seen. The textual and pictorial juxtaposition outlined here is crucial to Le Fanu's argument that modern medicine has bankrupted itself morally and intellectually by abandoning the primacy of clinical judgment and its focus on the individual case. His response is to call for a renewed acceptance that there are limits to what doctors can know; the rediscovery of the importance of that 'tacit' knowledge which can only be gained through experience; and a re-orientation of practice towards doing good in 'minute particulars' (Le Fanu 1999: 405–406).

Clinical judgement in medical law

Courts have also insisted that clinical decision making cannot be reduced to a mechanical exercise in rule following. As Lawton LJ put it in *Whitehouse v Jordan*, medicine:

> consists of the harmonious union of science with skill ... [it] has not yet got to the stage, and maybe it never will, when the adoption of a particular procedure will produce a certain result.[3]

The enduring role for 'skill' was explained by Scott LJ in *Mahon v Osborne* with reference to:

> (1.) [t]he multiform difficulties presented by the particular circumstances of the operation, (2.) the condition of the patient and the whole set of problems arising out of the risks to which he is being exposed, [and] (3.) the difficulty of the [doctor's] choice between risks.[4]

Cases were complex and varied greatly and each had to be treated as a whole. As a result, explicit rules could not be allowed to supplant the situated knowledge of the individual practitioner. Elsewhere Streatfield J argued that:

> [the relevant] textbook writers ... were writing of the subject generally. They were not writing of a particular patient.... [S]omething must be left to the judgment of the doctors on the spot, who did not have to treat a case of infective hepatitis only, but had a particular patient to treat.[5]

There was, therefore, a 'paramount need' for doctors' discretion in balancing risks and choosing a course of action to be unfettered.[6]

The importance of clinical judgement increases, rather than decreases, with progress in the science base of medicine. This perhaps unexpected conclusion was well explained by Lord Diplock in *Sidaway v Board of Governors of the Bethlem Royal Hospital*:

> unless the art in which the artificer claims to have acquired skill and judgment is stagnant so that no improvement in methods or knowledge is sought ... advances in the ability to heal resulting from the volume of research, clinical as well as technological, will present doctors with alternative treatments to adopt and a choice to select that treatment (it may be one of several) that is in their judgment likely at the time to prove most efficacious or ameliorating to the health of each particular patient.[7]

The proliferation of clinical guidance based on scientific studies thus adds to the complexity of decision making in health care (Vogd 2002). In effect practitioners are faced with two sources of indeterminacy: the variability of patients and the expansion of knowledge. As Miola suggests in relation to ethical guidance, deferring to the skill of doctors is a way of reducing this complexity and ensuring that decision making gets done in medicine and in law.[8]

This burden of judgement under conditions of uncertainty has been acknowledged by courts. According to Lord Donaldson in *Whitehouse v Jordan*:

doctors have to practise their profession on and beyond the frontiers of the unknown, ... they have sometimes to take calculated risks ... they have sometimes to make inspired guesses.[9]

The chance of harm resulting from such action, whether culpable or not, is 'almost always a matter of chance' and 'it ill becomes anyone to adopt an attitude of superiority'.[10] In the same case, Lord Denning drew clear parallels between lawyers and doctors in this regard:

> Whenever I give a judgment and it is afterwards reversed in the House of Lords, is it to be said that I was negligent? That I did not pay enough attention to a previous binding authority or the like? Every one of us every day gives a judgment which is afterwards found to be wrong.... So also with a barrister who advises that there is a good cause of action and it afterwards fails.[11]

His attempt on this basis to create a new category of 'errors of judgment' exempt from liability was rejected by the House of Lords. Reaffirming the objective, *Bolam* test of negligence, it held that a doctor would be liable if she had fallen below the standard of a responsible body of medical practitioners.[12] A similar attempt, in *Wilsher v Essex Area Health Authority*, to tailor the standard of care to the level of actual experience possessed by a trainee doctor, was equally rejected in favour of a more objective, uniform approach.[13] Nonetheless the dignity and prestige of medicine continued to be emphasized by courts. For example, Peter Pain J, concluding his judgment in *Clark v MacLennan*, expressed regret that he had to find the defendant gynaecologist liable in negligence and urged him to 'take comfort in the thought that even Apollo, the God of healing, and the father of Aesculapius, had his moment of weakness'.[14]

Reconstructing the art model of medicine

The art model of medicine has, thus, been influential in professional polemics and in the reasoning of common law courts. In this section I seek to elaborate key elements of that model, drawing on work in the philosophy of medicine. I hope to clarify the distinctive phenomenology and epistemology of medicine which it entails, as well as the ideal of medical training which it proposes.

A science of particulars

Courts and commentators have emphasized that clinical medicine is concerned with unique and variable phenomena. In an influential paper of 1976, Samuel Gorovitz and Alasdair MacIntyre built on this insight to distinguish medicine from the natural sciences. Motivated by a practical concern with the so-called malpractice crisis which had beset American medicine since the 1960s, they sought to engender more realistic expectations among both doctors and patients by clarifying three distinctive causes of medical mishaps. The first two are familiar: the culpable errors of practitioners and the under-developed state of scientific knowledge. The third source of error, which they claimed had been overlooked until then, lies in the unique complexity of each patient. Unlike physics or chemistry, which are concerned with universal phenomena, clinical medicine is a 'science of particulars' (Gorovitz and MacIntyre 1976: 51).

The objects of medicine – patients – are more like unique complex phenomena such as hurricanes or salt-marshes than chemical compounds, atoms or sub-atomic particles. As 'particulars', they cannot be understood in the abstract, but only through their distinctive histories and their evolving relations with the environment. The complexity, diversity and contingency of patients mean that they cannot be adequately comprehended in law-like generalizations. Any prediction regarding their future development, either with or without therapeutic intervention, is prone to an inevitable or 'necessary fallibility' (Gorovitz and MacIntyre 1976: 62). Thus, a diagnosis may be incorrect or a therapy may fail regardless of the care taken by the practitioner and irrespective of all possible scientific knowledge. Rather like Lord Denning in *Whitehouse v Jordan*,[15] they argued that accidents occurring under the third head imply no culpability and are not an appropriate focus for litigation.[16]

The insights of Gorovitz and MacIntyre were anticipated by and elaborated more fully in the work of the pioneering philosopher of science Ludwik Fleck.[17] Writing in the 1920s, he too argued against any reduction of clinical practice to the natural sciences:

> [While a] scientist looks for typical, normal phenomena … a medical man studies precisely the atypical, abnormal, morbid phenomena. And it is evident that he finds on this road a great wealth and range of individuality of these phenomena which form a great number, without distinctly limited units, and abounding in transitional, boundary states.
>
> (Fleck 1986: 39)

According to Fleck, this distinctive focus is reflected in the indeterminacy and instability of medical knowledge. No other discipline is characterized by such a proliferation of sub-types and exceptions, as is evident in the frequency with which clinical categories are qualified by the prefixes, for example, 'para-psoriasis' and 'pseudo-anaemia' (1986: 41). The complexity generated by the contingent and variable nature of medical phenomena is compounded by the fact they are connected to each other 'by means of a tremendous number of relations' (Fleck 1986: 43). Causal connections in medicine can, accordingly, be 'developmental, correlative, substituting, synergetic or antagonistic'. This double complexity drives an embarrassing wedge between theory and practice in medicine. As Fleck points out, whereas in the natural sciences no observation can be incompatible with theory, in medicine one commonly hears the saying 'impossible in theory although it comes up in practice' (1986: 42).[18] He asserts that it is easy in medicine to generate dogmatic, pseudo-logical explanations which hold for the short term, but (probably) impossible to reach general, embracing ideas. Indeed, given the variety of medical phenomena, it can be said that the more logical the therapy proposed, the worse the physician is likely to be (1986: 42).

Segmented knowledge

Fleck's argument would seem to deny a role for theory in medicine and to prioritize pure and unmediated clinical experience in accordance with traditional medical ideology discussed above. However, while he rejects dogmatism, Fleck does not embrace such a naïve position: 'an empty mind', he says, 'cannot see at all' (1981: 247). Instead he takes a constructivistic and pluralistic approach to medical knowledge (1981: 247). The latter is produced by multiple groups, or 'thought collectives', each with its own distinctive 'thought style'. This segmentation can be observed historically, for example, in the radical variation in the forms of anatomical drawing over the centuries. It is also evident across contemporary medicine. Due to increasing specialization, medicine is now composed of multiple sub-disciplines. Each has its own thought style, produced and maintained by groups of experts who share a point of view, a common terminology and a given set of research problems.[19] In joining a thought collective within medicine, a new member learns 'to see right' in accordance with the canons of that sub-discipline (1981: 251).

Thought styles are incommensurable: they cannot be reduced to common terms; one cannot be wholly explained wholly in terms of another. This is borne out by Annemarie Mol and Marc Berg's empirical study of how the meaning of 'anaemia' – ostensibly a single medical phenomenon – varies as between different sub-disciplines (1994). Thus patho-physiology is concerned with oxygen supply to the tissues; in the laboratory a statistical norm, with more or less arbitrary cut-off points, is imposed; while general practitioners only investigate for anaemia in the presence of indicative clinical signs and symptoms. These are rival, incompatible definitions which cannot be ranked on the same scale for precision or accuracy. Furthermore, as Mol and Berg note, this rivalry is less likely to be fought out to a decisive conclusion, for instance by reference to an overarching theory. In fact it is usually contained through a division of competencies, or jurisdictions, as between professional groups (Mol and Berg 1994: 258). As a result the segmentation of medicine is fairly stable and enduring.[20]

Exemplar reasoning and clinical prudence

We have seen that Fleck was one of the first philosophers to remark on the pluralism and incommensurability of medical knowledge. As a trained doctor, he was nonetheless aware that clinical decision making did (and had to) go on. For him the process of integrating the multiple perspectives, provided by the different sub-disciplines of medicine, in order to reach a clinical decision was ultimately opaque (1986: 45). More recently, Kenneth Schaffner has proposed a view of medical reasoning that incorporates complexity revealed in Fleck's work, but which also goes beyond its embrace of obscurity (1986: 63–80). Schaffner agrees that clinical concepts, such as different 'diseases', are characteristically overlapping, blurred at the edges, and linked by a series of family resemblances. As a result, unlike the natural sciences, clinical medicine cannot be completely represented in law-like terms, as the 'deductive systematization of a broad class of generalizations under a small number of axioms' (1986: 69). Instead he argues that 'exemplar' reasoning, based on analogy, and not deduction or induction, is central to medical practice.

Schaffner draws the meta-scientific notion of exemplars from the work of Thomas Kuhn (1996: 200). These are concrete problem solutions, or shared examples of how to get the job done, often provided as appendices to the discussions of general principles in biomedical texts. Doctors are also equipped with a rich stock of 'clinical exemplars' or 'cases' during their training on the wards and their post-qualification experience (Schaffner 1986: 71).[21] When confronted by a new case, they seek analogies with previous cases which they have studied or encountered. The relevant exemplar will indicate how to 'see' the patient at hand and, thus, what generalizations or 'laws' are applicable in that situation. Of course, it is common to seek scientific respectability for medicine by reconstructing and concealing the process of analogical reasoning 'so that it appears more like a deductive filling in of a general pattern' (Schaffner 1986: 70). But this is always secondary, since exemplars are cognitively prior to the axioms or principles which they are supposed to illustrate.

If medical knowledge is held in this form, how is it applied in the case of the particular patient? Edmund Pellegrino and David Thomasma answer this question by reminding us that the practice of medicine imposes a burden of decision making on the individual doctor which is quite absent from the work of the laboratory scientist (though not as we shall see from that of the common law judge). They argue that clinical reasoning always 'ends in a decision to act for and on behalf of a human who seeks to be healed' (Pellegrino and Thomasma 1981: 122). This goal imposes an 'atmosphere of prudence' on the whole process of diagnosis and recommendation of therapy. At each stage, a doctor seeks to weigh, balance and eliminate certain factors in a judicious manner which cannot be reduced either to logical reasoning or to technical competence (1981: 121). In that process the doctor is guided by a variety of prudential maxims, for example: 'act to optimize as many benefits, minimize as many risks as possible'; 'be wary of hunches and intuitions'; 'recognize one's own clinical style, prejudices, and beliefs about what is good for patients'; and so on (1981: 137). It is important to note, that these are only suggestions; they cannot be ranked in any hierarchical order and no single rule is indispensable to right clinical action. Furthermore, as the philosophers Michael Polanyi and Michael Oakeshott both argued, maxims are only useful when reintegrated into the practitioner's tacit or practical knowledge of the discipline.[22]

Personal knowledge – training by apprenticeship

The segmentation of medical knowledge into 'thought styles' (Fleck) and the importance of 'exemplars' in clinical reasoning (Schaffner) suggest that medical cognition is a mode of seeing correctly. In describing the development of this faculty, Polanyi gave the example of a medical student attending a course in the X-ray diagnosis of pulmonary diseases. Initially the novice is wholly puzzled by the pictures which he is asked to view:

> Then as he goes on listening for a few weeks, looking ever carefully at new pictures of different cases, a tentative understanding will dawn on him; he will gradually forget about the ribs and begin to see the lungs. And eventually if he perseveres intelligently, a rich panorama of significant details will be revealed to him: of physiological variations and pathological changes, of scars, of chronic infections and signs of acute disease. He has entered a new world.
>
> (Polanyi 1958: 101)

For Polanyi, neither this nor any other useful knowledge can be wholly specified in explicit detail. Much essential knowledge is held tacitly, without being fully present to the consciousness of the doctor when she is drawing on it.[23] Acquiring this 'embodied' knowledge is, as the quotation above suggests, the result of a process of personal change or 'self-modification' on the part of the knower (Polanyi 1958: 151).

Tacit knowledge and the skill of seeing correctly cannot be transmitted in rule form. Rather they are absorbed through observing more experienced practitioners. For Polanyi, then, a period of apprenticeship is essential to becoming a doctor or any other kind of professional:

By watching the master and emulating his efforts in the presence of his example, the apprentice unconsciously picks up the rules of the art including those which are not explicitly known to the master himself.

(1958: 153)

The relationship between master and student is necessarily hierarchical. To be initiated into the hidden wisdom of medicine is to submit to authority, to surrender oneself 'uncritically to the imitation of another' (Polanyi 1958: 53). Since true knowledge takes the form of embodied experience, the master attains to his position through longevity of practice. It follows that the most senior members of a profession are those best able to testify to successful and unsuccessful performance, to genuine and fake practice. Polanyi views the disciplines as closed spheres perpetuating themselves by co-option (1958: 244). Attempts by outsiders to regulate medicine on the basis of explicit rules, for example, through law or consumer activism, are bound to fail. In Oakeshott's words, 'we come to penetrate an idiom of activity in no other way than by practising the activity' (1991: 121). Professional autonomy, central to the art model of medicine, is thus justified on the basis of an anti-rationalist epistemology.

Elective affinities: the common law as practical knowledge

The view of medicine as an art sustained the law's deferral to professional opinion across a range of issues in medical law, as I argued above. In this section I seek to show that the plausibility of that representation of medicine has been reinforced by the remarkably similar understanding of the nature of the common law. There exists, in other words, a set of 'elective affinities' between the two disciplines as perceived by many leading practitioners and theorists of each.[24] I detail here the key elements of that legal self-understanding, paying particular attention to its correspondence with the description of medicine in the previous section. Consistent with my ambition in this book to locate medical law with reference to its historic, institutional and national contexts, I will focus specifically on the precedent-based system of reasoning used by lawyers in England and other common law jurisdictions. Of course the law in these jurisdictions is not wholly composed of case law. Statute law, including explicit codes of rights, and detailed regulations now abound. Nonetheless it is still true to say that case law methods are at the heart of juristic technique. As with clinical training in medicine, they are at the ideological core of what it is to be a common lawyer. University law students learn in the first instance how to interpret, apply and distinguish precedents (Atiyah 1987: 29). The key substantive areas of contract, tort, constitutional law, and criminal law are still significantly based on case law. Furthermore the meaning and scope of legislative enactments can only be known through the precedent cases in which they have been applied.

Priority of 'the case'

It is perhaps a truism to say that the common law is concerned with individual cases. As noted in Chapter 3, Tim Murphy has argued that the common law 'is geared to generating a situation of immediacy', a direct apprehension of individuals and their disputes (1997: 116). The parties and any witnesses to a dispute are brought in person before the court. The facts of the case are established through oral examination and the presentation of documentary evidence. Its outcome will often depend on the credibility of witnesses established in the presence of judge and jury. Through these individualizing processes:

> the knowledge of 'society', the management of disagreement, and the practical experience of the business of government are woven together in an indissoluble manner.
>
> (Murphy 1997: 88)[25]

As such, the common law can be contrasted with the statistically based social sciences, such as economics, which are both abstract and future oriented (Murphy 1997: 149).

It is of course true that decisions in individual cases furnish the normative stuff of the common law: precedents applicable in future cases with similar facts. Nonetheless, a certain methodological prudence has tended to favour the particularist framing and interpretation of judicial opinions.[26] English judges have usually been wary of establishing broad principles from which legal consequences can be drawn 'automatically', that is without reference to social consequences and without giving any consideration to the specific facts of possible future cases (Atiyah 1987: 15). At the extreme end of this particularism is Lord Halsbury's oft-quoted opinion that since 'a case is only an authority for what it actually decides' it cannot 'be quoted for a proposition that may seem to follow logically from it'.[27] To take one example, judicial shyness of generalization in the specific context of liability for negligence is attributed to the fact that:

> circumstances may differ infinitely and, in a swiftly developing field of law, there can be no necessary assumption that those features which have served in one case to create the relationship between the plaintiff and the defendant on which liability depends will necessarily be determinative of liability in the different circumstances of another case.[28]

Regional rationalities

This orientation to the individual case has strongly influenced the form taken by the common law. In particular it is reflected in the traditional view that the common law does not, in the first instance, constitute a system of clearly defined rules.[29] How is this seemingly counter-intuitive position reached? The reasoning in precedent cases is normally a close weave of facts and norms. Rules can be extracted from cases. But this is always a tentative process which does not furnish definitive statements of the law, but merely evidence or opinion as to what it might be. This is so since appellate court judges commonly offer divergent reasons for reaching the same outcome in the same case, and since the reasoning of any judge in any case is subject to interpretation and re-interpretation in future decisions (Stone 1964: 267). Thus, although the common law can be said to be composed of authoritative materials in the form of previous decisions, this increases, rather than eliminates, the scope for judicial creativity and conceptual instability (Stone 1964: 281). Precedent cases are, therefore, prior to the rules which they are taken to instantiate.

This embarrassment is increased by the fact that words in law as elsewhere may stand for a range of diverse, though related things (Perelman 1980: 126). In English law, for instance, the meaning of 'possession' varies significantly when used in relation to larceny, trespass, land tenure, or bailment (Twining and Miers 1991: 259).[30] Even in a single area of law, such as negligence, the particular instances of a general concept do not all exhibit a fixed set of universal features corresponding to those of an ideal entity. Rather, they are linked by similarities 'which some bear to others but not necessarily to all, like family resemblances' (Stone 1965: 478). If the common law is not composed in the first instance of clearly delimited rules, then it cannot be a system either. Indeed for Brian Simpson systematization is merely:

> the ideal of an expositor of the law, grappling with the untidy shambles of the law reports, the product of the common law mind which is repelled by brevity, lucidity and system, and it is no accident that its attraction as a model grows as the reality departs further and further from it.
>
> (1973: 99)[31]

The anti-system view is supported by Charles Sampford's critique of leading common law theorists (1989). To take one example, he rejects Ronald Dworkin's model of 'law as integrity', according to which legal rules and decisions are justified by a fairly coherent set of high-level principles, and ultimately by a theory of political philosophy.[32] Sampford shows that in practice the achievement of consistency or 'integrity' in law is impaired by the intractable heterogeneity of the very material of the common law: precedent cases establishing various rules are often actuated by opposing principles or policy considerations; judges are prone to distinguish and confine difficult precedents rather than to reject them openly on the basis of high-level principles. This is exacerbated by the fact that judges are engaged primarily in adjudication rather than justification (Sampford 1989: 87). Spurning the all-embracing idea, they generally seek what might be called a limited or 'regional' rationality, sufficient only to reach a decision in the particular case. As Lord Macmillan put it in *Read v Lyons* the task of the courts was 'to decide particular cases between litigants and ... [not] to rationalize the law of England'.[33]

This understanding of the nature of the common law is supported by Michael Lobban's study of the relationship between legal practice and legal theory in the late eighteenth and early nineteenth centuries. The most prominent jurisprudent of the time, Sir William Blackstone, had attempted 'to show that the common law could be seen to fit a deductive system of reasoning from natural law principles, which were essential and epistemologically correct' (Lobban 1991: 12). By contrast, in Jeremy Bentham's view, the common law could never be rationalized from within; to achieve the ideal rule-based code it was necessary to start anew, from first principles (Lobban 1991: 13). Notwithstanding this difference, however, both Blackstone and Bentham were equally out of step with the thinking of contemporary, and indeed, subsequent practitioners. They shared a holistic view of the law, which ran contrary to the prevailing view that:

> it was the function of the common law, not to apply eternal rules, nor to regulate society from above, but to provide useful, just and flexible solutions to individual cases.
>
> (Lobban 1991: 14–15)

Given this orientation to practice, Blackstone's work was fated to be read mainly as an introductory guide for students and gentleman scholars, a shorthand to memory, or a 'crib' to use Oakeshott's term (1991: 29). Bentham's was widely ignored (Lobban 1991: 47). On the orthodox view, the law was in the first instance a set of procedures and forms for laying out the facts of the case, and an array of techniques for drawing inferences from them with reference to precedents (which at that time were not strictly binding). The 'source of law lay in the way that judges thought about legal problems' (Lobban 1991: 7). It is to this distinctive style of thinking that I now turn.

Reasoning by analogy

Given the infinite variability of fact situations and the vagueness and imprecision of many legal concepts, we can expect deductive and syllogistic reasoning to play a subordinate role in the common law. It is true that there is a role for deduction where the rule forming the major premise of the relevant legal syllogism is clear, e.g. 'to be valid, contracts for the sale of land must be in writing; this contract is in writing; therefore, all else being equal, it is valid'. Most appellate cases arise, however, because just this clarity is missing, e.g. 'does writing include email'. In such cases, deduction is only of secondary importance (MacCormick 1978: 65). Rather the judge and advocates must use other heuristic techniques to construct out of the precedent cases a rule (i.e. a major premise) applicable to the facts of the case at hand, e.g. 'writing does not include email; therefore a contract for the sale of land in email form is not valid'. In the search for a major premise common lawyers seek:

> non-necessary truths [by] reflection on the likenesses and dissimilarities of particular instances either actual or hypothetical, particular to particular.
>
> (Stone 1965: 481)

To a significant, though neglected, degree then legal cognition is analogical cognition; e.g. 'email and paper documents are not substantially similar (analogous) in this context'.[34]

It is, of course, possible to analyse analogical reasoning in the law as a combination of deduction and induction (Levi 1948: 1).[35] Indeed judges commonly present their reasoning in this more pristine form as a token of their objectivity, maintaining 'the image of the rule of law [as] the law of rules' (Goodrich 1986: 156). Yet this process is commonly one of reconstruction, since the crucial moment in analogy is the seeing of a similarity (or similarities) between earlier and later cases (Stone 1964: 315). Only then can formal logical procedures be undertaken. The vital question at this point is how the lawyer, like the doctor, can be brought to see correctly. In other words, it is necessary to move beyond the empty formalism of the injunction that like be treated alike, and to inquire as to the procedures for determining what counts as similar, and what not.

Some writers suggest that analogy is only possible within an overarching rational context which links legal relationships among themselves 'harmoniously' (Zaccaria 1991: 57). Natural law theorists, for instance, affirm a realist ordering of things into 'natural classes'. Reference to these classes allows one to discriminate conclusively between the accidental and the essential features of any case and, thus, to reason analogically, i.e. to say that a later case is essentially similar and should be treated in the same way. However, as Maris correctly notes, any realist metaphysics would now be regarded as untenable and its revival would in any case cut across important normative understandings in liberal society, particularly those concerning pluralism and choice in matters of value (1991: 85). Rather, as

Sampford's critique discussed above suggests, the rational context of analogical reasoning in the common law is necessarily plural and regional. i.e.
specific to a given area of law.[36] Similarities are usually identified between
cases that are conceptually proximate (Maris 1991: 102). Clearly the more
problematic (i.e. novel) the case, the wider the judge will be tempted to
stray in search of analogous cases and relevant principles.[37] But this search
is never exhaustive (Twining and Miers 1991: 152).

Judgment, training and tradition

Reasoning in the common law thus very often involves a search for appropriate analogies. It requires the judge and advocates to consider and interpret competing precedents, to adopt some and reject others. The
foregoing discussion suggests that arguments in this mode are never
wholly compelling. As we saw in Chapter 1, theorists of rhetoric, such as
Chaïm Perelman, argue that, while legal decisions should be reasonable,
they cannot be rational (1980: 160). Given the impossibility of a 'mechanical jurisprudence', there remains a considerable role for the exercise of
the type of prudential judgment discussed above in the context of clinical
medicine (Postema 1986: 70). This is acknowledged by many writers. Clifford Geertz, for instance, saw lawyers as 'connoisseurs of cases in point,
cognoscenti of matters in hand' (1993: 168). For Julius Stone:

> wisdom, which has always been the governing, moderating and evalu-
> ating core of good judgment, is [an] intangible and inarticulate pre-
> supposition ... of the reasoning of lawyers and judges.
>
> (1964: 337)

This practical wisdom is sometimes referred to as the 'personal element'
in judicial work or, more bluntly by legal realist writers, as 'hunch' (Hutcheson 1929).[38]

It would, however, be incorrect to view the exercise of judgment in the
common law as a wholly subjective or discretionary affair. Though not
finally constrained by formal logic, it is nonetheless subject to a number of
less rigid normative, social and cultural controls (Simpson 1973: 95). Prudential maxims guide, although they do not compel, the reasoning of
legal practitioners. The best known are found in equity, that area of
English law historically most associated with the exercise of prudential reasoning; e.g. 'delay defeats the equities'; 'equity looks to the intent rather
than to the form', etc. Similar maxims guide statutory interpretation. In
the substantive common law too, judges rely explicitly or implicitly on
what Torstein Eckhoff called 'guiding standards' (1976). Karl Llewellyn
identified 14 such 'steadying factors' in common law decision making,
including: the mental conditioning of lawyers; prior identification and

sharpening of issues before trial; accepted ways of handling authoritative sources of law and of presenting arguments in court; constraints of group decision making and of publicity; judicial security and honesty (1960: 19ff.).

Moreover, as Simpson pointed out, within groups such as the legal profession, especially among its most powerful members, there exist strong pressures against innovation. Young members of the group must be effectively indoctrinated before they can achieve any position of influence; there should be a 'gerontocratic structure' which privileges the wisdom and experience of older members of the profession (Simpson 1973: 96). The apprenticeship method of training lawyers has traditionally guaranteed this effect.[39] In the common law, cohesion is thus preserved, not by rational means, but through a 'combination of institutional arrangements and conservative dogma' (Simpson 1973: 77).[40]

The importance of a suitable initiation is made clear when we recall the analogical style of reasoning characteristic of the common law. We noted that there were no explicit, immutable principles, and no realist metaphysics available to instruct the judge or lawyer in how to see resemblances between cases. Instead as Bankowski says:

> 'Same' is a public concept which makes sense only within the context of a particular form of life. Thus we do not understand the 'same' by adding any new facts but, by looking at it from within a context and tradition, we make valid and rational choices. It is within the context of this legal tradition then, with its interlocking network of principles, rules etc. that we find the conditions for making valid assertions of analogy and disanalogy. Analogy is at base a social concept.
>
> (1991: 208)

Training in law must, therefore, be an extended induction into the professional context, into the tradition which makes it possible to see resemblances between cases. To quote Bankowski again, it:

> is this knowing how of the practitioner which comes through socialization, a knowledge of the correct answer without necessarily being well-versed in the structure of the argument which is often evidence of a tradition.
>
> (1991: 211)

Conclusion

The practices of clinical medicine and the common law are thus seen to share a number of significant features. Both disciplines have a primary orientation to the individual case. The clinical gaze and the procedural forms of the common law create 'the case' and elevate it to phenomenological and ethical primacy. In this they differ from the aggregative social sciences which emerged in the nineteenth century and which are oriented to a collective field that they themselves call into being (Foucault 1979). The historical differences between clinical and, say, public health medicine, or between law and public administration are thus reproduced at the level of the phenomenological.

The case is also primary in the domain of epistemology. In both clinical medicine and the common law, the record or memory of cases has traditionally been the storehouse of disciplinary knowledge. Rules can be abstracted from various concatenations of cases, but this is always a contingent and revisable process. As a result, concepts are never wholly specifiable, having blurred and overlapping meanings, and neither discipline can be fully and exhaustively articulated as a system. Deductive or syllogistic reasoning plays a subordinate part in the procedures of each. Historically both doctors and common lawyers have contrasted the responsive pragmatism of their own practice with the inflexible dogmatism of rival practitioners. This is captured nicely in the comment of Jerome Frank that:

> The lawyer who is not moderately alive to the fact of the limited part that rules play is of little service to his clients, The judge who does not learn how to manipulate these abstractions will become like that physician ... 'who preferred that patients should die by rule rather than live contrary to it'.
>
> (1963: 141)

The margin of uncertainty freed up by the analogical style of thought allows the doctor or judge to attend to the particularity of the case at hand.

The primacy of the case, the non-systematic nature of disciplinary knowledge and the importance of exemplary precedents mean that there remains an important role for judgement in the practice of medicine and the common law. Practitioners draw upon a kind of prudential wisdom in deciding on right action in clinical or juridical matters. This judgement is guided by non-compelling maxims and principles, but also by certain social and cultural constraints. Both the faculty of judgement and its constitutive parameters are developed in the individual practitioner first during a period of apprenticeship to a more experienced practitioner, and later through constant practice. Only in this way do initiates acquire the needed stock of exemplary cases and, thus, the ability to see new cases in accordance with the traditions of the discipline.

The shared vision of medical and legal practice which has been developed in this chapter is both traditional and traditionalist. It has a distinctively pre-modern flavour and is obviously rooted in a general conservative and anti-rationalist philosophy as I noted above. The work of Polanyi and Oake-shott referred to earlier makes clear the connections between politics and epistemology in this context. Polanyi's theory of tacit knowledge, echoing Oakeshott's essays on practical knowledge, was developed out of a critique of what they diagnosed as the fallacious, but dominant positivism of the mid-twentieth century. This rested on the assumption that the world was com-pletely knowable and representable in terms of its exactly determined elements (Polanyi 1958: 139; Oakeshott 1991: 16). The ideal knower was free of bias and commitment, detached from the subject of her inquiries, and fully conscious of all she knew. The completeness and objectivity of this knowledge legitimated the aspirations of democrats and collectivists. Avail-able to expert and layperson alike, it could be used instrumentally by over-bearing regimes to remould the world.

Against this objectivism, Polanyi and Oakeshott argued that both per-sonal judgment and tradition were indispensable to knowing. In an irony writ large in the work of Edmund Burke 150 years earlier, they claimed that only self-selecting, self-sustaining elites of practitioners and scholars could guarantee the integrity and continued reproduction of the various disciplines and, thus, resist the drive to totalitarianism.[41] This irony was extended and intensified under the Keynesian welfare state which greatly widened access to health care, social support, education, housing and so on, but which made such access conditional on precisely the kind of unre-viewable professional judgment that medical leaders, the judiciary and conservative philosophers had prized. In the next chapter, I consider the challenge to this model of welfare delivery and to the underpinning phil-osophy, as it was articulated within the law, in the context of the broad shift to neo-liberalism.

Notes

1 See Whitley (1988: 403)
2 It is true that the British Medical Association vehemently opposed Bevan's plan. But this was based on an almost 'paranoiac' misreading of the proposals (Timmins 2001: 119).
3 *Whitehouse v Jordan* [1980] 1 All ER 650 (CA at 659).
4 *Mahon v Osborne* [1939] 2 KB 14 (CA at 31).
5 *Holland v The Devitt and Moore Nautical College, The Times*, 4 March 1960.
6 *Mahon v Osborne* [1939] 2 KB 14 (CA per Scott LJ at 31).
7 [1985] AC 871 (HL at 892–893).
8 See discussion of Miola in Chapter 2.
9 [1980] 1 All ER 650 (CA at 662).
10 *Whitehouse v Jordan* [1980] 1 All ER 650 (CA per Donaldson LJ at 666).
11 [1980] 1 All ER 650 (CA at 658).
12 *Whitehouse v Jordan* [1981] 1 All ER 267 (HL per Lord Edmund Davies at 276). The objective dimension of the *Bolam* test was emphasized in *Bolitho v City & Hackney Health Authority*, where it was held that the approach of the body of

practitioners relied on had to have a logical basis in so far as it proceeded from a conscious weighing of risks and benefits.

13 [1987] QB 730 (CA per Mustill LJ at 750–751).
14 *Clark v MacLennan* [1983] 1 All ER 416 (QB at 433).
15 [1980] 1 All ER 650 (CA at 658).
16 For critiques of this argument, see Bayles and Caplan (1978) and Minogue (1982).
17 For an overview, see Löwy (1988).
18 This inverts the title of a famous essay by Kant, 'On the Common Saying: "This May Be True in Theory, but It Does Not Apply in Practice"' (1793).
19 There are obvious affinities here with the later work of Thomas Kuhn, a debt acknowledged in Kuhn (1996: ix).
20 See Löwy (1988: 143).
21 On the acquisition of such exemplars in the course of medical training, see Atkinson (1997).
22 See Oakeshott (1991: 55); Polanyi (1958: 50).
23 See further Henry (2006).
24 The term 'elective affinities' comes from Goethe via the work of Max Weber, for example *The Protestant Ethic and the Spirit of Capitalism* (1958: 91–92). He defined it as the degree of correspondence between different social, cultural or economic forms which favour, more or less, each other's continuance. See Howe (1978).
25 See also Lobban (1991: 14–15).
26 See Sunstein (1995).
27 *Quinn v Leathem* [1901] AC 495 (HL at 506).
28 *Caparo v Dickman* [1990] 2 AC 605 (HL per Lord Oliver at 636).
29 See for example, Frank (1963: 134).
30 See also Hart (1958: 144).
31 The idea of law as a system can be traced to aesthetic understandings of law as geometry (seventeenth century) or as architecture (eighteenth century). See Stein (1961: 252).
32 For an early formulation see Dworkin (1967).
33 [1947] AC 156 (HL at 175).
34 See Kaufmann (1966); Sunstein (1993) and Postema (1986: 31ff.).
35 See also Horovitz (1972: 32).
36 See also Ladeur (1991: 17).
37 For a differential typology of analogies in the common law, see Lamond (2014).
38 See also Yablon (1990).
39 See Harrington and Manji (2003).
40 See also Kennedy (1986).
41 See Burke (1999).

References

Armstrong, D (1977) 'Clinical Sense and Clinical Science', 11 *Social Science and Medicine* 599.

Atiyah, PS (1987) *Pragmatism and Theory in English Law* (London, Stevens).

Atkinson, P (1997) *The Clinical Experience. The Construction and Reconstruction of Medical Reality*, 2nd edition (Aldershot, Hampshire, Ashgate).

Bankowski, Z (1991) 'Analogical Reasoning and Legal Institutions', in PJ Nerhot (ed.), *Legal Knowledge and Analogy. Fragments of Legal Epistemology, Hermeneutics and Linguistics* (Dordrecht, Kluwer) 198.

Bayles, MD and A Caplan (1978) 'Medical Fallibility and Malpractice', 3 *Journal of Medicine and Philosophy* 169.

Burke, E (1999) *Reflections on the Revolution in France* (Oxford, Oxford University Press).

Dworkin, RM (1967) 'The Model of Rules', 35 *University of Chicago Law Review* 14.

Eckhoff, T (1976) 'Guiding Standards in Legal Reasoning', 29 *Current Legal Problems* 205.

Fleck, L (1981) 'On the Question of Medical Knowledge', 6 *Journal of Medicine and Philosophy* 237.

Fleck, L (1986) 'Some Specific Features of the Medical Way of Thinking', in RS Cohen and T Schnelle (eds), *Cognition and Fact. Materials on Ludwik Fleck* (Dordrecht, Springer) 39.

Foot, M (1962) *Aneurin Bevan: A Biography. Volume One: 1897–1945* (London, MacGibbon and Kee).

Foucault, M (1979) *The History of Sexuality. The Care of Self* (vol I) (New York, Vintage Books).

Frank, J (1963) *Law and the Modern Mind* (New Brunswick, NJ, Transaction Publishers).

Geertz, C (1993) *Local Knowledge. Further Essays in Interpretive Anthropology* (New York, Basic Books).

Goodrich, P (1986) *Reading the Law. A Critical Introduction to Legal Method and Techniques* (Oxford, Blackwell).

Gorovitz, S and A MacIntyre (1976) 'Toward a Theory of Medical Fallibility', 1 *Journal of Medicine and Philosophy* 51.

Harrington, J and A Manji (2003) '"Mind with Mind and Spirit with Spirit": Denning and African Legal Education', 30 *Journal of Law and Society* 376.

Hart, HLA (1958) 'Dias and Hughes on Jurisprudence', 4 *Journal of the Society of Public Teachers of Law* 143.

Henry, SG (2006) 'Recognizing Tacit Knowledge in Medical Epistemology', 27 *Theoretical Medicine and Bioethics* 187.

Horovitz, J (1972) *Law and Logic. A Critical Account of Legal Argument* (New York, Springer-Verlag).

Howe, RH (1978) 'Max Weber's Elective Affinities: Sociology within the Bounds of Pure Reason', 84 *American Journal of Sociology* 366.

Hutcheson, JC (1929) 'The Judgment Intuitive: The Function of the "Hunch" in Judicial Decision', 14 *Cornell Law Quarterly* 274.

Kaufmann, A (1966) 'Analogy and the Nature of Things: A Contribution to the Theory of Types', 8 *Journal of the Indian Law Institute* 358.

Kennedy, D (1986) 'Freedom and Constraint in Adjudication: A Critical Phenomenology', 36 *Journal of Legal Education* 518.

Kuhn, TS (1996) *The Structure of Scientific Revolutions* (Chicago, University of Chicago).

Ladeur, KH (1991) 'The Analogy between Logic and Dialogic of Law', in PJ Nerhot (ed.), *Legal Knowledge and Analogy. Fragments of Legal Epistemology, Hermeneutics and Linguistics* (Dordrecht, Kluwer) 12.

Lamond, G (2014) 'Analogical Reasoning in the Common Law', 34 *Oxford Journal of Legal Studies* 567.

Lawrence, C (1985) 'Incommunicable Knowledge: Science Technology and the Clinical Art in Britain 1850–1914', 20 *Journal of Contemporary History* 503.

Lawrence, C (1994) *Medicine in the Making of Modern Britain 1700–1920* (London, Routledge).

Le Fanu, J (1999) *The Rise and Fall of Modern Medicine* (London, Abacus).

Levi, EH (1948) *An Introduction to Legal Reasoning* (Chicago, University of Chicago).

Llewellyn, K (1960) *The Common Law Tradition. Deciding Appeals* (Boston, MA, Little, Brown).

Lobban, M (1991) *The Common Law and English Jurisprudence 1760–1860* (Oxford, Clarendon Press).

Löwy, I (1988) 'Ludwik Fleck on the Social Construction of Medical Knowledge', 10 *Sociology of Health and Illness* 133.

MacCormick, N (1978) *Legal Reasoning and Legal Theory* (Oxford, Clarendon Press).

Maris, CW (1991) 'Milking the Meter: On Analogy, Universalisability and World Views', in PJ Nerhot (ed.), *Legal Knowledge and Analogy. Fragments of Legal Epistemology, Hermeneutics and Linguistics* (Dordrecht, Kluwer) 71.

Minogue, BP (1982) 'Error, Malpractice and the Problem of Universals', 7 *Journal of Medicine and Philosophy* 239.

Mol, A and M Berg (1994) 'Principles and Practices of Medicine: The Coexistence of Various Anaemias', 18 *Culture, Medicine and Psychiatry* 247.

Murphy, WT (1997) *The Oldest Social Science? Configurations of Law and Modernity* (Oxford, Clarendon Press).

Oakeshott, M (1991) *Rationalism in Politics and Other Essays* (Indianapolis, IN, Liberty Press).

Osborne, T (1998) 'Medicine and Ideology', 27 *Economy and Society* 259.

Pellegrino, ED and DC Thomasma (1981), *A Philosophical Basis of Medical Practice. Toward a Philosophy and Ethic of the Healing Professions* (Oxford, Oxford University).

Perelman, C (1980) *Justice, Law and Argument. Essays on Moral and Legal Reasoning* (Boston, Reidel).

Polanyi, M (1958) *Personal Knowledge. Towards a Post-Critical Philosophy* (London, Routledge and Kegan Paul).

Postema, GJ (1986) *Bentham and the Common Law Tradition* (Oxford, Oxford University Press).

Sampford, C (1989) *The Disorder of Law. A Critique of Legal Theory* (Oxford, Blackwell).

Schaffner, KF (1986) 'Exemplar Reasoning about Biological Models and Diseases: A Relation between the Philosophy of Medicine and the Philosophy of Science', 11 *Journal of Medicine and Philosophy* 63.

Simpson, AWB (1973) 'The Common Law and Legal Theory', in AWB Simpson (ed.) *Oxford Essays in Jurisprudence* (Second Series) (Oxford, Clarendon Press) 77.

Stein, P (1961) 'Elegance in Law', 77 *Law Quarterly Review* 242.

Stone, J (1964) *Legal System and Lawyers' Reasonings* (Stanford, CA, Stanford University Press).

Stone, R (1965) 'Ratiocination not Rationalisation', 74 *Mind* 463.

Sunstein, CR (1993) 'On Anological Reasoning', 106 *Harvard Law Review* 741.

Sunstein, CR (1995) 'Incompletely Theorized Agreements', 108 *Harvard Law Review* 1733.

Timmins, N (2001) *The Five Giants. A Biography of the Welfare State*, 2nd edition (London, Harper Collins).

Twining, W and D Miers (1991) *How to Do Things with Rules*, 3rd edition (London, Weidenfeld and Nicolson).

Vogd, W (2002) 'Professionalisierungsschub oder Auflösung ärztlicher Autonomie: die Bedeutung von Evidence-Based Medicine unter der neuen funktionalen Eliten in der Medizin aus system – und interaktionstheoretischer Perspektive', 31 *Zeitschrift für Soziologie* 294.

Weber, M (1958) *The Protestant Ethic and the Spirit of Capitalism* (New York, Scribners).

Whitley, R (1988) 'The Transformation of Expertise by New Knowledge: Contingencies and Limits of Skill Scientification', 27 *Social Science Information* 391.

Yablon, CM (1990) 'Justifying the Judge's Hunch: An Essay on Discretion', 41 *Hastings Law Journal* 231.

Zaccaria, G (1991) 'Analogy as Legal Reasoning: The Hermeneutic Foundation of the Analogical Procedure', in PJ Nerhot (ed.), *Legal Knowledge and Analogy. Fragments of Legal Epistemology, Hermeneutics and Linguistics* (Dordrecht, Kluwer) 42.

Chapter 8

Ethics

Introduction

The great questions of modern health care – abortion, euthanasia and organ transplantation, for example – now come before the law pre-packaged as moral problems. Consequently any legal response is expected first and foremost to be ethically sufficient. Judicial decisions and legislation are liable to be evaluated on this basis, not only by philosophers, but also by lawyers. Ethics is held to be the truth of the law in this area: that which the law must strive for, though often failing in doing so.[1] The reasons why this should be so are seldom explored. The connection between law and ethics is held by many scholars to be natural and inevitable.[2] Different theoretical styles, such as utilitarianism or Kantian deontology, are accepted or rejected, as are specific principles, such as the doctrine of double effect.[3] The direct normative relevance of ethics to medical law is, however, beyond question. Of course medical lawyers do not suggest that courts and legislators have always been guided by ethical principle in practice. Indeed scholars have defined as a key task for themselves precisely the labour of instructing, praising or condemning legal decision makers in this regard. Generally, however, the task is seen as one of revealing and elaborating a pre-existing link between the two disciplines. The purpose of this concluding chapter is to question that assumption and to investigate the specific historical and disciplinary contexts which have made ethics plausible as a higher instance for medical law reasoning. My objective is to offer a rhetorical reading of the emergence of a new, ethically informed medical law which has challenged the profession-centred model associated with the Keynesian welfare state model considered throughout this book.

Medical law practitioners and scholars do not, of course, ignore the contextual and historical dimensions of their work. Indeed medical law is often said to share with medical ethics a distinctive origin story by which it explains its emergence and its reasons for existing. In this narrative, the founding moment is often provided by the Nuremberg trial of Nazi doctors in 1945.[4] The horrific crimes committed by German doctors against prisoners of war and concentration camp inmates brought forth the ringing declaration of patients' rights in the decision of the US military tribunal.[5] Modern bioethics is then taken to develop, by way of reaction, as a means of ensuring that such violations never happen again. As at Nuremberg, law is the necessary instrument of this moral purpose. It is clear that the practices revealed by the Nuremberg trials are of profound and enduring salience in ethical and legal debate concerning medical practice. What may be reflected upon, however, is whether a direct causative link can be traced between the atrocities documented by the tribunal on the one hand, and the rise of a specific form of medical law and medical ethics in the post-war period on the other.

For one thing, it is widely accepted that these two related disciplines did not emerge in their present form until the period from the late 1960s to early-1980s.[6] If a climate of paternalism and unprincipled decision making had allowed the Nazi doctors to flourish, then such a climate continued to prevail in Britain and the United States three decades after their crimes were made known to the world at Nuremberg. Moreover, it can readily be argued that the traditional model of doctor–patient relations in Britain was strengthened, not weakened, by the revelations at Nuremberg. As discussed in earlier chapters, both conservative philosophers, such as Michael Polanyi, and socialist politicians, such as Aneurin Bevan, were of the view that it was precisely the self-selecting and self-governing nature of the British professions, including medicine, which had preserved their independence from the state.[7] By contrast the rule-based rationalism of medical practice on the continent had opened up the professions there to external political control, making them an instrument of totalitarian oppression and criminality. It is not possible here to establish the specific historical effectiveness of different approaches to medical governance in protecting British, German and other patients. The point is rather that the association of medical law and medical ethics cannot simply be seen as an inevitable reaction to the events of the Second World War and their aftermath. The interdependent relation between them was not pre-given, but created through persuasive work on the part of scholars and practitioners of both disciplines. Clearly the case of the Nazi doctors served as a powerful negative exemplar, but only when harnessed to arguments concerning developments within the legal system and in its broader social environment.

This chapter investigates the conditions under which the identification of medical ethics and medical law became plausible for lawyers and legal academics. As has been seen throughout this book, prior to the rise of ethics, and the creation of more modern medical law, courts and legislators deferred to clinical and professional judgment in deciding on legality in this area. Previous chapters have explored the manner in which that deferral to medical decision-making was *substantively* plausible in so far as it was justified by common-sense ideas of the national space, utopia, art and science. In the present chapter I move beyond this to explore the manner in which such deferrals were *formally* plausible in so far as they reflected broader developments in the nature of mid-twentieth century law. I hope to show that this *Bolam* regime was consistent with a shift away from abstract and universally applicable rules towards more open-ended standards, allowing high levels of executive discretion and professional autonomy under the Keynesian welfare state.[8] Having elaborated the key elements of this 'deformalization' of law, in the next section, I will trace them through the key features of medical law under *Bolam*. In subsequent sections I argue that the positions developed by early medical law scholars were informed by broader critiques of law in this mode. They argued in effect that *Bolam* constituted a violation of traditional rule-of-law values, opening the way to medical paternalism and a denial of patients' rights. In later sections I will argue that medical ethics played an important role in supporting these challenges and in articulating a response to them. In short it offered an aspirational goal for academic reformers: an ideal of law restored to its true form. This resonated with broader neo-liberal critiques of law in the welfare state and with proposals for a more autonomy-focused, contract-based legal order to come in its place. As such this final chapter offers a contextual and rhetorical reading of the origins of the 'new medical law' which is succeeding *Bolam*.

Law and welfare state: 'deformalization'

The diagnosis of a decline in formal legal values, or the 'deformalization of law', was developed by German jurists such as Franz Neumann, on the left, and Carl Schmitt, on the right, in the Weimar period.[9] These writers argued that the first half of the twentieth century had been marked by a shift in the predominant legal form away from the general, abstract norms applicable to all legal subjects which had been characteristic of liberal law in the nineteenth century. In its place law had been 'materialized' through 'a flight into general clauses', i.e. the increasing use of open-ended tests of good faith, good morals and so on (Hedemann 1933). The application of the latter was determined, not by deductive reasoning, but by the elaboration and balancing of policy concerns. Neumann associated this tendency with the decline of the liberal model of capitalism under which a system of formally rational and universally applicable legal norms provided certainty to autonomous participants in the market (1957: 40). The rise of 'monopoly capitalism' in its place saw competition between enterprises give way to the formation of large cartels in specific sectors under state guidance.[10] The contemporaneous extension of the franchise and the strength of the labour movement also meant that the state increasingly intervened directly in the economy, controlling prices and supervising wage agreements, for example (Neumann 1986: 268). These interventions were supported by a system of special tribunals tasked with settling disputes, for example between capital and labour or between enterprises themselves. Access to these tribunals and their determination of rights and duties was conditional on membership of a specific group. By contrast with the classical nineteenth-century model, rights and duties were 'no longer connected with the will of legally equal persons', but rather with the status which a given person, association or company possessed in society (Neumann 1957: 63).

New legal fields emerged to match the special substantive norms and dedicated tribunals that were established governing specific areas of economic activity, for example labour law (Teubner 1990: 37). Each increasingly identified more with policy imperatives in relation to the area of social activity with which it was concerned, than with those of the legal system as a whole. Distinctive sets of standards and tests allowed the concrete interests at stake in the relevant field to be identified, weighed and balanced (Teubner 1990: 30). This orientation to context and fact meant that law, rather than being 'a *formal* guideline for members of society, [became] a *material* part of social reality' (McCormick 2000: 1698, emphasis added). These developments were condemned by jurists for producing a fragmentation of the legal system and a decline in rule of law values: clarity and predictability, the formal equality of legal subjects and the coherence of law as a whole (Scheuerman 1994: 1).

Equivalent developments were also evident in the context of welfare provision, which expanded steadily from the late nineteenth century reaching its greatest extent in the decades after the Second World War. In form and function, welfare partook of the features of monopoly capitalism discussed above. As regards form, welfare in Britain and elsewhere was increasingly delivered by state agencies, often monopolies akin to those prominent in the industrial sector. The National Health Service established through a merger of existing private, voluntary and local authority health facilities in 1948 is a leading example of this tendency to concentration.[11] As regards function, the availability of unemployment assistance and national insurance, for instance, set limits to the operation of markets in labour and served to embed the capitalist economy in the wider society.[12] This was also true of the NHS. By predicating treatment on need rather than means to pay, it tempered the contradiction between formal equality, guaranteed by law under liberal capitalism, and substantive inequality as regards health status and access to care.

The functioning of the welfare state was also marked by high levels of professional discretion, for example in the field of family policy.[13] Thus, married women were excluded or disincentivized from undertaking formal employment, setting further limits to the scope of the market economy (Pateman 2000: 137). This was justified in the foundational Beveridge report on the basis that:

> the great majority of married women must be regarded as occupied on work which is vital though unpaid, without which their husbands could not do their paid work and without which the nation could not continue.
>
> (Beveridge 1942: 49)

The state, as interpreter and steward of the national interest, was bound to intervene deeply in many areas of life, constituting the family appropriately and securing the role of women within it (Wilson 1977: 89). As well as educationalists, social workers, psychologists and health visitors, doctors made a significant contribution to achieving this task. In a study carried out in the mid-1970s Michèle Barrett and Helen Roberts found that decisions on clinical diagnosis and therapeutics were oriented by a (non-medical) assumption that men:

> had a primary, 'natural' drive to support and cherish their wife and family [and] women had a similar drive to nourish and cherish their husband and family.
>
> (1978: 44)

Consequently men were offered medical help in dealing with occupational strains, whereas women were advised to give up paid work or seek psychiatric advice if all else failed.

Professionals not only implemented state policy, they also defined it at collective and individual levels, identifying need and determining the appropriate response to it (Poulantzas 1978: 218). This blurring of executive and legislative functions was sheltered by the operation of tests which predicated legality on broad standards such as 'best interests' or 'welfare'.[14] The application of these tests depended on factual and contextual evaluations which were strongly shaped by professional expertise. As a result, law in the welfare state was subject to the process of 'materialization' discussed above. The concrete situation of parties determined the allocation of rights and duties, powers and liabilities as between them. Not formal equality, but one's status as professional or client was increasingly decisive. Given the diversity of policy considerations and the variety of professional knowledge, welfare law was also marked by the tendency towards fragmentation which we noted above in the economic context.[15] In the next section, I will argue that this 'materialization' thesis also offers a productive means of understanding medical law under *Bolam*. This will require us to bear in mind the considerable affinities between the role of doctors in the NHS and that of other professionals in the rest of the welfare state as set out in this section. I will argue that the *Bolam* regime needs to be understood in terms of legal form and function within this broader context.

The form of medical law under *Bolam*

The *Bolam* test was initially adumbrated to determine the question of liability for medical negligence, but it was also extended to determine a wide range of issues beyond clinical malpractice. This process of 'Bolamization' meant that professional opinion functioned as a black box, to which the law could defer and through which it could conceal the indeterminacy of its own decision making in areas of moral and political controversy. This deferral was also consistent with the broader pattern of administrative discretion under the Keynesian welfare state. In sheltering medical judgment, the operation of the *Bolam* test exhibited several features of deformalized law, as diagnosed by Weimar jurists, which I will explore in this section: (1) the prominence of open-ended tests; (2) frequent reference to policy considerations in legal decision making; and (3) a decline in formal equality in favour of the differential status of legal subjects.

Bolamized medical law was marked by a preference among courts and legislators for broad standards over detailed rules. Thus Lord Diplock in *Sidaway* held that a doctor is subject to:

> a single comprehensive duty covering all the ways in which [he] is called upon to exercise his skill and judgment in the improvement of the physical or mental condition of the patient.... This general duty is not subject to dissection into a number of component parts to which different criteria of what satisfy the duty of care apply, such as diagnosis, treatment, advice.[16]

The scope of a doctor's duty to disclose information prior to treatment would be determined by the opinion of a responsible body of practitioners, i.e. in just the same manner as the scope of her duty to exercise care in carrying out that treatment. Subsequent courts declined to make an exception to this comprehensive application of *Bolam* to information disclosure in cases of elective procedures, such as contraceptive treatment and sterilization.[17] As Kerr LJ put it 'the *Bolam* test is all-pervasive' in the medical context.[18] This refusal to introduce distinctions was also evident in cases where sterilization was proposed for a person lacking capacity. In *Re B (A Minor) (Wardship: Sterilisation)*, Lord Hailsham explicitly refused to separate out non-therapeutic from therapeutic sterilization for purposes of determining the best interests of the patient in such cases.[19] The only practicable course, he held, was to apply a unitary test of the patient's welfare.[20] The failure to draw distinctions meant that judges treated the resolution of these cases as largely a matter of fact, i.e. concerning the clinical needs of, and prognosis for, the patient. Under *Bolam* the latter would be determined by expert medical opinion.[21]

Broad tests allowed the law to reflect the purposes of medicine, enabling the profession to discharge its role in shaping and implementing wider state policy for health and welfare. This was evident in the context of abortion, in which policy on the family and the role of women within it, as discussed above, were central to the justification for legislative reform in 1967. MPs emphasized that unwanted pregnancy threatened women's ability to care for existing children and their husbands.[22] This policy justification is also expressed in the terms of the Abortion Act 1967 itself. In determining whether there is a risk to the physical or mental health of the woman such as to justify termination, regard may be had to the 'woman's actual or reasonably foreseeable environment' (s 1(2)) and in particular the 'physical or mental health of ... any existing children' (s 1(1)(a)). These policy concerns are mediated by clinical judgment, since determination of the grounds for lawful termination is predicated upon the opinion of two medical practitioners (s 1).[23] In *R v Smith*, Lord Scarman affirmed that 'a great deal of social responsibility is [thus] placed on the shoulders of the medical profession'.[24] Once this responsibility is discharged through an authentic exercise of professional judgment, courts will not interfere with doctors' discretion.[25]

Policy considerations were also prominent in the *Gillick* litigation. At first instance, Woolf J, as he then was, quoted from the impugned Guidance allowing doctors to provide contraceptive treatment and advice to minors without informing their parents. This testified to the Department of Health and Social Security's understanding of the broader social problem:

> In 1972 there were 1,490 births and 2,804 induced abortions among resident girls aged under 16; these figures are vivid reminders of the need for contraceptive services to be available for and accessible to young people at risk of pregnancy irrespective of age.[26]

The pressing task of the law, in furthering public health policy through sheltering clinical judgment, is defined and defended rhetorically here through using the idiom of statistical recitation, with its connotations of objectivity, and through placing the extract at the start of the judgment. In his conclusion Woolf J re-emphasized the public health perspective in justification of his decision to uphold the lawfulness of the Guidance, mockingly contrasting it with the non-scientific perspective of its critics:

> The statistics to which I have referred ... indicate to those whose religious beliefs do not dictate the contrary, that some of those children

were, at any rate, very much in need of assistance in avoiding such pregnancies.[27]

A majority of the House of Lords was similarly persuaded: an under-16 could receive contraceptive advice and treatment as long as they had 'achieved sufficient understanding and intelligence to understand' what was proposed.[28] Lord Scarman admitted that determination of capacity according to such an open-ended test would 'leave the law in the hands of the doctors'.[29] But the alternative of imposing ' "a priori" legal lines of division [was] sure to produce in some cases injustice, hardship, and injury to health'.[30] The alignment of medical law with policy imperatives in this area was reaffirmed in the more recent case of *Axon*.[31] In rejecting a challenge very similar to that of Mrs Gillick, Silber J paid careful attention to testimony from the Deputy Chief Medical Officer regarding the negative public health consequences of allowing parents to be informed in such cases and to evidence that young women's use of contraceptive services had fallen by almost a third in the aftermath of the Court of Appeal decision in *Gillick* allowing confidentiality to be breached.[32]

Under 'Bolamized' medical law, the distribution of rights depended, not on universal criteria, with all being formally equal, but on the concrete location of the actor in relation to the medical enterprise. Legislative and judicial deference to clinical expertise created legal asymmetries between doctors and patients, as well as inconsistencies in the obligations of doctors and other professionals. Thus, as we saw in Chapter 6, the needs of a beneficent and pluralistic medical science were reflected in the terms of the *Bolam* test itself which allow a doctor to follow a minority of professional opinion without culpability. The tendency, exemplified in *Maynard v West Midlands Regional Health Authority*,[33] to accept such evidence without further scrutiny was exceptional as regards other professions, whose standard practice was always liable to be deemed negligent no matter how widely followed.[34] Admittedly attempts to take medical negligence law beyond this by excusing mere 'errors of judgment' or mistakes due to inexperience were rejected by the House of Lords.[35] However, the underlying goal of securing the central position of doctors within the NHS provided clear support for the *Bolam* test as it stood. This goal was also reflected in the legally superordinate status of doctors within the hierarchy of health professions. Thus, for example, in *Royal College of Nursing of the United Kingdom v Department of Health and Social Security*,[36] the House of Lords held that, in order to avoid criminal liability, nurses assisting at a termination of pregnancy had to be subject to the direction and control of a medical professional. The relationship would, in effect, be 'one in which the nurse is little more than the doctor's handmaiden' (Montgomery 1992: 145). As we have seen, the relationship between doctors and patients was similarly hierarchical. Access to treatment, whether routine or ethically sensitive, and the extent to which information had to be disclosed regarding the risks and incidents of treatment, were all made dependent on professional opinion.

The work of doctors also benefited, and still benefits, from certain role-specific exceptions to the general criminal law in key areas. The Abortion Act 1967, for example, is structured as an exception to ss 58 and 59 of the Offences Against the Person Act 1861.[37] As discussed above, terminations are only lawful where indicated by clinical judgment in relation to the applicability of the enumerated criteria and where carried out by or under the control of doctors. The issues in *Gillick* were also posed in terms of the criminal law. In his dissenting opinion, Lord Brandon had argued that a doctor providing an under-16 with access to contraceptive treatment would be liable as an accessory to statutory rape under the Sexual Offences Act 1956, s 6(1). It could not, he stated, 'make any difference that the person who promotes, encourages or facilitates the commission of such an act is a parent, or a doctor or a social worker'.[38] The majority took the opposite view, Lord Fraser ruling that:

> the only practical course is to entrust the doctor with a discretion to act in accordance with his view of what is best in the interests of the girl who is his patient.[39]

As Professor JC Smith argued, the effect of Lord Fraser's 'Guidelines' on the exercise of this discretion was to carve out an exception to the general criminal law, specific to medical practitioners, via an implicit application of the doctrine of necessity, premised on considerations of public health (1986: 117). The elevated status of doctors underpinning this derogation was plausible due to their key role in the Keynesian welfare state. But it was also secured rhetorically by the longer-established affinities between the common law and medicine, as 'noble professions' exhibiting the features of both art and science.

Critiquing *Bolam*: legal form and liberty

The challenge to *Bolam* developed by academic commentators from the late 1970s on was mounted in the name of substantive values, such as patient autonomy, dignity, justice in the allocation of resources and so on. However, much of its purchase also came from an intertwined critique of the formal properties of that legal regime. The terms of that critique are familiar from the work of the Weimar jurists discussed above, as I hope to show in this section through a detailed engagement with representative studies by Ian Kennedy and Sheila McLean, as well as contemporaneous work on the reform of mental health legislation. These interventions concerning the nature of medical law were not merely a matter of abstract speculation. Rather they need to be understood with reference to the crisis of the Keynesian welfare state in that period. Concerns about the degeneration of law were revived as a central part of neo-liberal explanations for the crisis and as a pointer to its resolution. This was the rhetorically salient conjuncture within which the re-foundation of medical law was proposed.

The first charge raised by medical law critics was that vague, open-ended tests had conceded special privileges to doctors, sheltering them from responsibility to the rest of society. According to Kennedy, the practice of medicine was thus inappropriately treated as a private matter, beyond the purview of the law (1983: 119–120). This ceding of legal sovereignty also entailed a loss of control over the quality of clinical decision making. Much had been left to the unarticulated judgment of doctors. As a result the position of patients was 'amorphous and unpredictable', prey to unstated assumptions, prejudices and 'the emotional baggage' of practitioners (McLean 1999: 105, 121). Clinical irrationality had been adopted into law by *Bolam*, with the result that 'medical fact' was privileged over 'legal coherence' (McLean 1999: 110). Thus, for Kennedy, the best interests test in medical law did not operate as a genuine test, but was instead:

> a somewhat crude conclusion of social policy [under which everything] ... is made to turn on the facts on which the judgment of best interests is to be made.
>
> (1991: 395–396)

The orientation to fact was reflected in the conservative and descriptive approach taken by judges and earlier writers on the subject. They had simply adopted the:

> traditional English approach to legal categories [which] are almost universally fact-based or contextual. Fact situations are shovelled under the heading of, for example, tort or contract, or property, almost as if by accident.... The search for an underlying conceptual framework is ignored as an empty exercise, something for idle hands. Continental Europeans shake their heads in disbelief.
>
> (Kennedy 1991: vii)

As this contrast between civil law and common law would suggest, Kennedy's aspiration was that English medical law should take the form of a system of legal norms, articulated hierarchically at progressively higher degrees of abstraction and generality. Codification would ultimately establish medical law on a rationally defensible basis (Kennedy 1983: 127). Even short of that, the factual complexity and variety of cases should not hinder lawmakers from establishing guidelines in advance or judges from treating cases in terms of general principles (Kennedy 1983: 96, 116). By way of example, he noted 'the splendid use of the natural law principles of freedom and privacy as found in the US constitution' by American courts in end-of-life cases such as that of Karen Quinlan[40] (Kennedy 1983: 89).

Both Kennedy and McLean thus proposed a re-foundation of medical law on the basis of principle. But this would involve a refurbishment or restoration of medical and legal decision making, rather than the imposition of something wholly extraneous and novel upon them. Doctors' decisions, they claimed, were already being taken on the basis of principles. The problem was that these were not articulated and argued over in an explicit process of weighing and balancing. Equally, principled reasoning was 'traditional' in law (Kennedy 1991: 158). Concepts of justice, rights and due process such as would allow for the explicit delineation and resolution of controversies in health care were already inherent in English law. Bolamization meant, however, that law had 'reneged on this promise' and turned away from its true nature (McLean 1999: 20). Thus, medical law as it stood was not really law at all. In the absence of an obligation to give reasons, the delivery of health care under *Bolam* was merely a matter of 'administration', to use Neumann's term, involving the bare exercise of executive power.[41] Were equivalent leeway accorded to policemen, Kennedy noted, the latter would be allowed to arrest citizens whenever they thought 'appropriate' (1991: 159). The consequences, not just for law's formal quality, but for the substantive liberty of citizens were obvious in both domains.

This link between legal rationality and patient rights is also evident in the critique of mental health law developed by scholars and activists between the 1960s and early 1980s. The Mental Health Act 1959 reflected a highpoint in medical influence over the treatment of psychiatric patients. In the spirit of *Bolam*, the Act conceded high levels of discretion to professionals, deliberately reducing the level of legal control over the admission, detention and treatment of patients which had marked previous legislation (Glover-Thomas, 2002: 27).[42] As Clive Unsworth pointed out, this approach was inspired by a concern to allow professionals to make best use of the expanding range of new pharmaceutical products without undue restraint (1987: 262). However, subsequent concerns about uncontrolled discretion, the vulnerable position of patients and the harm caused by institutionalization, as well as the rise of the so-called 'anti-psychiatry' movement, led to a growing challenge to the 'medicalism' of the 1959 Act (Glover-Thomas, 2002: 30ff.).[43] At bottom, this challenge was premised on the view, broadly shared by critics of *Bolam*, that:

> psychiatric coercion had to be assessed on legal, social and moral grounds rather than purely medical ones.
>
> (Glover-Thomas, 2002: 63)[44]

Instead the National Association for Mental Health (MIND) and other groups proposed a new 'legalism'. MIND's legal director at the time Larry Gostin argued that psychiatric decision making should be controlled by detailed rules and guidelines, that patients should have clearly defined and enforceable legal rights and retain their civil and social status as far as possible, notwithstanding their condition or treatment needs.[45] Gostin's recommendations were implemented to a significant degree in the Mental Health Act 1983.[46] Commentators noted that his approach was shaped by his training in US constitutional law, which, as we saw above, was also picked out as a model for general English medical law by Kennedy.[47]

Unsworth's study also points us towards the broader political and economic context of this shift in mental health law, and I would argue of medical law more broadly. He notes in particular the growing strength of libertarian and anti-paternalist thought on the ascendant right wing of British politics in the late 1970s:

> Just as the post-Second World War consensus in favour of moderate social interventionism furnished the political climate for the Mental Health Act 1959, so the reassertion of legalism may be linked to the dissolution of this consensus, with the apparent exhaustion of social democracy and the renewed fashionability of versions of liberalism.
>
> (1987: 343)

Of course, the complex arguments of commentators and reformers such as Kennedy, McLean and Gostin cannot be reduced to a matter of political affiliation. Nonetheless, their challenge to medical paternalism and intrusiveness clearly echoed influential critique of the Keynesian welfare state articulated most notably in the work of Friedrich Hayek.[48]

Concern about arbitrariness and irrationality in law was a central motivation for Hayek's rejection of post-war social democracy, of which the NHS was the most prominent institutional manifestation.[49] Like Schmitt, whose work he frequently invoked,[50] Hayek emphasized that the operation of the welfare state was marked by a crisis of legal form. As in the Weimar Republic, this had led to a blurring of the distinction between state and society, with governmental authority being handed over to competing organized interests such as trade unions and professional associations (Hayek 1973: 13). The resulting crisis of sovereignty was manifest in the industrial disputes of the 1970s, contests which extended to the NHS itself.[51] It was also evident in the apparently unchecked power of doctors over patients noted by other libertarian critics such as Thomas Szasz and Ivan Illich, whose work influenced the legal scholars under discussion here.[52] Hayek castigated the orientation to substantive equality of the welfare state as a threat to liberty. Only formal equality was genuine, and this depended on general rules of law and conduct.[53] Only generality would ensure that:

the coercive power of the state can be used only in cases defined in advance by the law and in such a way that it can be foreseen how it will be used.

(Hayek 1944: 83–84)

This position was echoed in McLean's demand that medical law:

should guarantee certainty of rule and rule enforcement, thereby informing people of the limits of their discretion and enhancing freedom by permitting them to take legal rules into account.

(1999: 131, quoting Robertson, 1975: 245)

In its rejection of formal legal values, post-war collectivism constituted a regression to pre-Renaissance irrationalism, according to Hayek.[54] His proposal that collectivism itself, along with state intervention in the economy, needed to be abandoned was increasingly embraced by British political leaders as the crisis of the 1970s deepened. It is true that leading British medical law scholars spurned this political position, declaring their allegiance to the NHS as an enduring national project.[55] However, their critique of the legal regime under which the Service then functioned derived much persuasive force from the terms of Hayek's polemics and their wider popular reception.

Moving away from *Bolam*

Academic critiques of Bolamized medical law have had significant influence over the last 15 years. While much of the case law and legislation discussed above remains in place, a number of clear tendencies away from the materialized form discussed above are apparent. Courts have become increasingly willing to introduce distinctions and qualifications in the operation of key tests. Thus, in *Bolitho v City and Hackney Health Authority*,[56] the House of Lords held that *Bolam* did not mandate simple acceptance of medical testimony regarding the standard of clinical care. Emphasizing the normative over the factual, Lord Browne-Wilkinson held that a 'responsible' body of opinion within the terms of the test had to have a 'logical basis'.[57] The experts supporting it must have directed 'their minds to the question of comparative risks and benefits and ... reached a defensible conclusion on the matter'.[58] The undifferentiated welfare test for the sterilization of incompetent adults set out by Lord Hailsham in *Re B* also yielded to a two-stage test in a series of influential Court of Appeal decisions.[59] The clinical acceptability of the procedure and the 'social, emotional and other interests' of the particular patient now need to be given separate consideration, as we saw in Chapter 2.[60] The tendency towards 'legalism' pioneered in the Mental Health Act 1983 is also evident in the detailed tests of capacity and best interests contained in the Mental Capacity Act 2005 and in the elaborate regulatory regime set out in the Human Tissue Act 2006, for example.[61] Most recently in *Montgomery v Lanarkshire Health Board*,[62] the Supreme Court preferred a patient-centred test of negligence in risk disclosure to Lord Diplock's 'Bolamized' approach in *Sidaway*. Like Kennedy and McLean, their Lordships represented this assertion of patients' rights not as an innovation, but as a return to fundamental principles immanent in the common law, most notably self-determination.[63] These developments are underpinned by a basic distinction, explicitly drawn by the Supreme Court in *Montgomery*,[64] between a zone in which the profession is largely free to determine technical matters and one in which non-technical choices are made by patients and supervised by the courts. This reduces, while not eliminating, the asymmetry in favour of medical practitioners produced by an undifferentiated application of the *Bolam* test.[65]

If status distinctions have diminished, policy remains an important feature of medical law. The manner in which it is defined and pursued has shifted, however, consistent with the decline of the paternalism and professional dominance typical of the Keynesian period. Thus, as Kenneth Veitch has argued, the rise to prominence of individual rights in health care and welfare more generally is far from being antithetical to the pursuit of wider state objectives (2010). On the contrary, the autonomous subject, cast as a consumer of services or burdened with responsibility for 'healthy choices', serves as the key vehicle for neo-liberal policies in favour of markets and reduced welfare expenditure. In formal terms, the domestication of the ECHR has allowed policy to be considered explicitly and weighed against the rights of patients and others, rather than simply being absorbed into clinical judgment (Wicks, 2007: 121–128). The decision in *Axon*, noted above, provides a good example. In that case Silber J itemized and explicitly balanced the rights and health policy concerns at stake in *Gillick*-type cases within the terms of sections I and II of Article 8 ECHR which guarantees, and provides for limits on, the right to privacy and family life.[66]

Admittedly the tendency away from 'materialized' medical law is far from complete. Thus, for example, an attempt to subject the law on abortion to the general law on informed consent by removing the requirement of two doctors' signatures as a condition of lawfulness failed in 2008 (Sheldon 2009). More generally, as we saw in Chapter 2, the expectation of principled coherence held out by academic reformers has not been realized. On the contrary, as Jonathan Montgomery has argued, the turn to 'legalism' has permitted the opportunistic and wholly instrumental use of law by activists (2006). In paradoxical fashion, the pursuit of formal rationality has produced its opposite. The result, he argues, has been a 'demoralization' of both professionals and the practice of medicine itself.

The source of these difficulties has been investigated by José Miola in his extensive study of the 'symbiotic' relationship between medical law and medical ethics (2007). Though holding out the promise of a reasoned philosophical grounding for the new medical law, Miola finds that ethics have functioned merely as 'fragments of discourse' which judges simply use piecemeal 'for their own ends' (2007: 84, 214). If anything, the result of this tendency has been to accentuate the paradoxical drift towards incoherence of reformed medical law identified by Montgomery. However, as I noted at the start of this chapter, ethics continue to be foundational for most medical lawyers. In the next section, I seek to explain this enduring popularity with reference to the style and form of medical ethics and its appeal to lawyers faced with the crisis of legitimacy of materialized law.

Ethics and legal form

Wiebren van der Burg provides a developmental perspective on the strong connection between medical law and ethics consistent with the historical and contextual approach taken in this chapter. He views both interventionist health law and liberal bioethics as emerging to challenge the paternalist medical practice and legal abstentionism prevalent for most of the twentieth century (Van der Burg 1997: 92). The early alliance between the disciplines was obviously strategic: ethics furnished reasoned arguments to law, which offered institutional authority and the prospect of enforcement in return. But they also had a shared intellectual style. Both took what he calls a 'product' approach, aimed at producing rules and principles in the first instance, rather than more open-ended practices of argumentation. Both sought to replace a largely implicit, common-sense approach to medicine with theoretically informed reflection (van der Burg 1997: 99, 101).[67]

Bioethics scholars have emphasized the foundational role of law in the constitution of their discipline from the late 1960s on. They take law to be responsible for the agenda and much of the terminology of bioethics (Annas 1988: 3). Law reform and the decision of court cases provide a practical goal for ethics scholarship, as well as furnishing a focus for teaching in the field (Capron and Michel 1993: 34). Much ethical argument is aimed at determining law-like precepts to guide conduct (Davis 1995). There are, of course, many opponents of this tendency who condemn the attendant impoverishment of ethical thought and its capacity to engage with the complexity of issues arising in health care.[68] The persistence and force of their criticisms, however, testifies to the profound entanglement of the two disciplines.

The idea of ethics played a similarly important role in the interventions of pioneer medical lawyers such as Kennedy and McLean. They deployed the term 'ethical', first to denote the non-medical elements of clinical decision making which went unmarked under *Bolam* (Kennedy 1983: 106). In this mode, 'ethics' identifies the normative terrain formerly ceded to professional opinion and over which legal sovereignty should be reclaimed. This jurisdictional connotation is bolstered by a suggestion that the first task of law is to 'reflect and promote good ethics', rather than, say, to advance policy as defined by doctors (Kennedy 1983: 125). In imposing the requirements of formal due process on decision-making in health care, the law would at the same time subject the 'gut responses' of professionals and administrators to the searchlight of critical moral reasoning' (McLean 1999: 111). This contribution would be well repaid since an understanding of the ethical themes running through medical practice would provide the law with 'the kind of internal coherence and consistency' which it then lacked (Kennedy 1991: 385). As this suggests, ethics and law are seen as substantially similar, at least in their ideal forms: the work of a well-functioning ethics committee involves articulating 'the kinds of standards for which we look to the law'; the task of academics and judges is to reassert the law's own 'internal ethics' (McLean 1999: 131, 20). Law should follow ethics in taking a principled approach to the promotion of fundamental values, chief of which is individual autonomy (Kennedy 1983: 121; McLean 1999: 19).

Ethics and law are thus neither wholly united nor completely separate. The relationship between them is, as Susan Wolf suggests, one of intimacy, more like a marriage than a merger (2004: 295). The combination of difference with a desire for unity in Wolf's image is evident in the work of Kennedy and McLean discussed above. There, ethics functions as an ideal for law to emulate. However, this ideal is not beyond the law, but is already within it. The role of ethics in these accounts is thus to remind law of its 'true nature'. It marks the formal values which had been obscured with the shift to open-ended tests, fact-driven argumentation and the status-based powers of professionals. It calls for a restoration of law's coherence, in the face of its social diffusion and fragmentation.

Conclusion: genre and rhetoric

I have argued in this chapter that the rise of a 'new' medical law from the 1970s on can be traced to a crisis of the legal form associated with the post-war Keynesian welfare state. This crisis was diagnosed and remedies proposed with reference to the key features of the dominant *Bolam* regime: the replacement of open-ended tests with increasingly elaborate sets of legal distinctions; the disciplining of policy considerations as interpreted by health professionals; and an equalization of status as between doctors and patients. In each case, what was sought was a restoration of qualities of law associated with nineteenth-century liberal ideals. Ethics played a key role in this transformation. Its contribution did not come, however, through providing clear answers to specific legal problems on the basis of a coherently ordered body of ethical norms. Rather, it functioned as a catalyst: an ideal 'self-description' of the legal system which would enable medical law to return to itself.[69]

The purchase of ethics thus derived from its formal properties more than its substantive content, which is persistently contested. (Indeed endemic dispute over the latter is a mark of vigour rather than failure in ethics as a discipline.) Ethics was plausible, I would argue, as a distinctive *genre* of writing: a set of routine conventions and constraints on the production of meaning (Frow 2006: 10). Genres are not rigidly fixed in advance; rather, they are performed anew in specific texts produced in specific contexts (Williams 1977: 180). As such the use or invocation of any genre is always thoroughly rhetorical: a strategic response to the demands of a given situation; a bid to secure the credibility of the writer and the plausibility of what they are arguing for (Miller 1994: 31). Frow suggests that there are three main features of a given genre by which such credibility is achieved (2006: 74–76). These are: its 'typical thematic content', i.e. which issues are most frequently addressed and which are overlooked; its 'structure of address', i.e. the relationship that the text produces between the author and their audience, as well as with other parties; and the 'mode of writing' adopted in the text, i.e. the tone and manner of expression, the figures and images characteristically deployed in such texts. Each of these features can be used to explain the generic appeal of ethics to medical lawyers.

The thematic focus of ethics, as I noted above, has been strongly influenced by the caseload of the courts and by the passage of new legislation related to health. Both law and ethics were clearly oriented to dilemmas arising in clinical medicine, paying less attention to societal and public health issues, though that has begun to change.[70] Ethics also offered a new model for the relationship between speaker, audience and third parties in medical law.[71] Under *Bolam*, lawyers and doctors were the privileged addressees of judicial speeches. As Sally Sheldon has shown, health care users and litigants, very often women, were ignored or belittled, their testimony often discounted as emotional and irrational (1998: 20–26). This rhetorically differentiated approach to the parties to litigation was an obvious manifestation of the triumph of status over equality typical of deformalized law. By contrast, the reformalization of medical law proposes a reconfiguration of this set of relationships. Judges are now careful to address the patient directly and to preface controversial judgments with expressions of sympathy and understanding.[72] Equally they show increasing awareness of the wider public as an audience not only for their decisions, but for the reasoning supporting them.

The shift in the structure of address is matched by a change in the 'mode of writing' in medical law. As we have seen in earlier chapters, many of the leading decisions associated with the *Bolam* regime were articulated in a distinctively British or English idiom. They drew on well-established images of medical and legal practice. They reproduced common-sense understandings of the NHS as a territorially defined enterprise. They borrowed from and invoked cultural and political texts. This was a concrete and situated rhetoric, most capable of persuading specific national and professional audiences. It contrasts sharply with the idiom of medical ethics favoured by reforming medical lawyers. In its dominant form, the latter adopts an Anglo-American 'ordinary language' style which is intended to be relatively accessible to specialist and non-specialist alike. To borrow from Roland Barthes, this:

> forgoes any elegance or ornament ... achieving a style of absence which is almost an ideal absence of style ... in which the social or mythical characters of language are abolished in favour of a neutral and inert state of form.
>
> (1968: 78, 77)

A non-figurative style tends to establish the 'irretrievable honesty' of the author in addressing 'fundamental problems' (Barthes 1968: 78). In its very lack of colour, it connotes objectivity and the general applicability of the arguments to which it gives form. As a generic exemplar for law, it suggests that the arguments of judges and academic medical lawyers are or should be addressed to a 'universal audience': anyone in any context should be capable of being convinced by their reasoning (Perelman 1982: 27).

Notes

1 This orthodoxy is critiqued by Montgomery (1989, 2000).
2 For example, Miola states that 'for as long as courts and ethics have existed, their interconnectivity has been nothing if not inevitable' (2006: 22).
3 For a recent review of this doctrine, see Billings (2011).
4 See the discussion in Miola (2007: 34–35).
5 For example, Annas and Grodin describe the trial as having a 'watershed nature ... for the history of medical ethics and law' (1999: 112).
6 See Wilson (2014).
7 See respectively Polanyi (1958: 244) and Bevan (1990: 112)
8 *Bolam v Friern Hospital Management Committee* [1957] 1 WLR 582 (McNair J). For further discussion of the test in *Bolam* and its extension beyond clinical malpractice, see Chapter 2.
9 See for example Neumann (1957) and Schmitt (2007).
10 See Jessop (1990: 32–34).
11 See Timmins (2001: 101–126).
12 See the discussion in Chapter 1.
13 For a contemporary critique, see Handler (1968).
14 See further Habermas (1996: 101).

15 See Teubner (1986).

16 *Sidaway v Board of Governors of the Bethlem Royal Hospital* [1985] AC 871 (HL per Lord Diplock at 893).

17 See *Gold v Haringey Health Authority* [1988] QB 481 (CA); *Blyth v Bloomsbury Health Authority* [1993] 4 Med LR 151 (CA).

18 *Blyth v Bloomsbury Health Authority* [1993] 4 Med LR 151 (CA at 157).

19 [1988] AC 199 (HL at 203–204).

20 *Re B (A Minor) (Wardship: Sterilisation)* [1988] AC 199 (HL per Lord Hailsham at 203).

21 See Miola (2007: 66).

22 For example, Dr John Dunwoody MP, HC Deb 22 July 1966, vol 732, col 1099; see further Thomson (1998) and the discussion in Chapter 2 above.

23 This is subject to the exception that, where the termination is immediately necessary to save the life or to prevent grave permanent injury to the woman, the requirement for the opinion of a second medical practitioner can be dispensed with, s 1(4).

24 *R v Smith* [1974] 1 All ER 376 (CA at 381).

25 *Paton v British Pregnancy and Advisory Service Trustees* [1979] QB 276 (Fam per Baker P at 282).

26 *Gillick v West Norfolk and Wisbech Area Health Authority* [1984] 1 QB 581 at 588 quoting Health Service Circular (Interim Series) (HSC (IS) 32) May 1974, para 40.

27 *Gillick v West Norfolk and Wisbech Area Health Authority* [1984] 1 QB 581 at 599.

28 *Gillick v West Norfolk and Wisbech Area Health Authority* [1986] 1 AC 112 (CA & HL per Lord Scarman at 188–189).

29 Ibid. (CA & HL at 191).

30 Ibid. (CA & HL per Lord Scarman at 191).

31 *R (Axon) v Secretary of State for Health* [2006] EWHC 37 (Admin), [2006] QB 539 (FamD).

32 *R (Axon) v Secretary of State for Health* [2006] EWHC 37 (Admin), [2006] QB 539 (FamD per Silber J at [67]–[69]). The decision of the Court of Appeal in *Gillick* was subsequently overruled by the House of Lords, *Gillick v West Norfolk and Wisbech Area Health Authority* [1986] 1 AC 112 (CA & HL).

33 [1984] 1 WLR 634 (HL).

34 *Edward Wong Finance Co Ltd v Johnson Stokes & Master* [1984] AC 296 (PC); *Cavanagh v Ulster Weaving Co Ltd* [1960] AC 145 (HL).

35 See *Whitehouse v Jordan* [1981] 1 WLR 246 (HL per Lord Edmund-Davies at 257–258); *Wilsher v Essex Area Health Authority* [1988] AC 1074 (HL per Lord Bridge at 1081).

36 [1981] AC 800 (HL).

37 Abortion Act 1967, ss 1 and 6.

38 *Gillick v West Norfolk and Wisbech Area Health Authority* [1986] AC 112 (HL per Lord Brandon at 196).

39 [1986] AC 112 (HL per Lord Fraser at 174), emphasis added.

40 *In re Quinlan*, 70 NJ 10, 355 A2d 647 (NJ 1976).

41 See Neumann (1957: 66).

42 The 1959 Act was defended by Jones (1980). It is worth recalling that the facts of *Bolam* itself concerned alleged negligence in the administration of electro-convulsive therapy for a psychiatric condition.

43 See for example Laing (1960) and Goffman (1968).

44 Glover-Thomas notes, however, that in practice many of the safeguards introduced in the 1983 Act ironically reinforced rather than limited medical power in this area (2002: 63).

45 See Gostin (1975).
46 See further Glover-Thomas (2002: 53ff.).
47 See Unsworth (1987: 336).
48 For a useful survey, see Gamble (1996).
49 See Hayek (1944: 61) and Scheuerman (1997: 178).
50 For example see Hayek (1944: 59).
51 See Klein (2013: c.4).
52 The most notable examples are Illich (1976) and Szasz (1961).
53 See Hayek (1960: 155); this positive aspect of liberal legalism was also noted from the left by Franz Neumann (1957: 66).
54 See Gamble (1996: 79).
55 See, for example, Kennedy (1983: 48).
56 [1998] AC 232 (HL).
57 *Bolitho v City and Hackney Health Authority* [1998] AC 232 (HL at 242).
58 Ibid. (HL per Lord Browne-Wilkinson at 242).
59 *Re A (Mental Patient: Sterilisation)* [2000] 1 FCR 193 (CA); *Re S (Adult Patient: Sterilisation)* [2001] Fam 15 (CA).
60 This formulation is taken from *Re SL (Adult Patient: Sterilisation: Patient's Best Interests)* [2001] Fam 15 (CA per Butler-Sloss LJ at 28).
61 See the criteria for best interests in the Mental Capacity Act 2005, s 4 – though note that these are open ended and need only be 'considered' e.g. see ss 4(3), 4(6) and 4(7).
62 [2015] UKSC 11, [2015] 2 WLR 768.
63 Ibid. (per Lords Kerr and Reed at [80]).
64 Ibid. (per Lords Kerr and Reed at [82]).
65 Against this trend, an attempt to remove the requirement that two doctors' signatures be obtained before an abortion could lawfully be carried out failed in 2008, see Sheldon (2009).
66 See *R (Axon) v Secretary of State for Health* [2006] EWHC 37 (Admin), [2006] QB 539 (FamD per Silber J at [118]–[152]).
67 See, for example, Clouser and Gert (1990).
68 See, for example, Ladd (1978: 4); Schneider (1994: 20).
69 See further Nobles and Schiff (2006: c.1).
70 See, for example, Farmer and Campos's trenchant criticisms of the 'quandary ethics' which dominated the field until recently (2004).
71 On the rhetorical creation and delimitation of audiences, see Black (1970) and Wander (1984).
72 See, for example, *R (on the application of Pretty) v DPP* [2002] 1 AC 800 (HL per Lord Bingham at 809); *R (on the application of Purdy) v DPP* [2009] EWCA Civ 92 455 (CA per Judge LJ at 459).

References

Annas, GJ (1988) *Judging Medicine* (Clifton, NJ, Humana Press).

Annas, GJ and M Grodin (1999) 'Medical Ethics and Human Rights: Legacies of Nuremburg', 3 *Hofstra Law and Policy Symposium* 111.

Barthes, R (1968) *Writing Degree Zero* (New York, Hill and Wang).

Barrett, M and H Roberts (1978) 'Doctors and their Patients: The Social Control of Women in General Practice', in C Smart and B Smart (eds), *Women, Sexuality and Social Control* (London, Routledge).

Bevan, A (1990) *In Place of Fear* (London, Quartet Books).

Beveridge, W (1942) *Report on Social Insurance and the Allied Services*, Cmnd. 6404 (London, HMSO).

Billings, JA (2011) 'Double Effect: A Useful Rule that Alone Cannot Justify Hastening Death', 37 *Journal of Medical Ethics* 437.

Black, E (1970) 'The Second Persona', 54 *Quarterly Journal of Speech* 109.

Capron, AM and V Michel (1993) 'Law and Bioethics', 27 *Loyola of Los Angeles Law Review* 25.

Clouser, D and B Gert (1990) 'A Critique of Principlism', 15 *Journal of Medicine and Philosophy* 219.

Davis, R (1995) 'The Principlism Debate: A Critical Overview', 20 *Journal of Medicine and Philosophy* 85.

Farmer, P and NG Campos (2004) 'New Malaise: Bioethics and Human Rights in the Global Era', 32 *Journal of Law, Medicine and Ethics* 243.

Frow, J (2006) *Genre* (London, Routledge).

Gamble, A (1996) *Hayek. The Iron Cage of Liberty* (Cambridge, Polity).

Glover-Thomas, N (2002) *Reconstructing Mental Health Law and Policy* (London, Butterworths).

Goffman, E (1968) *Asylums. Essays on the Social Situation of Mental Patients and Other Inmates* (London, Penguin).

Gostin, L (1975) *A Human Condition Volume 1. The Mental Health Act from 1959 to 1975: Observations, Analysis and Proposals for Reform* (London, MIND).

Habermas, J (1996) *Between Facts and Norms. Contributions to a Discourse Theory of Law and Democracy* (Cambridge, MA, MIT Press).

Handler, J (1968) 'The Coercive Child Care Officer', 314 *New Society* 12.

Hayek, FA (1944) *The Road to Serfdom* (London, Routledge & Kegan Paul).

Hayek, FA (1960) *The Constitution of Liberty* (London, Routledge & Kegan Paul).

Hayek, FA (1973) *Law, Legislation and Liberty. A New Statement of the Liberal Principles of Justice and Political Economy Volume 1: Rules and Order* (London, Routledge & Kegan Paul).

Hedemann, JW (1933) *Die Flucht in die Generalklauseln. Eine Gefahr für Recht und Staat* (Tubingen, Mohr, Gelbe Or-Broschur).

Illich, I (1976) *Limits to Medicine. Medical Nemesis: The Expropriation of Health* (London, Marion Boyars).

Jones, K (1980) 'The Limitations of the Legal Approach to Mental Health', 3 *International Journal of Law and Psychiatry* 1.

Jessop, B. (1990) *State Theory. Putting Capitalist States in their Place* (Cambridge, Polity Press).

Kennedy, I (1983) *The Unmasking of Medicine* (London, Granada).

Kennedy, I (1991) *Treat Me Right. Essays in Medical Law and Ethics* (Oxford, Clarendon).

Klein, R (2013) *The New Politics of the NHS. From Creation to Reinvention*, 7th edition (London, Radcliffe).

Ladd, J (1978) 'Legalism and Medical Ethics', in JW Davis, B Hoffmaster and S Shorten (eds), *Contemporary Issues in Biomedical Ethics* (New York, Humana Press) 1.

Laing, RD (1960) *The Divided Self* (London, Tavistock).

McCormick, J (2000) 'Schmittian Positions on Law and Politics: CLS and Derrida', 21 *Cardozo Law Review* 1693.

McLean, S (1999) *Old Law, New Medicine. Medical Ethics and Human Rights* (London, Pandora).

Miller, CR (1994) 'Genre as Social Action', in A Freedman and P Medway (eds), *Genre and the New Rhetoric* (London, Taylor and Francis) 22.

Miola, J (2006) 'The Relationship between Medical Law and Ethics', 1 *Clinical Ethics* 22.

Miola, J (2007) *Medical Ethics and Medical Law: A Symbiotic Relationship* (Oxford, Hart Publishing).

Montgomery, J (1989) 'Medical Law in the Shadow of Hippocrates', 52 *Medical Law Review* 566.

Montgomery, J (1992) 'Doctors' Handmaidens: The Legal Contribution', in S Wheeler and S McVeigh (eds), *Law, Health and Medical Regulation* (Aldershot, Hampshire, Dartmouth Publishing Company) 141.

Montgomery, J (2000) 'Time for a Paradigm Shift? Medical Law in Transition', 53 *Current Legal Problems* 363.

Montgomery, J (2006) 'Law and the Demoralisation of Medicine', 26 *Legal Studies* 185.

Neumann, F (1957) *The Democratic and Authoritarian State. Essays in Political and Legal Theory* (Glencoe, IL, Free Press).

Neumann, F (1986) *The Rule of Law. Political Theory and the Legal System in Modern Society* (Leamington Spa, Berg).

Nobles, R and D Schiff (2006) *A Sociology of Jurisprudence* (Oxford, Hart Publishing).

Pateman, C (2000) 'The Patriarchal Welfare State' in C Pierson and FG Castles (eds), *The Welfare State: A Reader* (Cambridge, Polity).

Perelman, C (1982) *The Realm of Rhetoric* (Notre Dame, IN, University of Notre Dame Press).

Polanyi, M (1958) *Personal Knowledge. Towards a Post-Critical Philosophy* (London, Routledge & Kegan Paul).

Poulantzas, N (1978) *State, Power, Socialism* (London, Verso).

Robertson, JA (1975) 'Involuntary Euthanasia of Defective Newborns: A Legal Analysis', 27 *Stanford Law Review* 213.

Scheuerman, WE (1994) *Between the Norm and the Exception. The Frankfurt School and the Rule of Law* (Cambridge, MA, MIT Press).

Scheuerman, WE (1997) 'The Unholy Alliance of Carl Schmitt and Friedrich A Hayek', 4 *Constellations* 172.

Schmitt, C (2007) *The Concept of the Political* (Chicago, University of Chicago Press).

Schneider, C (1994) 'Bioethics in the Language of the Law', 24 *Hastings Center Report* 16.

Sheldon, S (1998) ' "A Responsible Body of Men Skilled in That Particular Art": Rethinking the *Bolam* Test', in S Sheldon and M Thomson (eds), *Feminist Perspectives on Health Care Law* (London: Cavendish) 15.

Sheldon, S (2009) 'A Missed Opportunity to Reform an Outdated Law', 4 *Clinical Ethics* 3.

Smith, JC (1986) 'Case Comment: Sexual Offences Act 1956 s.6 – Doctor Prescribing Contraception for Girl under 16 without Parent's Consent – Whether Necessarily Unlawful', *Criminal Law Review* 113.

Szasz, T (1961) *The Myth of Mental Illness. Foundations of a Theory of Personal Conduct* (New York, Harper & Brothers).

Teubner, G (1986) *Dilemmas of Law and the Welfare State* (Berlin, Walter de Gruyter).

Teubner, G (1990) ' "And God Laughed": Indeterminacy, Self-Reference, and Paradox in Law', 7 *Stanford Literature Review* 15.

Thomson, M (1998) *Reproducing Narrative: Gender, Reproduction and Law* (Aldershot, Hampshire, Ashgate).

Timmins, N (2001) *The Five Giants. A Biography of the Welfare State*, 2nd edition (London, Harper Collins).

Unsworth, C (1987) *The Politics of Mental Health Legislation* (Oxford, Clarendon Press).

Van der Burg, W (1997) 'Bioethics and Law: A Developmental Perspective', 11 *Bioethics* 91.

Veitch, K (2010) 'The Government of Health Care and the Politics of Patient Empowerment: New Labour and the NHS Reform Agenda in England', 32 *Law and Policy* 313.

Wander, P (1984) 'The Third Persona: An Ideological Turn in Rhetorical Theory', 35 *Central States Speech Journal* 197.

Wicks, E (2007) *Human Rights and Health Care* (Oxford, Hart).

Williams, R (1977) *Marxism and Literature* (Oxford, Oxford University Press).

Wilson, D (2014) *The Making of British Bioethics* (Manchester, Manchester University Press).

Wilson, E (1977) *Women and the Welfare State* (London, Tavistock).

Wolf, S (2004) 'Law and Bioethics: From Values to Violence', 32 *The Journal of Law, Medicine and Ethics* 293.

Index

abortion: Abortion Act 1967 18, 29–32,
170; access to 8–9; deferral to clinical
judgment 36; doctor liability, and 30;
imposed Caesarian sections 80–1; law
reform 79–80; metaphorics of
visibility, and 31; natural temporal
trajectory 79; PVS, and 77–82; social
circumstances, and 29; threshold of
viability 79; women's rights, and 30
advertising: UK medical law, and 90
Alder, John 130
Aldred, Rachel 112
American revolution 56
appellate courts: modes of persuasion
in 48–9
apprenticeship 148–9, 155; lawyers 155
Arendt, Hannah 44, 56–7, 60–2
Aristotle 2, 4, 63; *Art of Rhetoric* 2
art 140–56; clinical work as 117;
'elective affinities' 149; model of
medicine 144–9; science of
particulars 144–6; segmented
knowledge 146–7; thought styles
146
artificial nutrition and hydration;
withdrawal of 77–8
asylum 43; deportation of HIV patient
43, 44–6, 53–4; inhuman and
degrading treatment, and 45; mortal
medical need 45
autonomy:patient *see* patient autonomy

Bakhtin, Mikhail 3
Balkin, Jack 12
Bankowski, Zenon 155
Barrett, Michèle 166
Barthes, Roland 5, 47, 48, 179
Bellamy, Edward 102

Bentham, Jeremy 3
Berg, Marc 146
Bernard, Claude 121–2, 134
Bevan, Aneurin 50, 98–9, 141; founding
of NHS and 96–7, 101
Beveridge report 1941 97, 166
Bingham, Lord 9–11
bioethics 13; *see also* ethics;
development 163
biomedical ethics 19
Blackstone, Sir William 152
*Bolam v Friern Hospital Management
Committee* 18, 123, 167–70; Bolam test
33; Bolamization 172; challenge to
170; critiquing 170–4; form of
medical law under 167–70; moving
away from 174–6; psychiatric
patients, and 173
Boltanski, Luc 57, 105, 111–12
Brazier report 91–2; *see also* surrogacy;
rhetoric in 93
Brecht, Bertolt 27
British Medical Association (BMA) 19;
Abortion Act 1967, and 30
Britishness 132
brokering: UK medical law and 90
Brown, Stephen LJ 51–2, 54, 60–1
Browne-Wilkinson, Lord 126
Bunyan, John 131
Burke, Kenneth 46
Butler, Judith 34

Caesarian sections 80–1; imposed 80–1;
'medical state of exception' 81–2
Cain, Maureen 26
capacity: fixed age for 75; imposed
Caesarian sections 80–1; sterilization,
and 167

capitalism: death of 7; 'disembedding'
    8; ecological model 8; flexibility 8;
    privatization 8; social embedding,
    and 8
Cardozo, Benjamin 130
case law: juristic technique, and
    149–50
Catholicism 132
Chadwick, Edwin 51
charities: politics of pity, and 57
Chiapello, Eve 105, 111–12
chemotherapy: funding 9
clinical judgment 142–4; chance of
    harm 144; clinical guidance, and 143;
    deferring to 18; discretion 143;
    'errors of judgment' 144; medical
    law, in 142–4; skill, role of 143
Clam, Jean 22–3
Clyde, Lord 125
Cochrane Collaboration 108
cognitive pluralism 124
Cold War 56
Colley, Linda 132
common law 128–31; civil law, contrast
    171; deduction, and 153; dissent and
    130; exercise of judgment in 154;
    individual cases 150; induction, and
    153; 'natural classes' 153; nature of
    152; practical knowledge, as 149–55;
    reasoning by analogy 152–4; regional
    rationalities 151; social sciences, and
    150
contingency: management of 24,
    29–35
contraception: under 16s, for 20, 23–4,
    73–7; see also Gillick v West Norfolk and
    Wisbech Area Health Authority
court procedures: time, and 72–3
criminal law 1; homicide, and 1
culpability 1

Denning, Lord 6–7, 124, 128, 144
Diplock, Lord 123–4, 167
dissenting judgments 130–1
Donaldson, Lord 20
Dostoyevsky, Fyodor 62, 105
drugs: development of 120–1;
    monopoly patent rights 42;
    randomized trials, introduction of
    141

Eckhoff, Torstein 154
electro-convulsive therapy (ECT) 123

Eliot, George 119
emergency medicine 73, 82;
    temporality and 69, 80, 82–3
ethics 1, 162–79; bioethics see bioethics;
    identity of speaker, and 2;
    implementing 2; legal doctrine, and
    1; legal form and 176–7; medical see
    medical ethics; paternalism, and 163;
    political control, and 163; relevance
    to medical law 162; renvoi 20;
    Second World War, and 163
ethos 48, 59
European Convention on Human
    Rights (ECHR) 45
European Court of Justice 55
European Union 28, 52
euthanasia 1

fertility treatment: access to 8–9
Fleck, Ludwik 145
Foundation Trusts 52
France; scientific idea of medicine 118
Frank, Jerome 156
Fraser, Nancy 53
French revolution 56
Frow, John 7, 178
Fuller, Steve 134

Geertz, Clifford 154
General Medical Council (GMC) 19
Gillick v West Norfolk and Wisbech Area
    Health Authority 20, 72, 168–9;
    minority in 74–5; time, and 73–7
globalization 52
Goodrich, Peter 3, 4
Gorovitz, Samuel 144–5
Gostin, Larry 173
Grear, Anna, 29–30; deparadoxification
    31–2

Hailsham, Lord 167
Hale, Baroness 54, 59
Hale, Matthew 74
Hamilton CJ 78
Harris, John 19
Harvey, David 50, 52, 91, 96, 103, 110
Hayek, Friedrich 173–4
health tourism 42; government funding
    of 55; immigration and asylum, and
    43; prohibited treatments 43
Healthcare Commission 108
HIV: deporting patient with see asylum;
    third world, in 60

Hobbes, Thomas 3
homicide 1; criminal law, and 1
Hope, Lord 53–4, 59
Horder, Lord 141–2
human rights law 28
Hutchinson, Allan 3, 5–6, 7, 18, 22;
    'good faith' in legal reasoning 22

Illich, Ivan 134
immigration 43
incompetent adults 20–1, 174
Ireland, Paddy 7
Irish Supreme Court 78

Jameson, Fredric 96
Jessop, Bob 8
Jones, Carol 124
judgement: clinical *see* clinical
    judgement; common law, in 154
judges: audience for legal arguments
    25–6; contribution 6; imagery, use of
    48–9
jurisprudence; time, and 72

Keown, John 30
Keywood, Kirsty 26, 35
knowledge, medical: application 147–8;
    thought styles 146, 148
Knudsen, Morten 25
Kuhn, Thomas 118; Popper, and 133–4;
    Schaffner and 147
Kumar, Krishan 103

labour law 165
law: activity, as 23; authority, and 3;
    'cognitively open', as 24;
    contingency, management of 24;
    contradictory developments 17;
    criminal *see* criminal law; demand for
    plausibility 25; 'deparadoxification'
    23, 26; evolution 128–9; foundation
    for 5–6; indeterminate nature of 18;
    instability of meaning in 5;
    interventions in 4; legal rhetoric 5–9;
    see also legal rhetoric; materialist
    understanding 7; medical *see* medical
    law; persuasion, and 4;
    'operationally' closed, as 22;
    'programmes' 23; progress in 132;
    'reparadoxification' 26; rhetoric, and
    3; valid operations 21–2; violence,
    and 22
Le Fanu, James 141–2

Lefebvre, Henri 49
legal rhetoric 5–9; capitalism, and 7;
    'good faith commitment' 6; judges,
    contribution 6; materialist
    perspective 7–9; precedents, and 6;
    time and 71–3; 'utterance', meaning
    of legal 6
legal temporality: models of 73–4
Levitas, Ruth 110
Lewis, Sir Thomas 142
Lim, Hilary 82
Linden, Allen 125–6
Lister, Joseph 119–20
Llewellyn, Karl 154
Lobban, Michael 152
Locke, John 3
logos 47
Lord's Resistance Army 44
Luhmann, Niklas 18, 21; law, on 21;
    model of social systems 21
Lyell, Charles 129

MacIntyre, Alasdair 144–5
McLachlan, Hugh 93–5
Maclean, Alasdair 72, 84
McLean, Sheila 135
Maine, Henry Sumner 128–9
malpractice 124–5; US crisis in 145
Marx, Karl 7, 101
medical ethics 19–21; deformalization
    164–7; founding moment 162–3;
    function 21; identification 163–4;
    married women, and 165–6;
    materialization of law, and 164; state
    involvement, and 165
medical law: anti-market prohibitions,
    and 90; arbitrariness 173; biomedical
    ethics, and 19; Bolam, under 167–70;
    see also Bolam; 'Bolamized' 169;
    broad tests, and 168; capitalist
    economy, and 36; change in 17;
    changing caseloads 42–3;
    chronopolitics of 82–4; clinical
    judgments in *see* clinical judgment;
    deferring to clinical judgments 18;
    dynamic of 13; failure of 17;
    founding moment 162–3;
    'materialized' 175; materialist
    perspective 7; mobility cases 43;
    modes for analysing 2; NHS, and 8;
    paradoxes and plausibility in 21–6;
    pathologies of 19; *pathos* 48; policy
    and 175; politics and history and 1;

medical law *continued*
  principle, and 172; privileged
  audiences 5; renvoi 20; rhetoric, as
  1–2, 5, 9–12; rhetorical analysis of,
  meaning 2; territory of UK and 43;
  time and *see* time; vague, open ended
  tests 171; welfare, and 8
mental health law 172–3
Milburn, Alan 109, 111
Miola, Jose 18; biomedical ethics, on
  19; incompetent adults, on 20–1; test
  of best interest 33
Mol, Annemarie 146
monologism 3; *R v Cambridge Health
  Authority*, and 10
Montgomery, Jonathan 17, 107, 169,
  175–6
Morris, William 101–2
Mrs Dalloway 70
Murphy, Tim 57
Mustill, Lord 78

National Association for Mental Health
  (MIND) 173
National Health Service (NHS) 8;
  access to care, and 11; accountability
  107–8; alienation, and 103; anti-
  market prohibitions, and 90;
  'apparatus of medicine' 105;
  authoritarianism, and 103–4;
  benefiting from treatment 100;
  British space, and 44; clinical
  relationship 107–8; collective
  planning 96; commodity form,
  imposing 107; consumerist world,
  and 109; creation 50, 96–7, 101; crisis
  of national space 52–3;
  decommodification of work, and 9;
  enclave, end of 109; external
  regulation 108; fixed-tariff system
  108–9; globalization, and 52; health
  tourism, and 55; industrial action
  104; inequality, and 165; moral
  renewal, and 98; national space, and
  49–53; neo-liberal order, under 42;
  post-war settlement, and 42;
  privatization 53, 104; public-private
  partnerships 108–9; *R v Cambridge
  Health Authority*, and 11; remaking
  108–9; resource allocation 51; social
  peace, and 95; sovereign patient-
  consumers 106; space, creation of
  50–1; standards of care 108; state

apparatus, as 50; structure, changes
  to 108–9; suppression of market
  place, and 69; surrogacy, and *see*
  surrogacy; Titmuss, Richard, and
  99–101; underwriting clinical
  practice 99; 'utopia', and 95; utopian
  enclave, as 97–103; withdrawal from
  roles 52
National Institute for Health and Care
  Excellence 53; cost-effectiveness
  guidelines 53; standards for care 108
negligence 6; attribution of liability
  150; doctor-centered test 127;
  responsible body of practitioners
  126; 'schools of thought' 126;
  standard of care, and 123; universal
  meaning 151
Neumann, Franz 164–5
Nicholls, Lord 54, 59–60
Norrie, Kenneth 125
nuisance 6
Nuremberg trials 162–3

Oakeshott, Michael 148–9, 152, 157
Ost, François 69, 72, 83–4
Owen, Robert 96

Parker, LJ 74–5
Pascal, Blaise 131
Pashukanis, Evegeny 107
patents: monopoly rights over drugs 42
pathos 47–8, 56; distance, and 63
patient autonomy 1
Pellegrino, Edmund 147–8
Perelman, Chaïm 3, 93, 151, 154, 179
Perez, Oren 22; 'local paradoxes' 22
permanent vegetative state (PVS):
  abortion, and 77–82; ANH,
  withdrawal of 77–8; unlawful killing
  78–9; withdrawal of tube feeding 27
pity: compassion, and 61; politics of
  56–8; pre-empting 58–9
pluralism 124; bounded 126–8;
  progress through 130–1
Polanyi, Michael 96, 148–9, 157
Pollock, Allyson 112
Popper, Karl 121–2, 132–3
possession 151; meaning 151
Poulantzas, Nicos 50
precedents, 6–7; determining
  subsequent cases 46; 'enduring time',
  and 74
Priban, Jiri 27

Private Finance Initiatives (PFI) 52
privatization 8; NHS, of 52–3
professional judgment *see also* clinical
   judgment; centrality of 117; ideology
   of profession, and 140–1
progress; idea of 131–3
Protestantism 132
psychiatric patients: patient rights and
   172–3
public-private partnerships 108–9

R v Cambridge Health Authority, ex parte B
   9–12; 'experimental' treatment 10,
   12; facts of case 9–10; judgment 10;
   'Keynesian' approach 11–12;
   monologism, and 10; NHS, and 11
rationality; patient rights, and 172
Rawls, John 3
refusal of treatment; minor, by 20
renvoi 20
rhetoric: anti-utopian 109; Brazier
   report, in 93; classical 2–3; complex
   articulation 48; 'cultural sociology' 5;
   ethos 48; genre and 177; law rhetoric
   5–9; *see also* legal rhetoric; legal texts,
   and 5; *logos* 47; meaning 2–5; modes
   of proof in 46–9; *pathos* 47; power of
   4; speaker and audience 62; speech,
   and 4; time as 69; ultrasound images,
   and 79; 'utopia' *see* utopia
Roberts, Helen 166, 174
Royal College of Obstetricians and
   Gynaecologists; Abortion Act 1967,
   and 30

Sampford, Charles 151
Scarman, Lord 24, 76–7, 125
Schaffner, Kenneth 147
Scheuerman, William 73, 81
Schmitt, Carl 81, 164, 173
science; attributes 122–2; change in
   121–2; characteristics of 122; clinical
   work as 117; common law, in 12,
   128–31; 3; conceptions of medicine
   118; dynamic of scientific progress
   121–6; logic of scientific discovery
   128; medical practitioners, and 127;
   medicine as progressive 118–21;
   political radicalism, and 119; radical
   critique, and 133–4; testing and 122
scientism 93
Sheldon, Sally 30
Simpson, Brian 151

Smith, JC 170
socialism; NHS, and 96
space; 'lived-in' 49; modes of
   specialization 49–50; state
   apparatuses 50; state, role of 50
Stäheli, Urs 21
state funding: health care, of 28
statute law: abundance of 149; time,
   and 73–4
sterilization: *Bolam* test 33, 34, 167, 174;
   disabled patients 32–5; 'radical
   dissent' 34; state-sponsored 33; test of
   best interest 33; therapeutic and
   non- 32
Stone, Julius 151–4
surrogacy 91–5; Brazier report 91–2;
   commercialization 91;
   'commodification of childbearing'
   92; freer market, and 93; legislation
   91; reform proposals 92; regulation
   of 92–3; rhetoric and 93; welfare of
   child, and 92
Swales, John Kim 93–5,

Teubner, Gunther 18, 21, 22, 24, 26,
   28, 34, 77, 165
theatre: court, as 58
theory: role in medicine 146
Thomasma, David 147–8
Thomson, Michael 28
thought styles 146, 148
time 69–84; arbitrary time frames 72;
   doctrine of precedent 74; external
   time frames 72; *Gillick v West Norfolk
   and Wisbech Area Health Authority*, and
   73–7; intertemporal struggle 72;
   jurisprudence, and 72; legal
   processes, and 72–3; legal rhetoric,
   and 71–3; medical law, and 71;
   models of legal temporality 73–4; *Mrs
   Dalloway*, in 70; non-legal 77–82;
   plural, as 69; rhetorical, as 69; social,
   as 69
Titmuss, Richard 99–101; altruism 100;
   Brazier report, and 99; enumeration
   of costs 101; NHS, and 100
topics (topoi): and clinical judgment
   32; in *ex parte B* 11; the gift 53, 62, 94;
   logos 47; national space 49;
   plausibility 12–13; progress 118;
   reduction of complexity 25–7, 29
training 154–5; apprenticeship, by
   148–9

tube feeding: withdrawal 27

Uganda 44–6
ultrasound images: rhetorical power of
    79
Unsworth, Clive 172–3
utopia: anti-utopia 103–8; Beveridge
    report, and 97; 'blueprint' 96–7;
    dystopia 106; enclaves, as 96, 106;
    NHS as 97–103; pre-figurative trait
    96; process-utopia 110–11; topos,
    without 109–10; use of term 93

Veitch, Kenneth 1, 17, 113, 134–5
Van der Burg, Wiebren 176
Virilo, Paul 82

Webster, Charles 51
welfare state 97, 100, 140, 157, 165
White, James Boyd 3
Williams, Raymond 9, 101
Wilson, Duncan 9
Wolf, Susan 177
Woolf, Virginia 70
world trade law 42